The Bible Speaks Today
Series Editors: J. A. Motyer (OT)
John R. W. Stott (NT)
Derek Tidball (Bible Themes)

The Message of
1 Timothy & Titus
Guard the Truth

Titles in this series

The Message of
1 Timothy & Titus

Guard the Truth

JOHN R. W. STOTT

IVP Academic
An imprint of InterVarsity Press
Downers Grove, Illinois

InterVarsity Press, USA
P.O. Box 1400, Downers Grove, IL 60515-1426, USA
World Wide Web: www.ivpress.com
Email: email@ivpress.com

Inter-Varsity Press, England
Norton Street, Nottingham NG7 3HR, England
Website: www.ivpbooks.com
Email: ivp@ivpbooks.com

InterVarsity Press® is the book-publishing division of InterVarsity Christian Fellowship/USA®, a movement of students and faculty active on campus at hundreds of universities, colleges and schools of nursing in the United States of America, and a member movement of the International Fellowship of Evangelical Students. For information about local and regional activities, write Public Relations Dept., InterVarsity Christian Fellowship/USA, 6400 Schroeder Rd., P.O. Box 7895, Madison, WI 53707-7895, or visit the IVCF website at <www.intervarsity.org>.

Inter-Varsity Press is closely linked with the Universities and Colleges Christian Fellowship (formerly the Inter-Varsity Fellowship), a student movement linking Christian Unions in universities and colleges throughout the United Kingdom and the Republic of Ireland, and a member movement of the International Fellowship of Evangelical Students. For information about local and national activities write to UCCF, 38 De Montfort Street, Leicester LE1 7GP, England, visit them on the web at www.uccf.org.uk, or email them at email@uccf.org.uk.

Cover design: Cindy Kiple
Image: Diana Ong/Getty Images

USA ISBN 978-0-8308-1247-9
UK ISBN 978-0-85111-172-8

Typeset in Great Britain
Printed in the United States of America ∞

British Library Cataloguing in Publication Data

A catalogue record for this book is available from the British Library.

Library of Congress Cataloging-in-Publication Data

Stott, John R. W.
  [Guard the truth]
  The message of 1 Timothy & Titus / John R. W. Stott
    p. cm. —(The Bible speaks today)
  Originally published: Guard the truth. ©1996.
  Includes bibliographical references..
  ISBN 0-8308-1247-4 (pbk. : alk. paper)
    1. Bible. N.T. Timothy, 1st—Commentaries.   2. Bible. N.T. Titus–Commentaries
    III. Title.   IV. Series.
BS2745.53 .S76 2001
227'.83077—dc21

2001024035

| P | 30 | 29 | 28 | 27 | 26 | 25 | 24 | 23 | 22 | 21 | 20 | 19 | 18 |
| Y | 30 | 29 | 28 | 27 | 26 | 25 | 24 | 23 | 22 | 21 | 20 | 19 | |

Author's preface

It was as a comparatively young man that I began a serious study of the Pastoral Letters, so that I found no problem in sitting beside Timothy and Titus, listening through their ears to the elderly apostle's admonitions. But now the situation has changed. I am almost certainly older than the apostle was, and it is natural for me to sit beside Paul. Not of course that I am an apostle. But I think I feel something of his concern for the future of the gospel and for the younger generation whose responsibility it is to guard it and pass it on. It is an interesting hermeneutical question whom one may or should identify with when reading Scripture.

My first attempt to expound all three Pastoral Letters was during the fall term of 1972, when I was invited to lecture on them at Trinity Evangelical Divinity School outside Chicago. But before that during the sixties I had preached through them in All Souls Church in London. Then 2 Timothy was the set text for the biblical expositions at the great student missionary convention at Urbana in 1967, and at the Keswick Convention in Britain in 1969. Those studies of 2 Timothy were expanded and published in 1973 as one of the early *Bible Speaks Today* books under the title *Guard the Gospel.* 1 Timothy then became my set text for the Australian Church Missionary Society's Summer Schools in 1986, and for 'Commission 88', the East African student missionary conference, which was held outside Nairobi at the end of 1988.

So this penultimate *Bible Speaks Today* book in the New Testament series (due to be completed with an exposition of Matthew's Gospel by Roy Clements and Peter Comont) focuses on 1 Timothy and Titus. I address the question of the authenticity of the Pastoral Letters in an introductory chapter. In this preface I limit myself to their relevance to the contemporary world and church, especially the relevance of 1 Timothy and Titus.

The relevance of 1 Timothy and Titus

To draw up a list of topics to which these two letters make a substantial contribution is to compile an extraordinarily heterogeneous assortment. I have sub-titled the exposition of 1 Timothy 'The life of the local church'. For it contains apostolic instruction on the priority of prayer, on gender roles in the conduct of public worship, on the relations between church and state, and on the biblical basis for world evangelization. The apostle goes on to write about local church leadership, the conditions of eligibility for the pastorate, and how young leaders can ensure that their ministry is accepted, and not despised or rejected on account of their youth. Other subjects include the doctrine of creation, and its application to our everyday behaviour, the principles governing the church's social work, the remuneration and disciplining of pastors, the superiority of contentment over covetousness, the call to radical holiness, and the dangers and duties of the rich.

The exposition of Titus I have sub-titled 'Doctrine and duty', for, although the context is still the local church, the emphasis has shifted. Paul's chief concern now is that, in the three spheres of the church, the home and the world, our Christian duties in this present age will be enforced by the comprehensive doctrine of salvation, and especially by the past and future appearings of Christ.

But the apostle's overriding preoccupation throughout all three Pastoral Letters is with the truth, that it may be faithfully guarded and handed on. The pertinence of this theme, at the end of the twentieth century, is evident. For contemporary culture is being overtaken and submerged by the spirit of postmodernism. Postmodernism begins as a self-conscious reaction against the modernism of the Enlightenment, and especially against its unbounded confidence in reason, science and progress. The postmodern mind rightly rejects this naïve optimism. But it then goes further and declares that there is no such thing as objective or universal truth; that all so-called 'truth' is purely subjective, being culturally conditioned; and that therefore we all have our own truth, which has as much right to respect as anybody else's. Pluralism is an offspring of postmodernism; it affirms the independent validity of every faith and ideology, and demands in shrill tones that we abandon as impossibly arrogant any attempt to convert somebody (let alone everybody) to our opinion.

In contrast to this relativization of truth, it is wonderfully refreshing to read Paul's unambiguous commitment to it. He has himself been appointed, he says, 'a teacher of the Gentiles in faith and truth' (1 Tim. 2:7, RSV); the church is 'the pillar and foundation of the truth' (1 Tim. 3:15); and it is the truth which 'leads to godliness' (Tit. 1:1). The false teachers, on the other hand, 'have wandered away from the truth' and even 'oppose the truth' (1 Tim. 6:21; 2 Tim. 2:18; 3:8; cf. 4:4).

As the apostle develops his thesis, we become aware of the

existence of four groups of people, and of the interplay between them, namely Paul and his fellow apostles, the false teachers, Timothy and Titus, and the pastors they are to select and appoint.

First, there is Paul himself, who styles himself at the beginning of all three letters an apostle of Jesus Christ, adding in two of them that his apostleship is by the will or the command of God. And all through these letters his self-conscious apostolic authority is apparent, as he issues commands and expects obedience. Also, again and again, he refers to what he calls indiscriminately 'the truth', 'the faith', 'the sound doctrine', 'the teaching' or 'the deposit'. The plain implication is that a body of doctrine exists, which, having been revealed and given by God, is objectively true. It is the teaching of the apostles. Paul constantly calls Timothy and Titus back to it, together with the churches they oversee.

Secondly, in opposition to Paul, there are the false teachers. They are *heterodidaskaloi* (1 Tim. 1:3; 6:3), engaged in teaching what is *heteros*, different from and alien to the teaching of the apostles. They are essentially deviationists, who have 'wandered' or 'swerved' from the faith (1 Tim. 1:6; 4:1; 2 Tim. 2:18). Paul does not mince his words. What they are spreading is not an alternative truth, but 'lies', 'godless chatter', 'myths' and 'meaningless talk'.[1]

Thirdly, there are Timothy and Titus. They stand between the apostle and the church, in the sense that they represent him and relay his teaching to the church. They have been appointed to oversee the churches in Ephesus and Crete respectively, yet their job specification has been written by Paul. Twice in his first letter to Timothy he tells him that he hopes to visit him soon (3:14; 4:13). Meanwhile, during his absence, Timothy is to devote himself on the one hand to the public reading of Scripture, basing his teaching and exhortation on it, and on the other to Paul's written instructions. Indeed, Paul's written teaching was, in the providence of God, a deliberate substitute for his personal presence and direction of the church. This is why as many as ten times in 1 Timothy and Titus Paul writes 'teach these things', 'command and teach these things', or 'give the people these instructions'.[2] On each occasion *tauta* ('these things') means the teaching which Paul is giving Timothy and Titus. They are not only to hold on to it themselves, guarding the precious deposit of truth (1 Tim. 1:19; 3:9; 6:20), and to fight for it against the false teachers (1 Tim. 1:18; 6:12), but also to pass it on faithfully to the church.

Fourthly, there are the true and trustworthy pastors whom Timothy and Titus are to appoint. In both letters Paul lays down

[1] 1 Tim. 1:4f.; 4:2, 7; 6:3ff., 20; Tit. 1:14; 3:9; *cf.* 2 Tim. 2:16; 4:4.
[2] 1 Tim. 3:14; 4:6, 11, 15; 5:7, 21; 6:2, 17; Tit. 2:15; 3:8.

the conditions of eligibility they must fulfil (1 Tim. 3 and Tit. 1). Apart from a consistent moral character and a Christian home life, they must also be loyal to the apostle's teaching and have a teaching gift, so that they will be able both to teach the truth and to confute error (1 Tim. 3:2; Tit. 1:9).

Here then are the three stages of teaching which lie behind the Pastoral Letters. Over against the false teachers, first, there is Paul's authoritative apostolic instruction, which he passes on to Timothy and Titus; secondly there are Timothy and Titus themselves, who teach 'these things' to others, especially the pastors they are to appoint; and thirdly there are these pastors whose task it is to 'encourage others by sound doctrine and refute those who oppose it' (Tit. 1:9). These stages are clearly set out in 2 Timothy 2:2, where what Timothy has heard from Paul he is to 'entrust to reliable men' (the pastors), who in their turn will 'also be qualified to teach others' (the churches). It is noteworthy that in this verse reliability (to the Word) and an ability to teach it are the two essential qualifications for the pastorate, which Paul has already laid down in 1 Timothy 3:2 and Titus 1:9.

In these three stages of instruction it is vital to preserve the gap between Paul on the one hand and Timothy, Titus, the pastors and the churches on the other. The true apostolic succession is a continuity not of order but of doctrine, namely the teaching of the apostles handed on from generation to generation. And what makes this doctrinal succession possible is that the teaching of the apostles was written down and has now been bequeathed to us in the New Testament. Just as Paul told Timothy, while he was absent, to attend to Old Testament Scripture and to his written instructions, so we must do the same. For Paul is now permanently absent. His approaching death looms behind all three Pastoral Letters, and especially behind 2 Timothy in which he states explicitly that the time of his departure has come (2 Tim. 4:6). So his paramount concern is to ensure the preservation of his teaching after his death. Now he has been dead a long time. And there is no living apostle who can take his place. Instead, we have his writings. Indeed we have the whole Bible, both the Old and the New Testaments, the written legacy of the prophets and the apostles.

'This ... is the difference beween the apostles and their successors,' wrote Calvin:

> The former were sure and genuine scribes of the Holy Spirit, and their writings are therefore to be considered oracles of God; but the sole office of others is to teach what is provided and sealed in the Holy Scriptures. We therefore teach that faithful ministers are now not permitted to coin any new doctrine, but that they are

simply to cleave to that doctrine to which God has subjected all men without exception.[3]

Much contemporary confusion in the church arises from our failure to make a clear enough distinction between the apostolic and the post-apostolic periods. Our forefathers understood it better than we do. Oscar Cullmann's explanation could hardly be improved:

> ... the infant church itself distinguished between apostolic tradition and ecclesiastical tradition, clearly subordinating the latter to the former, in other words subordinating itself to the apostolic tradition.[4]

> The fixing of the Christian canon of Scripture [*sc.* the New Testament] means that *the church itself*, at a given time, traced a clear and definite line of demarcation between the period of the apostles and that of the church, between the time of foundation and that of construction, between the apostolic community and the church of the bishops, in other words, between apostolic tradition and ecclesiastical tradition. Otherwise the formation of the canon would be meaningless.[5]

Finally, I thank Professor Stephen Williams and Nelson González for their kind help in compiling the bibliography. I am also grateful to Nelson, who has a most uncanny and disconcerting knack of spotting the weak places in my argument; to Dr Alastair Campbell of Spurgeon's College, who is himself writing on the Pastorals; to David Stone, who has produced another of his useful study guides; to Colin Duriez, IVP's ever-helpful General Books Editor; and to Jo Bramwell, for her meticulous copy-editing. They have all read the typescript and made suggestions, to virtually all of which I have tried to respond. Finally, I am extremely grateful to Frances Whitehead for crowning her forty years' service to All Souls Church and to me, by producing yet one more immaculate typescript.

New Year's Day, 1996   JOHN STOTT

---

[3] J. Calvin, *Institutes of the Christian Religion*, translated by F. L. Battles (Collins, 1986), IV.8.9.
[4] From 'The Tradition' in Oscar Cullmann, *The Early Church* (SCM, 1956), p. 87.
[5] *Ibid.*, p. 89.

Chief abbreviations

AV — The Authorized (King James) Version of the Bible (1611).

BAGD — Walter Bauer, *A Greek-English Lexicon of the New Testament and Other Early Christian Literature*, translated and adapted by William F. Arndt and F. Wilbur Gingrich, second edition, revised and augmented by F. Wilbur Gingrich and Frederick W. Danker from Bauer's fifth edition, 1958 (University of Chicago Press, 1979).

Eusebius — *Ecclesiastical History*, translated by G. A. Williamson (Penguin, 1965).

GNB — The Good News Bible (NT 1966–1992; OT 1976, 1992).

GT — C. L. W. Grimm and J. H. Thayer, *A Greek-English Lexicon of the New Testament* (T. and T. Clark, 1901).

Irenaeus — *Against Heresies*, translated by F. M. R. Hitchcock, in W. J. Sparrow Simpson and W. K. Lowther Clarke (eds.), *Early Church Classics* 2 (SPCK, 1916).

JB — The Jerusalem Bible (1966).

JBP — *The New Testament in Modern English* by J. B. Phillips (Collins, 1958).

Josephus, *Ant.* — *The Antiquities of the Jews, c.* AD 93–94, translated by William Whiston, 1737; from *Josephus: Complete Works* (Pickering and Inglis, 1981).

Josephus, *Wars* — *The Wars of the Jews, c.* AD 78–79, translated by William Whiston, 1737; from *Josephus: Complete Works* (Pickering and Inglis, 1981).

LXX — The Old Testament in Greek according to the Septuagint, third century BC.

Metzger — Bruce M. Metzger, *A Textual Commentary on the Greek New Testament* (United Bible Societies, 1971; corrected edition, 1975).

Moffatt — James Moffatt, *A New Translation of the Bible* (Hodder and Stoughton, Old and New Testaments

	in one vol. 1926; revised 1935).
MM	J. H. Moulton and G. Milligan, *The Vocabulary of the Greek New Testament*, 1930 (Hodder and Stoughton, 1949).
NEB	The New English Bible (NT, 1961, second edition 1970; OT, 1970).
NIV	The New International Version of the Bible (1973, 1978, 1984).
NRSV	The New Revised Standard Version of the Bible (1989, Anglicized edition, 1995).
REB	The Revised English Bible (1989).
RSV	The Revised Standard Version of the Bible (NT, 1946; second edition, 1971; OT, 1952).
RV	The Revised Version of the Bible (1881–1885).
TDNT	*Theological Dictionary of the New Testament*, ed. G. Kittel and G. Friedrich, translated by G. W. Bromiley, 10 vols. (Eerdmans, 1964–1976).
Trench	R. C. Trench, *Synonyms of the New Testament* (eighth revised edition, Macmillan, 1876).

Bibliography

Works referred to in the footnotes are cited there by author's surname, or surname and date.

Commentaries

Alford, Henry, *The Greek Testament*, vol. 3 (Rivington's, fourth edition, 1865).

Barclay, William, *The Letters to Timothy, Titus, and Philemon*, The Daily Study Bible (1956; revised edition, St Andrew Press, 1975).

Barrett, C. K., *The Pastoral Epistles*, The New Clarendon Bible (Oxford University Press, 1963).

Bengel, Johann Albrecht, *Gnomon of the New Testament*, vol. 4, trans. and ed. Andrew R. Fausset (1754; T. and T. Clark, sixth edition, 1866).

Calvin, John, *The Epistles of Paul to Timothy and Titus* (1548–50; Oliver and Boyd, 1964).

Chrysostom, St John, *The Homilies on the Epistles to Timothy and Titus* (probably preached in Antioch between 389 and 398); in Philip Schaff (ed.), *A Select Library of the Nicene and Post-Nicene Fathers*, vol. XIII (1843; Eerdmans, 1976).

Dibelius, Martin, and Hans Conzelmann, *A Commentary on the Pastoral Epistles*, Hermeneia: A Critical and Historical Commentary on the Bible (1955; fourth revised edition, 1966; Eng. trans. Fortress, 1972).

Ellicott, Charles J., *The Pastoral Epistles of St Paul* (Longmans, 1861; fifth edition, 1883).

Fairbairn, Patrick, *Commentary on the Pastoral Epistles* (T. and T. Clark, 1874; Zondervan, 1956).

Fee, Gordon D., *1 and 2 Timothy and Titus*, The New International Biblical Commentary (1984; revised edition, Hendrickson, 1988).

Gealy, F. D., and M. P. Noyes, 'The Pastoral Epistles', in *The Interpreter's Bible*, ed. G. A. Buttrick, vol. 11 (Abingdon, 1955).

Guthrie, Donald, *The Pastoral Epistles: An Introduction and*

Commentary, Tyndale New Testament Commentaries (IVP, revised edition, 1990).

Hanson, A. T., *The Pastoral Letters*, The Cambridge Bible Commentary on the NEB (Cambridge University Press, 1966).

———*The Pastoral Epistles*, The New Century Bible Commentary (Marshall Morgan and Scott, 1982).

Hendriksen, William, *A Commentary on the Epistles to Timothy and Titus* (1957; Banner of Truth, 1959).

Houlden, J. L., *The Pastoral Epistles*, the TPI (Trinity Press International) New Testament Commentaries (Penguin, 1976; revised edition, SCM and TPI, 1989).

Karris, Robert J., *The Pastoral Epistles*, New Testament Message vol. 17 (Michael Glazier, 1979).

Kelly, J. N. D., *The Pastoral Epistles*, Black's New Testament Commentaries (A. and C. Black, 1963).

Knight, George W., *The Pastoral Epistles*, New International Greek Testament Commentary (Paternoster, 1992).

Liddon, H. P., *Explanatory Analysis of St Paul's First Epistle to Timothy* (Longmans, 1897).

Lock, Walter, *A Critical and Exegetical Commentary on the Pastoral Epistles*, The International Critical Commentary (T. and T. Clark, 1924).

Oden, Thomas C., *First and Second Timothy and Titus*, Interpretation (John Knox, 1989).

Plummer, Alfred, *The Pastoral Epistles*, The Expositor's Bible (Hodder, 1888).

Quinn, J. D., *Titus*, Anchor Bible (Doubleday, 1990).

Simpson, E. K., *The Pastoral Epistles: The Greek Text with Introduction and Commentary* (Tyndale, 1954).

Spicq, C., *Saint Paul: Les Epitres Pastorales* (1947; Paris: J. Gabalda, fourth edition, in 2 vols., 1969).

Towner, Philip H., *1 and 2 Timothy and Titus*, IVP New Testament Commentaries (IVP, 1994).

Ward, Ronald A., *Commentary on 1 and 2 Timothy and Titus* (Word, 1974).

White, Newport J. D., *The First and Second Epistles to Timothy and the Epistle to Titus*, in *The Expositor's Greek Testament*, vol. 4 (Hodder, 1910; reprint, Eerdmans, 1920).

Other works

Aitken, Canon W. Hay M. H., *The School of Grace: Expository Thoughts on Titus 2:11–14* (J. F. Shaw and Co., 1880).

Bassler, Jouette M., 'The Widows' Tale – A Fresh Look at 1 Tim 5:3–16', *Journal of Biblical Literature* 103.1 (1984).

Bailey, Kenneth E., 'Women in the New Testament: A Middle Eastern Cultural View', *Anvil* 11.1 (1994).

Campbell, R. Alastair, 'Leaders and Fathers: Church Government in Earliest Christianity', *Irish Biblical Studies* 17 (January 1995).

Collins, John N., *Diakonia: Re-interpreting the Ancient Sources* (Oxford University Press, 1990).

Donelson, Lewis R., *Pseudepigraphy and Ethical Argument in the Pastoral Epistles* (Tübingen: J. C. B. Mohr, 1986).

Ellis, E. Earle, 'The Pastorals and Paul,' *Expository Times* 104 (1992–3).

————'Pseudonymity and Canonicity of New Testament Documents', in M. J. Wilkens and T. Paige (eds.), *Worship, Theology, and Ministry in the Early Church, JSOT* Supplement Series 87 (Sheffield Academic Press, 1992).

————'Pastoral Letters', in Gerald E. Hawthorne, Ralph P. Martin and Daniel G. Reid (eds.), *Dictionary of Paul and his Letters* (IVP, 1993).

Fee, Gordon D., *Gospel and Spirit: Issues in New Testament Hermeneutics* (Hendrickson, 1991).

————*God's Empowering Presence: The Holy Spirit in the Letters of Paul* (Hendrickson, 1994).

France, R. T., *Women in the Church's Ministry: A Test-Case for Biblical Hermeneutics* (Paternoster, 1995).

Fuller, J. William, 'Of Elders and Triads in 1 Timothy 5:19–25', *New Testament Studies* 29.2 (1983).

Guthrie, Donald, *The Pastoral Epistles and the Mind of Paul* (Tyndale, 1956).

————'The Development of the Idea of Canonical Pseudepigrapha in New Testament Criticism', *Vox Evangelica* 1 (1962).

Hanson, Anthony T., *Studies in the Pastoral Epistles* (SPCK, 1968).

Harrison, P. N., *The Problem of the Pastoral Epistles* (Oxford University Press, 1921).

————*Paulines and Pastorals* (Villiers, 1964).

Hurley, James B., *Man and Woman in Biblical Perspective: A Study in Role Relationships and Authority* (IVP, 1981).

Karris, Robert J., 'The Background and Significance of the Polemic in the Pastoral Epistles', *Journal of Biblical Literature* 92.4 (1973).

Kidd, Reggie M., *Wealth and Beneficence in the Pastoral Epistles: A 'Bourgeois' Form of Early Christianity?* (Scholars, 1990).

Kirk, J. Andrew, 'Did "Officials" in the New Testament Church Receive a Salary?' *Expository Times* 84 (1972–3).

Knight, George W., *The Faithful Sayings in the Pastoral Letters* (J. H. Kok N.V. Kampen, 1968; Baker, 1979).

————'*Authenteō* in Reference to Women in 1 Timothy 2:12', *New Testament Studies* 30.1 (1984).

Kroeger, R. C., and C. C. Kroeger, *I Suffer not a Woman: Rethinking 1 Timothy 2:11–15 in Light of Ancient Evidence* (Baker, 1992).

Longenecker, Richard N., 'On the Form, Function and Authority of the New Testament Letters', in D. A. Carson and John D. Woodbridge (eds.), *Scripture and Truth* (IVP, 1983).

Metzger, Bruce M., 'A Reconsideration of Certain Arguments Against the Pauline Authorship of the Pastoral Epistles', *Expository Times* 70.11 (1958).

————'Literary Forgeries and Canonical Pseudepigrapha', *Journal of Biblical Literature* 91 (1972).

Mickelsen, Alvera (ed.), *Women, Authority, and the Bible* (Marshall, Morgan and Scott, 1987).

Moo, Douglas J., '1 Timothy 2:11–15: Meaning and Significance', *Trinity Journal* 1.1 (1980).

————'The Interpretation of 1 Timothy 2:11–15 – A Rejoinder', *Trinity Journal* 2.1(1981).

Moule, C. F. D., *The Birth of the New Testament* (1964; A. and C. Black, third revised edition, 1981).

————'The Problem of the Pastoral Epistles – A Reappraisal', *Essays in New Testament Interpretation* (Cambridge University Press, 1982).

Padgett, Alan, 'Wealthy Women at Ephesus – 1 Tim 2:8–15 in Social Context', *Interpretation* 41.1 (1987).

Payne, Philip B., 'Libertarian Women in Ephesus: A Response to Douglas Moo's Article "1 Timothy 2:11–15: Meaning and Significance"', *Trinity Journal* 2.1 (1981).

Pierson, Lance, *In the Steps of Timothy* (IVP, 1995).

Piper, John, and Wayne Grudem (eds.), *Recovering Biblical Manhood and Womanhood: A Response to Evangelical Feminism* (Crossway [USA], 1991).

Richards, E. Randolph, *The Secretary in the Letters of Paul* (Tübingen: J. C. B. Mohr, 1991).

Scholer, D. M., '1 Timothy 2:9–15 and the Place of Women in the Church's Ministry', in Alvera Mickelsen (ed.), *Women, Authority, and the Bible* (Marshall, Morgan and Scott, 1987).

Thurston, Bonnie B., *The Widows: A Women's Ministry in the Early Church* (Fortress, 1989).

Towner, Philip H., *The Goal of Our Instruction: The Structure of Theology and Ethics in the Pastoral Epistles* (JSOT Press, 1989).

————'The Present Age in the Eschatology of the Pastoral Epistles', *New Testament Studies* 32.2 (1986).

Verner, David C., *The Household of God: The Social World of the Pastoral Epistles* (Scholars, 1983).

Wilson, Stephen G., *Luke and the Pastoral Epistles* (SPCK, 1979).

Winter, Bruce W., *Seek the Welfare of the City: Christians as Benefactors and Citizens* (Paternoster, 1994).

Wright, David F., 'Homosexuals or Prostitutes? The Meaning of ARSENOKOITAI (1 Cor. 6:9; 1 Tim. 1:10)', *Vigiliae Christianae* 38.2 (1984).

————'Homosexuality: The Relevance of the Bible', *Evangelical Quarterly* 61:4 (1989).

Young, Frances, *The Theology of the Pastoral Letters* (Cambridge University Press, 1994).

The authenticity of the Pastoral Letters

Ever since F. C. Baur of Tübingen rejected the Pauline authorship of all three Pastoral Letters in 1835, the voices of critical orthodoxy have confidently followed this tradition. The letters are declared to be pseudonymous or deutero-Pauline, that is to say, composed by a disciple of Paul who attributed them to the pen of his master.

Yet the older view that these letters are authentically Pauline refuses to go away. During the twentieth century, and particularly during its last fifty years, a vigorous defence has been mounted by both Protestant and Catholic scholars. Some of the most notable are Newport J. D. White (1910), Walter Lock (1924), Joachim Jeremias (1934), C. Spicq (1947), E. K. Simpson (1954), Donald Guthrie (1957), William Hendricksen (1957), J. N. D. Kelly (1963), Gordon D. Fee (1984), Thomas C. Oden (1989), George W. Knight (1992) and Philip H. Towner (1994).

Perhaps the most helpful way to handle this controversy here will be to rehearse briefly the case for and against Pauline authorship, and for and against pseudonymity, and then to consider the possible contribution to the writing of Paul's letters made by his amanuensis.

1. The case for Pauline authorship

This case has always rested on two grounds – internal (the claims which the letters make that they were written by the apostle) and external (the acceptance of the letters as genuine by the church from the earliest days until the last century).

a. Internal evidence

The internal evidence is plain, and is so comprehensive that the theory of pseudonymity would credit Paul's imitator with historical and literary genius. All three letters begin with the announcement of Paul's name as author, and go on to identify him as 'an apostle of Jesus Christ'. Both letters to Timothy add that his apostleship is by God's 'command' or 'will'. The letters then purport to be addressed to Timothy and Titus, whom Paul has stationed in Ephesus and

Crete respectively, in order to silence false teachers (1 Tim. 1:3ff.) and appoint true teachers in their place (Tit. 1:5ff.). Paul also indicates his affectionate relationship with his delegates by calling each either his 'dear son' or his 'true son'. This is the framework; are we really to believe that it was all fabricated?

1 Timothy and Titus, with which we are concerned in this book, contain apostolic directions relating to the doctrinal, ethical and pastoral welfare of the churches. This is especially the case in 1 Timothy in which Paul twice states his intention to visit Timothy personally (3:14; 4:13) – a statement which Professor Moule calls 'a piece of gratuitous irony and in bad taste' if it was made up by a pseudonymous writer.[1] Interspersed with his instructions to Timothy the apostle makes a number of personal references to his ordination (1:18; 4:14), his youthfulness (4:11ff.) and his gastric problems (5:23), as also to his own former violent persecution of the church and marvellous conversion and commissioning by the sheer mercy of God (1:12ff.). He concludes his letter with a poignant appeal to Timothy to lead a life appropriate to a man of God (6:11ff.) and especially to guard the deposit of truth committed to him (6:20).

In the letter to Titus, which probably comes next chronologically, there are fewer personal references. Yet Paul carefully adapts his instructions to Titus' particular circumstances in Crete (1:10ff.), and seeks to regulate the Christian behaviour of different groups in the church (2:1ff.). He ends his letter with specific messages to or about four named individuals. He is proposing to send either Artemas or Tychicus to Titus to relieve him, so that he can join Paul in Nicopolis (3:12), and Titus is to help Zenas and Apollos on their way (3:13).

The second letter to Timothy is the most personal of the three; it claims to be the apostle's farewell message to Timothy shortly before his anticipated execution (1:13; 2:2; 3:14; 4:1ff., 6ff.). In addition, he recalls Timothy's tears, the faith and ministry of his mother and grandmother (1:4ff.), and his personal knowledge of the apostle's teaching, lifestyle and sufferings (3:10ff.). He begs Timothy twice to come to him, especially before winter will make navigation impossible (4:9, 21). He then mentions no fewer than seventeen friends by name, adding either news of them or requests or greetings to them.

Are we to suppose that all these specific and personal references were made up? Some scholars do not hesitate to say so. Here, for example, is L. R. Donelson: 'In the interest of deception he [sc. the pseudonymous author] fabricated all the personal notes.'[2] Others defend their authenticity, but have to resort to ingenious theories as to how they were first preserved and then incorporated into the

[1] Moule, p. 128.   [2] Donelson, p. 24.

letters. It is much more natural to hold that all the specifics about Paul, Timothy, Titus, Ephesus, Crete and other people, places and situations, are authentic parts of an authentic letter. Above all, as Bishop Handley Moule wrote about 2 Timothy: '*The human heart* is in it everywhere. And fabricators, certainly of that age, did not well understand the human heart.'[3]

b. External evidence

Turning now to the external evidence for the Pauline authorship of the Pastorals, we find that their genuineness was almost universally accepted by the church from the beginning. The first probable allusions to them are to be found in letters from Clement of Rome to the Corinthians (*c.* AD 95), from Ignatius of Antioch to the Ephesians (*c.* AD 110), and from Polycarp to the Philippians (*c.* AD 117). Then towards the end of the second century there are a number of indisputable quotations from all three Pastorals in Irenaeus' work *Against Heresies*. The *Muratorian Canon* (*c.* 200 AD), which lists the books of the New Testament, ascribes all three letters to Paul. The only exception to this positive witness occurs in Marcion, who was excommunicated as a heretic in 144 AD in Rome, on account of his rejection of most of the Old Testament and of Old Testament references in the New Testament. So he had theological grounds for repudiating the Pastorals, not least their teaching about the goodness of creation (1 Tim. 4:1ff.).

This external witness to the authenticity of the three Pastoral Letters continued as an unbroken tradition until Friedrich Schleiermacher rejected 1 Timothy in 1807 and F. C. Baur rejected all three letters in 1835. The question now is whether the case against the Pauline authorship can overthrow the strong internal and external evidence for it.

2. The case against Pauline authorship

The arguments put forward against the Pauline authorship of the Pastorals may be summed up as historical, linguistic, theological and ethical. We need to consider each in turn.

a. History

As we have seen, the text of 1 Timothy and Titus claims to furnish readers with the information they need about the historical circumstances of their composition.

[3] *The Second Epistle to Timothy* (Religious Tract Society, 1905), p. 21.

Paul states that, when he went into Macedonia, he urged Timothy to stay in Ephesus in order to curb its rampant heresy, and that similarly he had left Titus in Crete in order to complete what had been left incomplete, especially in the appointment of suitable elders in every town. But when did these events take place, involving Macedonia, Ephesus and Crete? When too did Paul winter in Nicopolis (Tit. 3:12), leave his cloak and scrolls behind in Troas (2 Tim. 4:13), and abandon Trophimus in Miletus when he was ill (2 Tim. 4:20)? It is simply not possible (though valiant attempts have been made) to fit Pauline visits to these places into Luke's record in the Acts. And where are we to place his stay, imprisonment and trial in Rome (2 Tim. 1:16ff.; 4:16ff.)?

It is this difficulty of reconciling the historical and geographical references in the Pastorals with Luke's narrative which has led some scholars to reject the notion that they have been invented and to revive instead the chronology developed by Eusebius in his famous fourth-century *Ecclesiastical History*. He wrote that Paul was released at the end of his two-year period of house arrest, where Luke takes leave of him,[4] and that he then resumed his missionary travels, penetrating even as far as Spain as he had hoped,[5] before being re-arrested, re-imprisoned, re-tried and finally condemned and beheaded. Although this reconstruction is somewhat speculative, depending almost entirely on Eusebius, it provides a framework into which the historical allusions in the Pastorals can quite easily be fitted, without needing to accuse the author of blunder, fiction or romance.

b. Vocabulary

In 1921 P. N. Harrison's book *The Problem of the Pastoral Epistles* was published. It is very largely a linguistic study. He advances four main arguments against Pauline authorship.

First, of 848 words which occur in the Pastorals as many as 306 are not to be found in the other ten letters attributed to Paul. Further, there is in the Pastorals a higher number (175) of hapaxes (*hapax legomena*, words occurring only once) than in any other Pauline letter. These linguistic peculiarities of the Pastorals create 'very serious doubts indeed' about common authorship.

Secondly, only 542 words occur in both the Pastorals and the other ten Pauline letters. This extraordinarily small common usage strongly suggests that the Pastorals were written by another hand.

Thirdly, the number of genuinely Pauline words which are absent from the Pastorals is 1,635, of which 580 are peculiar to Paul. This

---

[4] Acts 28:20.   [5] Rom. 15:24, 28.

omission of so much distinctively Pauline terminology 'constitutes a very serious objection indeed' to an acceptance of the Pauline authorship of the Pastorals.[6]

Fourthly, if instead of comparing the vocabulary of the Pastorals with that of the other ten Pauline letters, it is compared with that of the apostolic fathers and the apologists of the first half of the second century AD, the opposite result is obtained. Of the 175 hapaxes in the Pastorals, as many as 94 recur in the early church fathers. Thus, 'the author of the Pastorals does speak the language of the apostolic fathers and the apologists, while diverging from that of the other New Testament writers'.[7]

P. N. Harrison's main argument is linguistic, both in *The Problem of the Pastoral Epistles* (1921) and in his 'companion volume and supplement', *Paulines and Pastorals*, forty-three years later (1964). His painstaking statistical tables, when one recalls that he had no access to a computer, must be judged a *tour de force*. At the same time, he was a great deal too self-confident when he pronounced his conclusion 'rigorously proved scientific fact'.[8]

Harrison has had as many critics as converts. Dr Bruce Metzger took him to task in 1958 for ignoring the work of British, German and Swedish scholars who had questioned the validity of arguments which are based purely on statistical study of literary vocabulary, and which are applied to 'relatively brief treatises'.[9] Similarly, Professor C. F. D. Moule has written that 'there is no cogent reason for denying Pauline authorship to a letter merely because its vocabulary and style mark it as different from others which are firmly established as genuine'.[10] For there are several possible reasons for changes in Paul's language and style. Donald Guthrie summed these up as 'dissimilarity of subject matter', 'advancing age', 'change of environment' and 'difference in the recipients'.[11] Besides, as Harrison himself conceded, complete uniformity of vocabulary and style must not be expected in every author, 'least of all in one with a mind so versatile, pliable, original, fresh, impressionable and creative as the apostle'.[12] So saying, he seems to contradict his own thesis. As E. K. Simpson justly observed, 'great souls are not their own mimes'.[13]

There are two other possible explanations of the linguistic peculiarities of the Pastorals. The first is Paul's use of a secretary in his correspondence, to which I will return later. The second is the surprising degree to which, especially in 1 Timothy, Paul made use of 'pre-formed' material such as doxologies, credal confessions, and

---

[6] Harrison (1921), pp. 33–34.   [7] *Ibid.*, p. 70.   [8] *Ibid.*, p. 84.
[9] Metzger (1958), p. 94.   [10] Moule, p. 115.   [11] Guthrie (1990), p. 240.
[12] Harrison (1921), p. 45.   [13] Simpson, p. 15.

hymns, much of it introduced by tell-tale formulae like 'this is a trustworthy saying' or 'knowing this'. Dr Earle Ellis, who has drawn attention to this phenomenon, calculates that pre-formed material accounts for about 43% of 1 Timothy, 46% of Titus and 16% of 2 Timothy.[14]

c. Doctrine

Some scholars are quite rude in their evaluation of the theology (or lack of it) which they discern in the Pastorals. A. T. Hanson, for example, declares that 'there is a complete absence of unifying theme' in the Pastorals, even 'an impression of relative incoherence'. And the reason for this, he continues, is that the author of the Pastorals 'had no theology of his own. He is a purveyor of other men's theology.'[15] But this uncomplimentary judgment has been challenged by other scholars, including Dr Frances Young, who finds little difficulty in assembling the theological teaching of these three letters.

Some critics complain that they cannot find in the Pastorals either the trinitarian doctrine of the earlier letters, or the gospel of salvation. But without question the Pastorals set forth the gracious, redeeming initiative of 'God our Saviour', who gave his Son to die as our ransom, to redeem us from all evil, and to purify a special people for himself. He justifies us by his grace and renews us by his Spirit, in order that we may live a new life of good works. Dr Philip Towner has argued that salvation as a present reality is the 'centre point' of the message of the Pastorals;[16] and that the present age, which is the age of salvation, is illumined and inspired by the incarnation and the parousia, the Christ-events which inaugurate and terminate it.[17]

Very different is the assessment of Professor Ernst Käsemann who writes that he cannot regard as Pauline letters in which the church has become 'the central theme of theology', 'the gospel is domesticated', and Paul's image has become 'heavily daubed by church piety'.[18] One can only respond that this is an extremely subjective judgment. Paul's earliest letters already evidenced his high doctrine of church and ministry, and Luke tells us it was his policy to ordain elders in every church from the first missionary journey onwards.[19] His further instructions in the Pastorals about the selection and appointment of pastors, about the conduct of public worship in the local church, and about the maintenance of sound

---

[14] Ellis (1993), pp. 664–665.   [15] Hanson (1968), p. 110.
[16] Towner (1989), pp. 118–119.   [17] Towner (1986), pp. 427–428.
[18] *Jesus Means Freedom* (SCM, 1969), pp. 89, 97.   [19] Acts 14:23.

doctrine, are entirely compatible with this. It is simply not true that the church structures envisaged by Paul in the Pastorals are those of the second century, including the rise of the monarchical episcopate associated with Bishop Ignatius (c. AD 110). In the Pastorals there is no threefold order of bishops, presbyters and deacons, for bishops and presbyters are still the same person and office.

d. Ethics

It was Martin Dibelius who first applied the epithet 'bourgeois' to the Christian lifestyle envisaged in the Pastorals. And 'of course if bourgeois', Professor J. H. Houlden added, 'then certainly *petit* bourgeois'.[20] Robert Karris has also written about the 'middle-class ethic' of the Pastorals.[21] What these scholars are referring to is the atmosphere of respectability, of conformity to prevailing social values, which they feel permeates the ethical instruction of the Pastorals. And it is quite true that the author is concerned about the church's public image, and about its *eusebeia*, which sometimes means personal godliness but at other times seems to be a synonym for 'religion'.

On the other hand, there is great emphasis in the Pastorals, as in all Pauline letters, on the paramount Christian qualities of faith and love, and on the purity, the good works and the future hope to which they give rise. Commitment to Christ still has radical consequences; we are pilgrims travelling home to God, and summoned to live this life in the light of the next (*e.g.* 1 Tim. 4:8; 6:7f., 19).

Dr Towner, in his monograph *The Goal of Our Instruction*, subtitled *The Structure of Theology and Ethics of the Pastoral Epistles*, registers a salutary protest against those who interpret the Pastorals as giving evidence of a 'bourgeois Christianity', 'a Christianity which sought little more than to live comfortably in the world',[22] and a self-centred Christianity without mission. On the contrary, the 'Christian existence' for which Paul called is a combination of theology and ethics, which originates in the Christ-event and the salvation he achieved, and which directly counters the perversions of behaviour introduced by the false teachers. Instead, it lays down concrete duties for different groups, and is constantly motivated by the Christian mission.[23]

Having considered the language, doctrine and ethics of the Pastoral Letters, we should be able to agree with Dr J. N. D. Kelly that 'the

---

[20] Houlden, pp. 64–65.   [21] Karris (1979), p. 64.   [22] Towner (1989), p. 9.
[23] Another critique of Dibelius' use of the epithet 'bourgeois' is given by Kidd. He finds 'three layers of meaning' in Dibelius' understanding of 'bourgeois' Christianity,

anti-Pauline case has surely been greatly exaggerated'.[24] The differences of vocabulary do not necessarily demand a different author; there are other possible explanations. In regard to theology too, 'the critics seem to have overplayed their hand. Not only are the discrepancies fewer than they claim, but several of the more important are found on inspection to represent developments of ideas already present in the earlier correspondence.'[25]

There is still the possibility of pseudonymity, however, to which we now turn.

3. The case for and against a pseudonymous author

Everybody is agreed that in the Graeco-Roman world the practice of pseudonymity, that is, the false attribution of literary works to a great teacher of the past, was widespread. What is not so generally agreed is whether pseudonymous writing was always with a view to deception.

a. An attempted reconstruction

P. N. Harrison posited as the pseudonymous author of the Pastorals 'a devout, sincere and earnest Paulinist', who lived in Rome or Ephesus, and who wrote the Pastorals at the beginning of the reign of the Emperor Hadrian (AD 117). He knew and had studied every one of the ten Pauline letters, and in addition he had access to 'several brief personal notes' written by Paul to Timothy and Titus. 'He believed honestly and wholeheartedly the Pauline gospel as he understood it.'[26] Faced with the doctrinal and ethical challenges of false teaching, he and 'the best minds in the church' longed for 'a return of the old apostolic fervour and sanctity' and for 'a rekindling of the heroic courage' of Paul. They considered that the best way to promote this would be 'a letter written in the spirit, bearing the name, and recalling the very familiar words, of the great apostle'.[27] If this is correct, the Pastoral Letters are 'neither "genuine" (meaning the firsthand work of St. Paul), nor "spurious" (meaning the work of a forger), but "pseudonymous" (meaning the work of one who made no secret of the fact that he was writing under an assumed name)'.[28]

---

namely that it is (a) 'socially ascendant' (emerging from the poverty which characterized the first Christians), (b) 'culturally accommodative' (conforming to the prevailing culture, instead of criticizing it), and (c) 'unheroically conservative' (in contrast to the radical challenge of authentic Christian ethics). Dr Kidd makes a careful evaluation of these three elements in the course of assessing the socio-economic status of the churches supervised by Timothy and Titus.

[24] Kelly, p. 30.   [25] *Ibid.*, p. 31.   [26] Harrison, (1921), p. 9.   [27] *Ibid.*, p. 10.
[28] Harrison (1964), p. 14.

P. N. Harrison was also convinced that the very personal passages in the three Pastoral Letters were not fiction, composed by the pseudonymous author, but genuine Pauline fragments which the author, not knowing their original contexts, incorporated into his work. Harrison thought he detected five of these and suggested how they could all be fitted into the Acts narrative.

b. Pseudonymity in the ancient world

Dr Bruce Metzger has distinguished between 'a literary forgery' and 'a pseudepigraphon'. The former 'is essentially a piece of work created or modified with the intention to deceive'.[29] To which of these two categories would the Pastorals belong if they are pseudonymous? Scholars tend to insist that 'forgery' is an inappropriate word to use. Like P. N. Harrison they hold that the pseudonymous author of the Pastorals 'was not consciously deceiving anybody; it is not indeed necessary to suppose that he did deceive anybody'.[30] In this way Christian scholars defend the concept of pseudepigraphy on the ground that it was an accepted literary genre and a wholly innocent practice. Professor C. F. D. Moule writes of 'what may be called well-intentioned pseudonymity. With no intention to deceive', according to those who hold this view, 'the pseudonymist writes in the name of the apostle, genuinely believing that he is conveying a message that would have been acceptable to the master . . .'[31] But he goes on to write of the insoluble problem of reconciling this concept of 'honest' pseudonymity with the fabrication of the personal Pauline references in the Pastorals.

Dr Metzger too has serious qualms about pseudepigraphy. He asks three searching questions. Ethically, 'is a pseudepigraphon compatible with honesty and candour, whether by ancient or modern moral standards?' Psychologically, 'how should one estimate an author who impersonates an ancient worthy . . . ?' Theologically, 'should a work that involves a fraud, whether pious or not, be regarded as incompatible with the character of a message from God?'[32]

It is difficult to maintain the notion of pseudonymity as an accepted and innocent literary procedure.

c. Contemporary Christian responses

First, although it has become a commonplace ever since Baur for defenders of pseudonymity to maintain that it was an acceptable

---

[29] Metzger (1972), p. 4.   [30] *Ibid.*, p. 15.   [31] Moule, p. 116.
[32] Metzger (1972), p. 4.

practice, and that there was no intention to deceive, they yet offer 'no historical evidence for their assertions that New Testament pseudepigrapha were recognised as such and were regarded as innocent compositions . . .'[33] On the contrary, as Dr L R. Donelson concedes, 'we are forced to admit that in Christian circles pseudonymity was considered a dishonourable device'.[34] A pseudonymous work was either believed and therefore esteemed, or exposed and therefore condemned. There seems to be no evidence that some pseudonymous works were both exposed and esteemed. Several commentators quote the judgment of Serapion, the early third-century bishop of Antioch. Concluding that the *Gospel of Peter* was not genuine, he stated this principle: 'We, brothers, receive both Peter and the other apostles as Christ. But pseudepigrapha in their name we reject . . .'

Secondly, the claim that a pseudepigrapher did not intend to deceive, and indeed did not deceive, appears to be self-defeating. If nobody was deceived, what was the point of the subterfuge?

Thirdly, in spite of confident assurances about the innocence of pseudepigraphy, many of us find that our consciences are not so readily pacified. We remember that Scripture lays constant emphasis on the sacredness of truth and the sinfulness of false witness. We are not comfortable with the notions of a deceit which does not deceive and a pseudepigraphon which is not a forgery. 'The dictionary definition of "forgery" is fraudulent imitation,' writes Dr J. I. Packer, whatever people's aims and incentives may be. 'Frauds are still fraudulent, even when perpetrated from noble motives.'[35]

4. The case for an active amanuensis

A number of scholars refer to a work by Otto Roller whose short title is *Das Formular* (1933). It investigates Paul's letters in the light of letter-writing practices in antiquity, especially his use of an amanuensis. I rely on Professor Moule's summary.[36] Roller's conclusion was that verbatim dictation would have been too laborious for most authors, and extremely inhibiting to 'a torrential thinker like Paul'. It is more probable, therefore, first that the apostle would write part of each letter in his own hand (as at the end of Galatians), secondly that elsewhere he would tell his amanuensis what he wanted to say, letting him frame it in his own words, and thirdly that

---

[33] Ellis (1992), p. 217.
[34] Donelson, p. 16. See also J. S. Candlish, 'On the Moral Character of Pseudonymous Books', *The Expositor* 4 (1891), p. 103.
[35] *'Fundamentalism' and the Word of God* (IVF, 1958), pp. 183–184.
[36] Moule, pp. 129–131.

the apostle would read the end-product, amend it as necessary, and sign it personally. Professor Moule proposes this as a solution to the linguistic problem of the Pastorals, in that Paul would have allowed his secretary to fluctuate between free composition and a near-verbatim reproduction of Paul's own phraseology.

This general thesis has been considerably elaborated by Dr E. Randolph Richards in his work *The Secretary in the Letters of Paul* (1991). From a thorough study of letter-writing practices in Graeco-Roman antiquity, and especially of the letters of Cicero, he demonstrates that the writer 'could grant to the secretary complete, much, little or no control over the content, style and/or form of the letter'.[37] He then reduces this spectrum into a fourfold classification. The secretary might serve as 'recorder' (taking down the author's dictation verbatim), 'editor' (working from his instructions, or from an oral or written draft supplied by him), 'co-author' (co-operating with him fully in content, style and vocabulary), or 'composer' (having the whole task delegated by him). The first procedure Dr Richards calls 'author-controlled', the fourth 'secretary-controlled' and the middle two 'secretary-assisted'.[38]

For our purposes the first is eliminated, since verbatim dictation would leave no room for changes in vocabulary. So is the last, since a free composition would destroy Pauline authorship altogether, whereas we are asking whether the secretary hypothesis could explain the phenomenon of Pauline and non-Pauline words alongside one another. The reality is likely to be found in the middle two 'secretary-assisted' processes. The difference between them is only one of degree,[39] yet the second ('editor') seems to me to take precedence over the third ('co-author') for a reason we must now consider.

It has often been observed that in most of Paul's letters he associates a colleague with him in its writing, *e.g.* Sosthenes,[40] Timothy,[41] and Silas and Timothy.[42] Although Paul calls his missionary associates 'co-labourers', it would be misleading to call them 'co-authors'. For Paul was careful to affirm his own apostolic authority as the author, and to distinguish his colleagues from him (since they were not apostles) by referring to them as 'our brother Sosthenes' or 'Timothy our brother'. The Thessalonian letters are significant in this respect. Although they both begin with 'Paul, Silas and Timothy', and although the first person plural 'we' is used much of the time, it is nevertheless plain that the leadership role and

[37] Richards, p. 23.   [38] *Ibid.*, pp. 23–53.   [39] *Ibid.*, p. 200.
[40] 1 Cor. 1:1.   [41] 2 Cor. 1:1; Phil. 1:1; Col. 1:1.
[42] 1 Thes. 1:1; 2 Thes. 1:1. Otto Roller suggested that amanuenses were deliberately identified by and in the greetings. See Longenecker, pp. 107–109.

apostolic authority were Paul's. So he frequently lapses from 'we' to 'I'.[43] The end of the second letter puts the matter beyond doubt: 'I, Paul, write this greeting in my own hand, which is the distinguishing mark in all my letters. This is how I write.'[44] So the letter was essentially *his* letter, written with *his* apostolic authority. Paul, Silas and Timothy were not joint authors, although there is no reason to deny that Paul may have involved them in the writing process, by encouraging them to contribute their thoughts to it.

An amanuensis, however, was different. Not only did he undertake the actual mechanics of the writing, but Paul may have given him some liberty in clothing the apostle's thought with words. It is possible that this was the arrangement when Tertius wrote down the letter to the Romans.[45] But the only specific New Testament reference to this practice is the apostle Peter's statement that he had written his first letter 'with the help of Silas',[46] literally 'through Silas', whom he regarded, he adds, as 'a faithful brother'.

However much or little an amanuensis would contribute to the letter, we may assume that the apostle read it when it was complete, amended what needed to be changed, and endorsed its final form by his personal signature, so that the letter was decidedly his and not somebody else's. Each author-amanuensis duo would develop differently, and presumably the more 'faithful' the brother was perceived to be, the more responsible his contribution would become. A. T. Hanson was a bit cynical to write about the Pastorals that 'the more you attribute to the secretary, the less Pauline they are'.[47] But the principle is clear: we expect that the amanuensis contributed enough to explain the variations in style and language, but not enough to take over from Paul either the authorship or the authority of the letters.

So who was the amanuensis in the writing of the Pastorals?

P. N. Harrison asked himself in 1921 whether Paul's amanuensis on this occasion might have been Luke, since nobody else was with him.[48] But he raised the possibility only to dismiss it. So Professor C. F. D. Moule, who had already in his book *The Birth of the New Testament* (1962) asked himself if there might have been some Lucan involvement in the writing of the Pastorals, developed in a 1964 lecture a theory of Luke's 'free composition' of the Pastorals. He suggested 'that Luke wrote all three Pastoral epistles . . . during Paul's lifetime, at Paul's behest, and, in part (but only in part) at

---

[43] *E.g.* 1 Thes. 2:18; 3:1, 5; 5:27 ('I charge you . . .'); 2 Thes. 2:5.
[44] 2 Thes. 3:17; *cf.* 1 Cor. 16:21; Gal. 6:11; Col. 4:18; Phm. 19. This apostolic authentication of his letters was necessary because of the circulation of forgeries (2 Thes. 2:2).
[45] Rom. 16:22.   [46] 1 Pet. 5:12.   [47] Hanson (1982), p. 9.   [48] 2 Tim. 4:11.

Paul's dictation'.[49] He then went on to list some very interesting parallels between Luke-Acts and the Pastorals[50] – 'significant words' (e.g. soundness, godliness and honour), 'significant phrases' (e.g. love of money, true and false riches, Christ the judge of the living and the dead, and the athlete finishing the race), and 'significant ideas' (e.g. the 'triple phrase of majesty', angels being mentioned with God and Christ, and a retributive notion of justice). Perhaps then Luke could be called the 'framer' of the Pastorals.[51] Pseudepigraphs were normally composed after the death of the person named, whereas Luke wrote (according to this theory) in Paul's lifetime and at his behest.

Other scholars have taken up and developed Professor Moule's suggestion that Luke was Paul's amanuensis in drafting the Pastorals. Particular mention should be made of Dr Stephen Wilson's book *Luke and the Pastoral Epistles* (1979). He builds on Professor Moule's theory, although he thinks that the Luke who wrote the Acts and later the Pastorals was not Paul's companion of the same name. He draws attention to similarities of language and style between Luke-Acts and the Pastorals, and to a number of theological parallels (though with differences of emphasis), e.g. eschatology, salvation, Christian citizenship, church and ministry, Christology, law and Scripture. His over-confident conclusion is that 'certainly, given a choice between Paul and Luke as the author of the Pastorals, Luke is a far more likely candidate'.[52] His tentative hypothesis is that Luke wrote the Pastorals a few years after Acts, making use of Paul's 'travel notes' which he had found. In this way the Pastorals were volume 3 of a trilogy, following the publication of Luke's Gospel and Acts. The alternative would be 'common authorship' with Luke writing under Paul's direction, as Professor Moule had proposed.

Conclusion

Our investigation leads us to a fourfold conclusion.

(1) The case for the Pauline authorship of the Pastorals still stands. Both the internal claims and the external witness are strong, substantial and stubborn. The burden of proof rests on those who deny them.

(2) The case against the Pauline authorship is far from watertight. The arguments adduced – historical, linguistic, theological and ethical – can all be answered. They are not sufficient to overthrow the case for the Pauline authorship.

(3) The case for pseudonymous authorship is unsatisfying. The

---

[49] Moule (1964), p. 117.   [50] *Ibid.*, pp. 123–126.   [51] *Ibid.*, p. 127.
[52] *Ibid.*, p. 136.

belief that well-intentioned, even transparently innocent, pseudepigraphy was acceptable lacks evidence. It also raises serious moral questions about the practice of deliberate deceit.

(4) The case for Paul's constructive use of an amanuensis (whether Luke or Tychicus or somebody else) is reasonable, and may well account for some variations in style and vocabulary. At the same time, the amanuensis must not be allowed to oust the author, nor the author be robbed of his leadership role and apostolic authority.

The most likely scenario is that Paul the apostle wrote the three Pastorals, towards the end of his life, addressing contemporary issues, and communicating through a trusted amanuensis.

A. The Message of 1 Timothy
The life of the local church

1 Timothy 1:1–2
Introduction

Paul, an apostle of Christ Jesus by the command of God our Saviour and of Christ Jesus our hope,

²To Timothy my true son in the faith:

Grace, mercy and peace from God the Father and Christ Jesus our Lord.

Most readers find Timothy a very congenial character. We feel that he is one of us in all our frailty. He was very far from being a stained-glass saint. A halo would not have fitted comfortably on his head. No, the evidence is plain that he was a real human being like us, with all the infirmity and vulnerability which that entails.

To begin with, he was still comparatively young when Paul addressed this letter to him, for he told him not to let anyone look down on him on account of his youth (4:12), and some two years later he urged him to 'flee the evil desires of youth' (2 Tim. 2:22). So how old was he? It seems unlikely that the apostle would have invited Timothy to join his mission team before he had reached his late teens or early twenties,[1] in which case now, about thirteen or fourteen years later, he would be in his mid-thirties. The ancients regarded this as being still within the limits of 'youth' (*neotēs*). According to Irenaeus, 'thirty is the first stage of a young man's age, and extends to forty, as all will admit'.[2] Nevertheless, Timothy evidently felt inexperienced and immature for the heavy responsibility which Paul was laying upon him.

Secondly, he was temperamentally shy, needing affirmation,

---

[1] Acts 16:1ff. Those who would like to get to know Timothy as a person would do well to read Lance Pierson's *In the Steps of Timothy* (IVP, 1995). Claiming to be the first biography of Timothy to be written for nearly 1,000 years, and firmly based on the biblical data, it also uses inference, surmise and 'reasonable speculation' to reconstruct Timothy's life and ministry.

[2] Irenaeus, II.22.5.

encouragement and reassurance. So a few years previously Paul had urged the Corinthians to 'put him at his ease' when he came to them.[3] And in his second letter to Timothy he felt the need to exhort him not to be ashamed of Christ, since God had not given us 'a spirit of timidity' (1:7f.). It is not unfair, therefore, to think of him as 'timid Timothy'.

Thirdly, Timothy was physically infirm, and suffered from a recurrent gastric problem. For Paul referred to his habitual ailments, in particular to his stomach. He even prescribed a little medicinal alcohol: 'Stop drinking only water, and use a little wine because of your stomach and your frequent illnesses' (5:23).

So this is the profile of Timothy which we can construct from a number of Paul's references to him. He was young, diffident and frail. These three handicaps might have been thought to disqualify him from taking charge of the churches in and around Ephesus. But they endear him to us, and the grace of God was sufficient for his need: 'You then, my son, be strong in the grace that is in Christ Jesus' (2 Tim. 2:1).

Paul was expecting to visit Timothy in Ephesus soon, and would then of course, as an apostle, assume responsibility for the churches. But he seems to have anticipated the possibility of being delayed, and so sends Timothy these written instructions, so that during his absence Timothy would know how to regulate the life of the churches (3:14f.; 4:13). This letter, therefore, although addressed to Timothy personally, is not a private communication. It is written to him in his official capacity, and throughout it Paul is looking beyond Timothy to the churches. One clear hint of this is that his final greeting is couched in the plural: 'Grace be with you' (*meth' hymōn*, 6:21). Augustine in the fourth century and Thomas Aquinas in the thirteenth both used the adjective 'pastoral' in relation to one or other of these letters, although not until 1703 did D. N. Berdot refer to the three of them as 'the Pastoral Epistles'.

It is an appropriate expression, since the letters are concerned with the pastoral care and oversight of local churches. The apostle addresses six main topics. The first is the church's *doctrine* and how to preserve it intact, uncorrupted by false teaching (1:3–20). The second is the church's *public worship*, its global intercession for all humankind, together with the roles of men and women in the conduct of it (2:1–15). Thirdly, the apostle writes about the church's *pastorate*, and in particular the conditions of eligibility for presbyters and deacons (3:1–16). Fourthly, after outlining the church's moral instruction, which arises naturally from the doctrine of creation and calls for personal godliness (4:1–10), Paul addresses himself to the

[3] 1 Cor. 16:10, REB.

church's *local leadership*, specially how younger leaders can ensure that their teaching is listened to and not despised (4:11 – 5:2). Fifthly, the apostle handles the church's *social responsibilities*, not only to widows, but also to elders and to slaves (5:3 – 6:2). His sixth and final concern, in reaction to those who think 'that godliness is a means to financial gain', is the church's attitude to *material possessions* (6:3–21); he addresses both the covetous and the wealthy.

Here is wisdom for the local church in every generation and every place. Let no-one say that Scripture is out of date. Calvin, when dedicating his commentary to the Duke of Somerset in 1556, called this letter 'highly relevant to our own times'.[4] More than 400 years later we can make the same claim. Truly 'the Bible speaks today'.

The beginning of the letter is conventional. Paul announces himself as the author, Timothy as his correspondent, and God as the source of the grace, mercy and peace which he wishes him to enjoy. He thus describes the letter's three *dramatis personae*. He is not content, however, with a bare greeting like 'Paul to Timothy: grace'; each of the three persons involved is elaborated.

In nine out of his thirteen New Testament letters Paul designates himself *an apostle of Christ Jesus*, and usually adds a reference to the call, commission, command or will of God. Here it is *by the command of God our Saviour and of Christ Jesus our hope* (1). Thus Paul claims to be an apostle of Christ on a level with the Twelve, whom Jesus had named 'apostles',[5] with all the teaching authority which this represented. He had emphatically not appointed himself. Nor had he been appointed by the church. He was not one of the 'apostles of the churches',[6] whom today we might call 'missionaries'. On the contrary, he was an apostle of Christ, chosen, called, appointed, equipped and authorized directly by Christ, without any ecclesiastical mediation. To put the matter beyond dispute or misunderstanding, Paul adds that God the Father was involved with Christ Jesus in commissioning him; it was by their command that he was an apostle. This formula *by the command of (kat' epitagēn)* was apparently used on official notices, meaning 'by order of',[7] and Lock says it 'suggests a royal command which must be obeyed'.[8]

Further, Paul locates his apostleship in a historical context, whose beginning was the saving activity of *God our Saviour* in the birth, death and resurrection of Jesus, and whose culmination will be *Christ Jesus our hope*, his personal and glorious coming, which is the object of our Christian hope, and which will bring down the curtain on the historical process. Paul may even imply that the interval

---

[4] Calvin, p. 182.   [5] Lk. 6:13.   [6] *E.g.* 2 Cor. 8:23; Phil. 2:25.
[7] Simpson, p. 24.   [8] Lock, p. 5.

between these two termini will be filled with the spread of the apostolic gospel throughout the world.

Paul now designates *Timothy* as *my true son in the faith*. For if Paul is an authentic apostle of Christ, Timothy is an authentic son of Paul. *Gnēsios* ('true' or 'genuine') was used literally of children 'born in wedlock, legitimate' (BAGD). It is possible, therefore, that Paul is hinting at the circumstances of Timothy's physical birth. Since his father was a Greek, Jewish law will have regarded him as illegitimate. Spiritually, however, Timothy is Paul's genuine child, partly because he was responsible for his conversion and partly because Timothy has faithfully followed his teaching and example.[9] By affirming Timothy's genuineness Paul aims to reinforce his authority in the church.

After describing himself and Timothy, Paul refers to the God who binds them together in his family. What unites them is their common share in *grace, mercy and peace*. Each word tells us something about the human condition. For 'grace' is God's kindness to the guilty and undeserving, 'mercy' his pity on the wretched who cannot save themselves, and 'peace' his reconciliation of those who were previously alienated from him and from one another. All three issue from the same spring, namely *God the Father and Christ Jesus our Lord* (2b). Thus Father and Son are now bracketed as the single source of divine blessing, as they were in verse 1 as the single author of the divine command which constituted Paul an apostle.

---

[9] *Cf.* 1 Cor. 4:17; Phil. 2:22; 2 Tim. 3:10ff.

1 Timothy 1:3–20
1. Apostolic doctrine

As I urged you when I went into Macedonia, stay there in Ephesus so that you may command certain men not to teach false doctrines any longer ⁴nor to devote themselves to myths and endless genealogies. These promote controversies rather than God's work – which is by faith. ⁵The goal of this command is love, which comes from a pure heart and a good conscience and a sincere faith. ⁶Some have wandered away from these and turned to meaningless talk. ⁷They want to be teachers of the law, but they do not know what they are talking about or what they so confidently affirm.

⁸We know that the law is good if one uses it properly. ⁹We also know that law is made not for the righteous but for law-breakers and rebels, the ungodly and sinful, the unholy and irreligious; for those who kill their fathers or mothers, for murderers, ¹⁰for adulterers and perverts, for slave traders and liars and perjurers – and for whatever else is contrary to the sound doctrine ¹¹that conforms to the glorious gospel of the blessed God, which he entrusted to me.

This opening section sets the historical and geographical scene for the letter. It speaks of a visit by Paul to Macedonia and of a stay by Timothy in Ephesus. Since these events cannot be fitted into Luke's narrative in Acts, commentators have assumed from the earliest days of the church that Paul was released after those two years under house arrest in Rome, in which Luke takes leave of him,[1] and that he resumed his travels. *I went into Macedonia,* he writes, and at the same time *I urged you* to *stay there in Ephesus* (3a). We cannot say for certain whether Paul was himself in Ephesus when he exhorted Timothy to stay there. What is clear is that, however and whenever Paul issued his original spoken appeal to Timothy, he is now confirming it in writing. The reason for this arrangement was in general that Timothy might regulate the affairs of the churches of

---

[1] Acts 28:30–31.

Ephesus, and in particular that he might *command certain men not to teach false doctrines any longer* . . . (3b).

Paul's preoccupation in this first chapter is with the importance of maintaining true or 'sound' doctrine, and of refuting 'false' doctrine. This differentiation strikes a discordant note at the end of the twentieth century. It is not only that most societies are increasingly pluralistic in fact (an ethnic and religious mix), but that 'pluralism' as an ideology is increasingly advocated as 'politically correct'. This affirms the independent validity of every religion as a culturally conditioned phenomenon, and frowns on any attempt to convert people. Indeed, one of the chief tenets of 'postmodernism' is that there is no such thing as objective truth, let alone universal and eternal truth. On the contrary, everybody has his or her own truth. You have yours, and I have mine, and they may diverge widely from each other, even contradict each other. In consequence, the most prized virtue is tolerance. It tolerates everything except the intolerance of those who insist that certain ideas are true and others false, while certain practices are good and others evil.

No follower of Jesus Christ can possibly embrace this complete subjectivism. For he said he was the truth, that he had come to bear witness to the truth, that the Holy Spirit is the Spirit of truth, and that the truth will set us free.[2] So truth matters, the truth which God has revealed through Christ and by the Spirit. Jesus also told us to beware of false teachers. So did his apostles.

Indeed, Paul urges Timothy to stay in Ephesus precisely in order to stop the spread of false teaching. He calls these teachers' activity *heterodidaskaleō* (a verb he may well have coined), teaching doctrine which is *heteros*, which means not primarily that it is 'false' (NIV) or 'strange' (JB) or 'erroneous' (REB) or 'new' (JBP), but that it is 'different' (NRSV) from the teaching of the apostles. Similarly, Paul complained that the Galatians had deserted the grace of Christ for 'a different gospel'[3] and that the Corinthians were being led astray to a 'different Jesus', 'a different Spirit' and 'a different gospel' from those they had first received.[4]

The verb *heterodidaskaleō*, which Paul uses both in 1:3 and in 6:3, clearly indicates that there is a norm of doctrine from which the false teachers had deviated. It is variously designated in the Pastorals. It is called 'the faith',[5] 'the truth',[6] 'the sound doctrine',[7] 'the teaching'[8] and 'the good deposit'.[9] In nearly every one of these expressions the

---

[2] Jn. 14:6; 18:37; 16:13; 8:32.   [3] Gal. 1:6.   [4] 2 Cor. 11:1ff.
[5] 1 Tim. 1:3, 19; 3:9; 4:1, 6, 21; 2 Tim. 3:8; 4:7; 6:10, 12, 21; Tit. 3:15.
[6] 1 Tim. 2:4, 7; 3:15; 4:3; 6:3, 5; 2 Tim. 2:18, 25; 3:7–8; 4:4; Tit. 1:1, 14.
[7] 1 Tim. 1:10; 6:3; 2 Tim. 1:13; 4:3; Tit. 1:9; 2:1.   [8] Tit. 1:9; 1 Tim. 6:1.
[9] 1 Tim. 6:20; 2 Tim. 1:4 (literally).

noun is preceded by the definite article, indicating that already a body of doctrine existed which was an agreed standard by which all teaching could be tested and judged. It was the teaching of Christ[10] and of his apostles.[11]

What Paul does in this first chapter is to refer successively to three teachers or groups of teachers. First, he describes the false teachers and their misguided use of the law (3–11). Secondly, he alludes to himself, previously a persecutor of Christ but now an apostle of Christ, and to the gospel he preached (12–17). Thirdly, he addresses Timothy and urges him to fight the good fight of the truth (18–20). Moreover, the whole passage is extremely personal. Paul begins each paragraph with a verb in the first person singular: 'I urged you . . .' (3), 'I thank Christ Jesus our Lord' (12), and 'I give you this instruction' (18).

1. The false teachers and the law (1:3–11)

Paul's prediction some five years previously that 'savage wolves' would enter and devastate Christ's flock in Ephesus[12] had come true. But who were they? And what were they teaching?

Paul writes that they *want to be teachers of the law* (7). Thus the *heterodidaskaloi* (false teachers) are now identified as *nomodidaskaloi* (law-teachers). This latter word can denote a perfectly legitimate ·activity, however. Luke uses it of the scribes who taught the Mosaic law[13] and even of the illustrious Gamaliel.[14] So what is wrong with teaching the law? There is actually a great need in our day for Christian teachers of the moral law (the Ten Commandments as expounded by Jesus in the Sermon on the Mount), for it is through the teaching of the law that we both come to a consciousness of our sin and learn the implications of loving our neighbour.[15] Indeed, *we know that the law is good if one uses it properly* (8).[16] Evidently, then, there is both a right and a wrong, a legitimate and an illegitimate, use of the law. First, we ask what were the false teachers doing with the law which was wrong?

a. The wrong use of the law

Timothy is to command the false teachers not to *devote themselves to myths and endless genealogies* (4). *Mythoi* meant legends or fables, which Paul later categorized as 'godless myths and old wives' tales' (4:7), as 'Jewish myths',[17] and as an alternative to 'the truth'.[18] The

---

[10] 1 Tim. 6:3.   [11] 1 Tim. 1:11; 2:7; 2 Tim. 1:13; 2:2; 3:10, 14.
[12] Acts 20:29ff.   [13] Lk. 5:17.   [14] Acts 5:34.   [15] Rom. 3:20; 13:8ff.
[16] *Cf.* Rom. 7:12, 16.   [17] Tit. 1:14.   [18] 2 Tim. 4:4.

word *genealogies*, on the other hand, most naturally refers to those in Genesis, which trace the descent and so the pedigree of the patriarchs. Lock may well be right to urge that these two words 'be taken closely together, *muthoi* being defined by *genealogiai*, legendary stories about genealogies', which were handed down in the Haggada or rabbinical tradition.[19]

Two ancient Jewish documents may throw light on what Paul is referring to. The first is *The Book of Jubilees*,[20] which is dated between 135 and 105 BC, and which retells from a Pharisaic perspective the Old Testament story from the creation of the world to the giving of the law at Mt. Sinai. It divides this history into 'jubilees' (periods of forty-nine years) and asserts the uniqueness of Israel among the nations. The second book is *The Biblical Antiquities of Philo*,[21] although M. R. James calls its attribution to Philo 'wholly unfounded and quite ridiculous'.[22] Dating from soon after the destruction of Jerusalem in AD 70, it retells even more of the Old Testament story, from the creation of Adam to the death of Saul. Its chief objective is to maintain the eternal validity of the law against the encroachments of Hellenism.

So both books are tendentious rewrites of a section of Old Testament history. Both stress the indestructibility of Israel and of the law. And both embellish their story with fanciful additions. The author of *The Biblical Antiquities* supplements the biblical narrative 'by means of his fabulous genealogies',[23] which occupy chapters 1, 2, 4 and 8. Similarly *The Book of Jubilees* supplies us with the names of all the children of Adam and Eve, of Enoch's family, of Noah's predecessors and descendants, and of the seventy people who went down into Egypt.

It may be, then, that it is to this kind of fanciful literature that Paul is referring when he writes of law, myths and genealogies. It certainly seems that the false teaching was primarily a Jewish aberration, which is confirmed by the naming of 'the circumcision group'.[24] At the same time, the law-teachers were not the 'Judaizers' whom Paul had opposed in Galatians, and who taught salvation by law-obedience, for there is no hint in the Pastorals of a recurrence of this controversy. They may have been allegorizers. They were certainly speculators. They treated the law (that is, the Old Testament) as a happy hunting-ground for their conjectures. To Paul their whole approach was frivolous; God had given his law

---

[19] Lock, p. 8.
[20] *The Book of Jubilees* or *The Little Genesis*, translated, edited and introduced by R. H. Charles (A. and C. Black, 1902).
[21] Translated, edited and introduced by M. R. James (SPCK, 1917).
[22] *Ibid.*, p. 7.   [23] *Ibid.*, pp. 33–34.   [24] Tit. 1:10.

to his people for a much more serious purpose.

At the same time, the false teachers showed Gnostic as well as Jewish tendencies. For example, they were forbidding marriage and enjoining abstinence from certain foods (4:3f.). This indicated a false asceticism which was incompatible with the doctrine of creation and symptomatic of the Gnostic rejection of matter as evil. Some of the early church fathers, especially Irenaeus and Tertullian, followed up this clue. Both claimed that Paul was referring in 1 Timothy 1 to the full-blown Gnosticism of their day at the end of the second century, and both mentioned by name the learned Gnostic leader from Egypt, Valentinus. 'When he [sc. Paul] mentions endless genealogies, we recognise Valentinus,' writes Tertullian.[25] Both also gave a brief account of the Gnostic system: that matter is evil; that the supreme God could therefore not have been the Creator; that the gulf between him and the world was spanned by a succession of intermediaries called 'aeons'; that one of them was far enough removed from God to create the material world; and that these constituted 'the fabulous genealogy of thirty aeons'.[26]

There are two main problems with this reconstruction. The first is that Paul was not predicting the future phenomenon of developed second-century Gnosticism, but was describing a reality with which Timothy had to deal in his own day, in which Gnosticism had only begun to develop. Secondly, there is no evidence that the Gnostics ever referred to the aeons as 'genealogies', as Irenaeus and Tertullian do. All we can say in conclusion is that Paul's references suggest a false teaching which combined Jewish and Gnostic elements, either 'a Gnosticizing Judaism' or 'Judaizing forms of Gnosticism'.[27]

Paul now indicates two consequences of the false teaching, which are enough in themselves to condemn it. It obstructs both faith and love. Myths and genealogies *promote controversies* (4), he writes. The word is *ekzētesis* which can mean either 'controversy' (NIV)[28] or 'useless speculation' (BAGD). In fact, it seems to combine both notions.

On the one hand, false teaching promotes 'speculation' *rather than God's work - which is by faith* (4b). 'Work' translates *oikonomia*, which can be rendered either 'stewardship' or 'plan' (REB). The reference seems to be to God's revealed plan of salvation, of which we are stewards, and to which we must respond by faith. For speculation raises doubts, while revelation evokes faith.

On the other hand, false teaching promotes 'controversies',

[25] Tertullian's *Prescriptions against Heretics* 33, translated by H. Bindley, in W. J. Sparrow Simpson and W. K. Lowther Clarke (eds.), *Early Church Classics* 1 (SPCK, 1914); cf. Irenaeus.
[26] Tertullian, *op. cit.*   [27] Dibelius and Conzelmann, p. 17.   [28] Cf. Tit. 1:9.

'arguments and quarrels about the law',[29] whereas *the goal of this command*, or perhaps 'the end of all Christian moral preaching',[30] *is love, which comes from a pure heart and a good conscience and a sincere faith* (5). Such love, issuing from the inner springs of our heart, conscience and faith, is uncontaminated by false or even mixed motives. *Some have wandered away from these* (the pure heart, clear conscience and genuine faith) *and turned to meaningless talk*. Both verbs mean either to 'swerve' (*astocheō*) or to 'turn aside' (*ektrepō*) and indicate the importance of maintaining a straight course.

Thus Paul paints a double contrast, between speculation and faith in God's revelation, and between controversy and love for one another. Here are two practical tests for us to apply to all teaching. The first is the test of faith: does it come from God, being in agreement with apostolic doctrine (so that it may be received by faith), or is it the product of fertile human imagination? The second is the test of love: does it promote unity in the body of Christ, or if not (since truth itself can divide), is it irresponsibly divisive? 'Faith' means that we receive it from God; 'love' means that it builds up the church. 'He judges doctrine by its fruit.'[31] The ultimate criteria by which to judge any teaching are whether it promotes the glory of God and the good of the church. The doctrine of the false teachers did neither. It promoted speculation and controversy instead.

b. The right use of the law

We turn now from the wrong use of the law to its right use. The false teachers, who *want to be teachers of the law . . . do not know what they are talking about or what they so confidently affirm* (7, 'about which they are so dogmatic', REB). In contrast to their ignorance, however, Paul sets his knowledge. *We know that the law is good if one uses it properly* (8, *nominōs*, 'lawfully'). *We also know that law is made . . . for lawbreakers* (9, *anomois*, 'for the lawless'). Putting together these two truths which, Paul says, *we know*, we reach the striking statement that the lawful use of the law is for the lawless. All law is designed for those whose natural tendency is not to keep it but to break it. 'Not the saint but the sinner is the law's target.'[32]

It may be helpful to approach this question historically, for the Reformers struggled much over the true purpose of the law. Luther expressed his position in his *Lectures on Galatians* (1535). 'The law was given for two uses,' he wrote. The first was 'political' or 'civil'; the law was a bridle 'for the restraint of the uncivilised'.[33] The second

---

[29] Tit. 3:9.   [30] Lock, p. 10.   [31] Calvin, p. 190.   [32] Simpson, p. 31.
[33] *Luther's Works* 26, ed. Jaroslav Pelikan (Concordia, 1963), pp. 274–275, *cf.* pp. 308–310.

and 'principal' purpose of the law was 'theological' or 'spiritual'. It is a mighty 'hammer' to crush the self-righteousness of human beings.[34] For 'it shows them their sin, so that by the recognition of sin they may be humbled, frightened, and worn down, and so may long for grace and for the Blessed Offspring [sc. Christ]'.[35] It is in this sense that 'the law was our schoolmaster to bring us to Christ'.[36] Elsewhere Luther indicates that the law has a third use; we have 'to teach the law diligently and to impress it on the people', although he does not emphasize this.[37]

The Formula of Concord (1577), however, which settled Lutheran doctrine in disputed areas after Luther's death, clearly specified in its sixth article a threefold use of the law. It is a means to the preservation of human society,[38] a summons to repentance and faith[39] and a direction for the church.[40] These came to be called the *usus politicus* (to restrain evil), the *usus pedagogus* (to lead to Christ) and the *usus normativus* (to determine the conduct of believers).

Calvin agreed with these three functions of the law, but changed the order of the first two, and laid his emphasis on the third. Book II, chapter 7, of the *Institutes* is devoted to a consideration of why the law was given. First, it has a 'punitive' purpose, for it 'renders us inexcusable' and so drives us to despair. Then, 'naked and empty-handed', we 'flee to his [sc. God's] mercy, repose entirely in it, hide deep within it, and seize upon it alone for righteousness and merit'.[41]

Secondly, the law restrains evildoers, especially 'by fright and shame', from daring to do what they want to do, and so protects the community. In this sense the law acts as an external deterrent, while leaving the heart unchanged.[42]

'The third and principal use' of the law, indeed its 'proper purpose', according to Calvin, is the one which Luther somewhat neglected, namely 'its place among believers in whose hearts the Spirit of God already lives and reigns'. The law is 'the best instrument' both to teach us the Lord's will and to exhort us to do it. For 'by frequent meditation upon it' believers will 'be aroused to obedience, be strengthened in it, and be drawn back from the slippery path of transgression'.[43] Indeed it is in this 'joyous obedience' that authentic 'Christian freedom' is to be found.[44]

Thus the law's three functions according to Calvin are punitive (to

---

[34] *Ibid.*, pp. 309–316.   [35] *Ibid.*, p. 327.   [36] Gal. 3:24, AV.
[37] *Lectures on Genesis, Luther's Works* 3, ed. Jaroslav Pelikan (Concordia, 1961), p. 85.
[38] Rom. 13:1ff.   [39] Gal. 3:24.   [40] Rom. 8:4; 13:8.
[41] J. Calvin, *Institutes of the Christian Religion*, translated by F. L. Battles (Collins, 1986), II.7.1–9.
[42] *Ibid.*, II.7.10–11.   [43] *Ibid.*, II.7.12.   [44] *Ibid.*, II.19.1–5.

condemn sinners and drive them to Christ), deterrent (to restrain evildoers) and specially educative (to teach and exhort believers).

To which of these three purposes was Paul referring in his first letter to Timothy? Of which of them could it be said that 'the lawful use of the law is for the lawless'? Certainly the second, relating to the restraint of evildoers. Calvin wrote: 'The apostle seems specially to have alluded to this function of the law when he teaches "that the law is not laid down for the just but for the unjust and disobedient" . . . (1 Tim. 1:9, 10)'.[45] But Paul's words seem to apply to the first and third purposes of the law as well, since the law exposes and condemns the lawless,[46] and then, after they have fled to Christ for forgiveness, it directs them into a law-abiding life. In other words, all three functions of the law relate to lawless people, unmasking and judging them, restraining them, and correcting and directing them.

It is only because as fallen human beings we have a natural tendency to lawlessness (for 'sin is lawlessness')[47] that we need the law at all. The key antithesis, that the law is *not for the righteous but for lawbreakers* (9), cannot refer to those who are righteous in the sense of 'justified', since Paul insists elsewhere that the justified do still need the law for their sanctification.[48] Nor can it be taken to mean that some people exist who are so righteous that they do not need the law to guide them, but only that some people think they are. Similarly, when Jesus said, 'I have not come to call the righteous, but sinners to repentance',[49] he did not mean that there are some righteous people who do not need to be called to repentance, but only that some think they are. In a word, 'the righteous' in these contexts means 'the self-righteous'.

The fundamental principle that the law is for the lawless applies to every kind of law. For example, the reason we need speed limits is that there are so many reckless drivers on the roads. The reason we need boundaries and fences is that it is the only way to prevent unlawful trespass. And the reason we need civil rights and race relations legislation is in order to protect citizens from insult, discrimination and exploitation. If everybody could be trusted to respect everybody else's rights, laws to safeguard them would not be necessary.

The same is true of God's law. Its prohibitions and sanctions relate to the lawless. And Paul proceeds at once to illustrate the principle of 'law for the lawless' with eleven examples of law-breaking. The first six words, which he sets in pairs, appear to be more general than specific. The *law is made*, he writes, . . . *for lawbreakers and rebels* (JBP 'who have neither principles nor self-control'), *the ungodly and*

[45] *Ibid.*, II.7.10. [46] Rom. 3:20. [47] 1 Jn. 3:4. [48] *E.g.* Rom. 8:4; 13:8.
[49] Lk. 5:32.

48

sinful (who dishonour God and depart from righteousness), and *the unholy and irreligious* (who are devoid of all piety and reverence). These clearly refer to our duty to God, at least in general. But because the next five words are extremely specific in relation to our duty to our neighbour, it is natural to ask whether the first six may be meant to be specific in relation to our duty to God. George W. Knight suggests that they are.[50] Working backwards from the allusion to our father and mother, he proposes that *irreligious* (*bebēlos*) means profane in the sense of sabbath-breaking (the fourth commandment), that *unholy* (*anosios*) designates those who take God's name in vain (the third commandment), that *sinful* (*hamartō-los*) alludes to idolaters (the second commandment), and that *ungodly* (*asebēs*) denotes those who flout the first commandment to love God exclusively. This leaves the words *lawbreakers* (*anomos*) and *rebels* (*anypotaktos*), which seem to be introductory and to describe those who reject all law and discipline. This reconstruction is certainly ingenious, and may be correct, although it has to be declared unproved.

The next five words, however, do evidently allude to commandments five to nine. *Those who kill their fathers and mothers* of course break the fifth commandment to honour our parents; the expression is so extreme that Simpson is probably correct in understanding the reference to 'smiters of fathers or mothers, adjudged a capital crime in Ex. 21:15'.[51] *Murderers* break the sixth commandment, 'You shall not kill', while *adulterers and perverts* (heterosexual and homosexual offenders) break the seventh. At least the former certainly do ('You shall not commit adultery'), and the latter may be said to do so also if we understand the prohibition as intended to restrict sexual intercourse to the context of heterosexual marriage. 'Perverts' (NIV, REB) is not the best translation, nor is 'sodomites' (NRSV), for both terms nowadays carry assumptions and overtones which could express the kind of 'homophobia' which Christians should avoid. The Greek word *arsenokoitēs*, which occurs only here and in 1 Corinthians 6:9, is a combination of *arsēn* (male) and either *koitē* (bed) or *keimai* (to lie). It probably refers back to the Leviticus texts which prohibit 'lying with a man as one lies with a woman';[52] it denotes practising male homosexuals.[53] *Slave traders* (NIV) or 'kidnappers' (RSV) are guilty of the most heinous kind of stealing,

[50] Knight (1992), pp. 84–85. [51] Simpson, p. 31. [52] Lv. 18:22; 20:13, LXX.
[53] The attempts by Robin Scroggs in *The New Testament and Homosexuality* (Fortress, 1983) and John Boswell in *Christianity, Social Tolerance and Homosexuality* (University of Chicago Press, 1980) to argue that the *arsenokoitēs* was either an active male prostitute or a pederast have proved unsuccessful. See the refutation in Wright (1984), and my own reference to this question in *The Message of Romans* (IVP, 1994), pp. 77–78.

and both *liars and perjurers* break the ninth commandment not to bear false witness against our neighbour. The tenth commandment prohibiting covetousness is not included in Paul's catalogue, perhaps because it is a sin of thought and desire, not of word or deed. But in order to make his list comprehensive he concludes that the law is also made for *whatever else is contrary to the sound doctrine* (10). What is this? It is doctrine which *conforms to the glorious gospel* (literally, 'the gospel of the glory') *of the blessed God, which he entrusted to me* (11).

It is particularly noteworthy that sins which contravene the law (as breaches of the Ten Commandments) are also contrary to the sound doctrine of the gospel. So the moral standards of the gospel do not differ from the moral standards of the law. We must not therefore imagine that, because we have embraced the gospel, we may now repudiate the law! To be sure, the law is impotent to save us,[54] and we have been released from the law's condemnation, so that we are no longer 'under' it in that sense.[55] But God sent his Son to die for us, and now puts his Spirit within us, in order that the righteous requirement of the law may be fulfilled in us.[56] There is no antithesis between law and gospel in the moral standards which they teach; the antithesis is in the way of salvation, since the law condemns, while the gospel justifies.

2. The apostle Paul and the gospel (1:12–17)

I thank Christ Jesus our Lord, who has given me strength, that he considered me faithful, appointing me to his service. [13]*Even though I was once a blasphemer and a persecutor and a violent man, I was shown mercy because I acted in ignorance and unbelief.* [14]*The grace of our Lord was poured out on me abundantly, along with the faith and love that are in Christ Jesus.*

[15]*Here is a trustworthy saying that deserves full acceptance: Christ Jesus came into the world to save sinners – of whom I am the worst.* [16]*But for that very reason I was shown mercy so that in me, the worst of sinners, Christ Jesus might display his unlimited patience as an example for those who would believe on him and receive eternal life.* [17]*Now to the King eternal, immortal, invisible, the only God, be honour and glory for ever and ever. Amen.*

Turning away from the false teachers and their misuse of the law, Paul now writes about himself and the gospel which has been entrusted to him. He makes an extremely personal statement. He retells the story of his conversion and commissioning, sandwiching

[54] Rom. 8:3.   [55] Rom. 6:15; 7:6; 8:1–2.   [56] Rom. 8:3–4.

it between two paeans of praise. 'I thank Christ Jesus', he begins (12), and ends: 'Now to the King of the ages be glory and honour' (17). His whole life is permeated with thanksgiving, not only for his salvation but also for the privilege of having been made an apostle.

In particular Paul mentions three related blessings. First, *I thank Christ Jesus our Lord, who has given me strength* . . . (12a). It is striking that he refers to the inner strength Christ has given him, even before he specifies the ministry for which he needed to be strengthened. The appointment would have been inconceivable without the equipment. Secondly, *I thank Christ* . . . *that he considered me faithful* (12b). This cannot mean that Jesus Christ trusted him because he perceived him to be inherently trustworthy; his fitness or faithfulness was due rather to the inner strength he had been promised. Thirdly, *I thank Christ* . . . for *appointing me to his service* (12c). *Diakonia* is a generic word, and there are many forms which Christian service or ministry takes. But Paul is clearly referring to his commissioning as apostle to the Gentiles.

He now gives further substance to his thanksgiving by reminding Timothy what he had been, how he received mercy, and why God had had mercy on him.

First, he uses three words to describe what he had been: *I was once a blasphemer and a persecutor and a violent man* (13a). His 'blasphemy' was that he spoke evil of Jesus Christ; he also 'tried to force them [*sc.* his disciples] to blaspheme'.[57] His persecution of the church was pursued 'intensely', for he 'tried to destroy it',[58] and in persecuting it he did not realize that he was persecuting Christ.[59] Then behind both the blasphemy and the persecution there was *a violent man* (*hybristēs*), *hybris* being a mixture of arrogance and insolence, which finds satisfaction in insulting and humiliating other people.[60] Perhaps the apostle was intending to portray an ascending scale of evil from words (of blasphemy) through deeds (of persecution) to thoughts (of deep-seated hostility).

Secondly, Paul describes how he received mercy. Humanly speaking, there was no hope for someone as malicious and aggressive as he was. But he was not beyond the mercy of God. Twice he uses the same verb *I was shown mercy* (13b, 16a), or literally, as Thomas Goodwin the Puritan put it, 'I was bemercied'.[61] To 'mercy' Paul now adds 'grace', having already bracketed them in his opening greeting (1:2). *The grace of our Lord was poured out on me abundantly, along with the faith and love that are in Christ Jesus* (14). That is, grace 'overflowed' (NRSV) like a river in spate, which cannot be contained, but bursts its banks and carries everything

[57] Acts 26:9, 11.   [58] Gal. 1:13.   [59] Acts 9:4.
[60] See Trench, pp. 99–100.   [61] Quoted by Simpson, p. 34.

before it, sweeping irresistibly on. What the river of grace brought with it, however, was not devastation but blessing, in particular the 'faith' and the 'love' to which Paul has already assigned a primacy (4, 5). 'The Nile overflows; the crops abound. Grace overflowed, and faith and love sprang up.'[62] Grace flooded with faith a heart previously filled with unbelief, and flooded with love a heart previously polluted with hatred. It was, in the words of Bunyan's autobiography, *Grace Abounding to the Chief of Sinners*; he borrowed both parts of his title from verses 14 and 15.

No wonder Paul goes on to quote the first of the five 'trustworthy sayings' which occur in the Pastorals.[63] On each occasion the saying is pithy, almost proverbial, is perhaps a familiar quotation from an early hymn or creed, and is given by Paul his own apostolic endorsement. Indeed, since he constantly uses *pistos* ('trustworthy') of God, he is declaring that the aphorism is 'a faithful presentation of God's message'.[64]

This first 'faithful saying' is a concise summary of the gospel. *Here is a trustworthy saying that deserves full acceptance: Christ Jesus came into the world to save sinners – of whom I am the worst* (15). First, the content of the gospel is true and trustworthy, in distinction to the speculative nonsense of the false teachers and (we might add today) the lies of secular propaganda. Secondly, the offer of the gospel is universal. To be sure, NIV, REB and NRSV all put that it deserves 'full' acceptance, meaning 'complete' in the sense of 'unreserved'. But JBP renders it 'this statement is completely reliable and should be universally accepted'. This fits the context, since Paul argues in chapter 2 that the gospel must be made known to the nations. Thirdly, the essence of the gospel is that Christ came to save sinners. The law is meant for the *condemnation* of sinners; the gospel for their *salvation*. That Christ 'came to save' sounds like one of his own statements.[65] It alludes to both his incarnation and his atonement, and clearly implies his pre-existence. Indeed, after a careful examination of all the salvation passages in the Pastoral Letters Dr Philip Towner concludes that salvation as a present reality, though yet to be consummated, is 'the centre point of the message' and so of 'the sound teaching' of the apostles.[66]

Fourthly, the application of the gospel is personal. The universal offer is one thing ('worthy of all acceptation', AV); its individual acceptance is another ('of whom I am the worst'). He has already

---

[62] Ward, p. 37.   [63] The others are 3:1; 4:9; 2 Tim. 2:11 and Tit. 3:8.

[64] Knight (1992), p. 99. He argues that the words 'This is a faithful saying' represent 'a combined citation-emphasis formula', which both draws attention to the saying being quoted and affirms its reliability (Knight, 1968, 1979, pp. 19–20).

[65] *E.g.* Lk. 19:10; Jn. 3:13; 12:46; 17:18; *cf.* 11:27.

[66] Towner (1989), pp. 118–119.

called himself 'the least of the apostles'[67] and 'less than the least of all God's people';[68] he now humbles himself further as the 'chief' (AV), the 'foremost' (NRSV), 'the greatest' (JB) or 'the worst' (NIV) of sinners. Indeed, that is what *I am*, he writes, not simply what 'I was'.

But can he mean it? Are we to understand him literally? This is an interesting hermeneutical question. Common sense tells us not to take his statement as a precise, scientific fact. For he had not investigated the sinful and criminal records of all the inhabitants of the world, carefully compared himself with them, and concluded that he was worse than them all. The truth is rather that when we are convicted of sin by the Holy Spirit, an immediate result is that we give up all such comparisons. Paul was so vividly aware of his own sins that he could not conceive that anybody could be worse. It is the language of every sinner whose conscience has been awakened and disturbed by the Holy Spirit. We may begin like the Pharisee in Jesus' parable, 'God, I thank you that I am not like other men', but we end like the tax collector who beat his breast and said (literally), 'God have mercy on me, *the* sinner.'[69] The Pharisee indulged in odious comparisons; as far as the tax collector was concerned, however, there were no other sinners with whom to compare himself; he was the one and only.

We may now summarize what this first and pregnant 'trustworthy saying' tells us about the gospel. It is true and trustworthy. It is intended for everybody. It concerns Jesus Christ and his work of salvation. And it must be received by each of us individually.

One cannot reflect on this faithful saying without remembering the story of Thomas Bilney, who was converted through it. Elected in 1520 a Fellow of Trinity Hall, Cambridge, 'little Bilney' (as he was called on account of his shortness of stature) was searching for peace but could not find it.

'But at last', he wrote, 'I heard speak of Jesus, even then when the New Testament was first set forth by Erasmus . . . And at the first reading (as I well remember) I chanced upon this sentence of St. Paul (O most sweet and comfortable sentence to my soul!) in 1 Timothy 1. "It is a true saying, and worthy of all men to be embraced, that Christ Jesus came into the world to save sinners; of whom I am the chief and principal." This one sentence, through God's instruction and inward working, which I did not then perceive, did so exhilarate my heart, being before wounded with the guilt of my sins, and being almost in despair, that even immediately I seemed unto myself inwardly to feel a marvellous comfort and quietness, insomuch that "my bruised bones leaped

---

[67] 1 Cor. 15:9.   [68] Eph. 3:8.   [69] Lk. 18:9ff.

for joy" (Psalm 51). After this, the Scripture began to be more pleasant unto me than the honey or the honey-comb . . .'[70]

Perhaps Bilney's most notable convert was Hugh Latimer, who later became the popular preacher of the English Reformation. Latimer greatly admired the courage with which Bilney went to the stake for his evangelical faith; he referred to him in his sermons as 'St Bilney'.

Having considered Paul's descriptions of what he had been before his conversion and how he received mercy, we are ready in the third place to ask why God had mercy on him. The only possible answer is 'because God is a merciful God'. Ultimately, there is no other explanation. His merciful forgiveness originates not within us, as if we had any merit which inclined (let alone obliged) God to show mercy, but within his own merciful character, 'whose property is always to have mercy', as the Prayer Book says. Nevertheless, Paul mentions two factors which in his case might be said to have 'predisposed' God to be merciful.

The first concerned his past ignorant unbelief: *I was shown mercy because I acted in ignorance and unbelief* (13b). As he put it elsewhere, 'I . . . was . . . zealous for God' and 'convinced that I ought to do all that was possible to oppose the name of Jesus of Nazareth'.[71] Mind you, his conviction and zeal, his ignorance and unbelief were still culpable. He is not saying that his ignorance established a claim on God's mercy (or mercy would no longer be mercy, nor would grace be grace), but only that his opposition was not open-eyed and wilful, or it would have been the sin against the Holy Spirit and would have disqualified him from receiving mercy. It is similar to the familiar Old Testament distinction between 'unintentional' and 'defiant' disobedience.[72] We may still pray for others what Jesus prayed from the cross, 'Father, forgive them, for they do not know what they are doing',[73] providing we remember that we all still need to 'repent', even of sins committed 'in ignorance'.[74]

If Paul's ignorant unbelief in the past was one reason why God had mercy on him, a second related to the faith of others in the future: *But for that very reason I was shown mercy so that in me, the worst of sinners, Christ Jesus might display his unlimited* ('inexhaustible', REB, JB) *patience as an example for those who would believe on him and receive eternal life* (16). Although Paul's conversion had a number of unique features (the heavenly light, the audible voice, the Hebrew language, Paul's fall and blindness), it was also a 'prototype'

---

[70] *The Acts and Monuments of John Foxe* (1563), fourth edition, revised by Josiah Pratt, vol. 4 (Religious Tract Society, 1877), p. 635.
[71] Acts 22:3; 26:9.   [72] E.g. Nu. 15:22ff.   [73] Lk. 23:34.   [74] Acts 3:17, 19.

(*hypotypōsis*, BAGD) of all subsequent conversions, because it was an exhibition of Christ's infinite patience. In fact the conversion of Saul of Tarsus on the Damascus road has proved to be just that. It remains a standing source of hope to otherwise hopeless cases. Paul seems to speak to us across the centuries: 'Don't despair! Christ had mercy even on *me*, the worst of sinners; he can also have mercy on *you*!'

To sum up, although Paul had been a blasphemer and a violent persecutor, the grace of Christ had overwhelmed him. He received mercy partly because of his ignorant unbelief and partly in order to display for the benefit of future generations the limitless patience of Christ. It was this experience of Christ's grace, mercy and patience which underlay Paul's evangelistic enthusiasm. Just so, nobody can share the gospel with passion and power today who has not had a comparably personal experience of Christ.

No wonder Paul broke out into a spontaneous doxology, in which, however (as in the similar verse, 6:15), he made use of some phrases from an early liturgical form, which seems to indicate that liberty and liturgy are not necessarily incompatible. He addressed God as *the King*, the sovereign ruler of all things, who not only reigns over the natural order and the historical process, but has also established his special kingdom through Christ and by the Spirit over his redeemed people. The divine King is now characterized by four epithets. First, he is *eternal*, literally 'king of the ages' (as in Rev. 15:3), beyond the fluctuations of time. Secondly, he is *immortal*, beyond the ravages of decay and death. Hence the folly of idolaters who have 'exchanged the glory of the immortal God for images made to look like mortal man and birds and animals and reptiles'.[75] Thirdly, he is *invisible*, beyond the limits of every horizon. For 'nobody has ever seen God',[76] and indeed nobody 'can see' him (6:16); all that human beings have ever glimpsed is his 'glory', which has been defined as 'the outward shining of his inward being'. His glory is displayed in the creation,[77] in both the heavens and the earth,[78] and reached its zenith in the incarnate Son, who is 'the image of the invisible God'.[79] Fourthly, the King is *the only God*. The addition of the adjective 'wise' in the Textus Receptus used in the AV is 'no doubt a scribal gloss derived from Romans 16:27'.[80] What Paul is affirming is not the uniqueness of God's wisdom, but the uniqueness of his being. He has no rivals. 'I am the LORD', he declares, 'and there is no other.'[81] To this great *King, eternal, immortal, invisible, the only God*, Paul now ascribes (as is most justly due) all *honour and glory for ever and ever. Amen* (17).

---

[75] Rom. 1:23.   [76] Jn. 1:18; 1 Jn. 4:12.   [77] Rom. 1:20.   [78] Ps. 19:1; Is. 6:3.
[79] Col. 1:15.   [80] Metzger, p. 639.   [81] Is. 45:18.

3. Timothy and the good fight (1:18–20)

Timothy, my son, I give you this instruction in keeping with the prophecies once made about you, so that by following them you may fight the good fight, [19]holding on to faith and a good conscience. Some have rejected these and so have shipwrecked their faith. [20]Among them are Hymenaeus and Alexander, whom I have handed over to Satan to be taught not to blaspheme.

So far Paul has referred both to the teachers of the law (and their false gospel) and to himself as an apostle of Jesus Christ (and the true gospel). Now Timothy has to choose which of the two he is going to follow. On the one hand, the apostle is urging him to silence the false teachers; on the other he must feel the insidious influence of their speculations. He cannot remain neutral, and sit on the fence, even though he is young, inexperienced, impressionable and retiring. Now as then the truth demands a verdict.

Paul begins by describing the context in which he is writing. He reminds Timothy both of the special father-son relationship which bound them together and of the circumstances of his ordination: *Timothy, my son, I give you this instruction in keeping with the prophecies once made about you, so that by following them you may fight the good fight* (18). We are not told the substance of these prophecies. Nor is it clear whether they were directed to the church or to Timothy (declaring him called by God to his task, *cf.* Acts 13:1ff.) or to Paul (declaring Timothy a suitable addition to his mission team). What seems at least probable is that the occasion was his 'ordination'. For it was then that a 'gift' was given to Timothy, 'a prophetic message' was spoken, and 'the body of elders laid their hands' on him (4:14). Together these solemnly set him apart for his ministry, gifting and authorizing him to exercise it. It was *by following* these prophecies (RSV 'inspired by them') that Timothy would and could *fight the good fight.* Such at least was Paul's *instruction* to him. The word is again *parangelia,* 'command', as in verses 3 and 5. 'As often in military contexts . . . it conveys a sense of urgent obligation.'[82]

What this 'good fight' is Paul does not specify. But since in 6:12 he urges Timothy to 'fight the good fight of the faith', it is reasonable to conclude that he means the same thing here. Certainly to defend the revealed truth of God against those who deny or distort it, and to 'demolish strongholds' of error,[83] is to engage in a dangerous and difficult fight, which demands spiritual weapons, especially 'the sword of the Spirit, which is the word of God'.[84]

In particular, Timothy must keep *holding on to faith and a good*

[82] Guthrie (1990), p. 77.   [83] 2 Cor. 10:4.   [84] Eph. 6:17.

conscience (19a). Although here 'faith' does not have the definite article in the original, it does at the end of the verse (literally, 'suffered shipwreck concerning *the* faith'). So surely we must assume it at the beginning of the verse as well. Timothy possesses two valuable things which he must carefully guard, an objective treasure called 'the faith', meaning the apostolic faith, and a subjective one called 'a good conscience'. Moreover, they need to be preserved together (as in 1:5 and 3:9), which is exactly what Hymenaeus and Alexander have failed to do. This Hymenaeus is presumably the same heretic who taught that the resurrection had already taken place.[85] But Alexander was a common name, and there is no reason to identify this one with 'the metalworker' who did Paul 'a great deal of harm',[86] and who does not seem to have been a Christian at all.

Whoever these two men were, what we are told about them is that 'by rejecting conscience, certain persons have suffered shipwreck in the faith; among them are Hymenaeus and Alexander' (19b–20a, NRSV). The NIV rendering *some have rejected these* is unwarranted. What the heretics had rejected is clearly singular, not plural. The word used for their rejection of conscience (*apōtheō*) means to push something or someone away, to repudiate. It implies 'a violent and deliberate rejection'.[87] Having done this to their conscience, they have *shipwrecked their faith*. Conversely, it is precisely by preserving a good conscience that Timothy will be able to keep the faith. Thus belief and behaviour, conviction and conscience, the intellectual and the moral, are closely linked. This is because God's truth contains ethical demands. As Jesus said, 'if anyone chooses to do God's will, he will find out [or "know"] whether my teaching comes from God . . .'[88] In other words, doing is the key to discovering, obedience the key to assurance. By contrast, it is when people are determined to live in unrighteousness that they suppress the truth.[89] So if we disregard the voice of conscience, allowing sin to remain unconfessed and unforsaken, our faith will not long survive. Anybody whose conscience has been so manipulated as to be rendered insensitive is in a very dangerous condition, wide open to the deceptions of the devil (4:1–2). 'A bad conscience is the mother of all heresies,' Calvin wrote.[90] This may not be an invariable rule, but it is often true. I have myself known Christian leaders who once were faithful teachers, but who, as a result of some stubborn disobedience in their lives, turned aside from the truth and so ruined their ministry.

So serious was the apostasy of Hymenaeus and Alexander that Paul wrote of them: *whom I have handed over to Satan* (20). This is

---

[85] 2 Tim. 2:18.   [86] 2 Tim. 4:14.   [87] Guthrie (1990), p. 78.   [88] Jn. 7:17.
[89] Rom. 1:18.   [90] Calvin, p. 202.

almost certainly an allusion to excommunication, because Paul used the identical expression in relation to the incestuous offender at Corinth. 'Hand this man over to Satan', he wrote,[91] and then explained his meaning: 'Expel the wicked man from among you.'[92] Since the church is the dwelling-place of God, it follows that to be ejected from it is to be sent back into the world, the habitat of Satan. Radical though this punishment is, it is not permanent or irrevocable. Its purpose is remedial, 'in the hope that through this discipline' (REB) the offenders may *be taught not to blaspheme* (20). The implication is that, once the lesson has been learned, the excommunicated persons may be restored to the fellowship.

In this first chapter, which concerns the place of doctrine in the local church, Paul gives valuable instruction about false teaching. Its essential nature is that it is *heterodidaskalia*, a deviation (*heteros*) from revealed truth. Its damaging results are that it replaces faith with speculation and love with dissension. Its fundamental cause is the rejection of a good conscience before God.

What then should Timothy do in such a situation? Paul does not tell him to secede from the church, which would have been one extreme reaction. But neither may he remain silent in the face of heresy, let alone compromise with it, which would have been the opposite extreme. Instead, he was to stay at his post, and to fight the good fight of the faith, both demolishing error and contending earnestly for the truth.

---

[91] 1 Cor. 5:5.   [92] 1 Cor. 5:13.

1 Timothy 2:1–15
2. Public worship

In this pastoral letter Paul is looking beyond Timothy, to whom it is addressed, to the local churches he has been called to supervise. The apostle is concerned through Timothy to regulate the life of the church. He began with doctrine (chapter 1), urging Timothy to counter false teaching and to remain himself loyal to the apostolic faith. He continues now with the conduct of public worship (chapter 2).

As he had 'urged' Timothy (*parakaleō*) to remain in Ephesus to combat error (1:3), so now he exhorts him to give priority to public worship: *I urge* (*parakaleō* again), *then, first of all, that . . . prayers . . . be made for everyone.* 'First of all' refers 'not to primacy of time but primacy of importance'.[1] For the church is essentially a worshipping, praying community. It is often said that the church's priority task is evangelism. But this is really not so. Worship takes precedence over evangelism, partly because love for God is the first commandment and love for neighbour the second, partly because, long after the church's evangelistic task has been completed, God's people will continue to worship him eternally, and partly because evangelism is itself an aspect of worship, a 'priestly service' in which converts 'become an offering acceptable to God'.[2]

This emphasis on the priority of worship has particular importance for us who are called 'evangelical' people. For whenever we fail to take public worship seriously, we are less than the fully biblical Christians we claim to be. We go to church for the preaching, some of us say, not for the praise. Evangelism is our speciality, not worship. In consequence either our worship services are slovenly, perfunctory, mechanical and dull or, in an attempt to remedy this, we go to the opposite extreme and become repetitive, unreflective and even flippant.

Paul alludes to two main aspects of the local church's worship,

[1] Guthrie (1990), p. 74.   [2] Rom. 15:16.

which divide the chapter in half. First he considers its scope, and emphasizes the need for a global concern in public worship (1–7), and secondly he considers its conduct, and addresses the question of the respective roles of men and women in public worship (8–15).

1. Global concern in public worship (2:1–7)

I urge you, then, first of all, that requests, prayers, intercession and thanksgiving be made for everyone – [2]for kings and all those in authority, that we may live peaceful and quiet lives in all godliness and holiness. [3]This is good, and pleases God our Saviour, [4]who wants all men to be saved and to come to a knowledge of the truth. [5]For there is one God and one mediator between God and men, the man Christ Jesus, [6]who gave himself as a ransom for all men – the testimony given in its proper time. [7]And for this purpose I was appointed a herald and an apostle – I am telling the truth, I am not lying – and a teacher of the true faith to the Gentiles.

What stands out in this paragraph is the universal range of the church's responsibility. In contrast to the élitist notion of the Gnostic heretics, that salvation was restricted to those who had been initiated into it, Paul stresses that God's plan and therefore our duty concern everybody. Four times the same truth is emphasized. First, prayers are to be offered *for everyone* (1). Secondly, God our Saviour *wants all men* (NRSV 'desires everyone') *to be saved* (3–4). Thirdly, Christ Jesus *gave himself as a ransom for all men* (6, NRSV 'for all'). Fourthly, Paul was *a teacher of the true faith to the Gentiles* (7), that is, to all the nations or to everyone. There can be no doubt that this repetition is deliberate. These four truths belong together in Paul's mind. It is because God's desire and Christ's death concern everybody that the church's prayers and proclamation must concern everybody too.

a. The church's prayers should concern all people (2:1–2)

Paul mentions four different kinds of worship (*requests, prayers, intercession* and *thanksgiving*), three of which he has already brought together in an earlier letter.[3] Most commentators suggest that the first three are almost synonymous and cannot be neatly distinguished from one another. 'I admit', wrote Calvin with humility, 'that I do not completely understand the difference' between them. Then, after mentioning one attempt to do so, he continued: 'But I myself do not go in for subtle distinctions of that

---

[3] Phil. 4:6.

kind.'[4] Indeed, he is content with the broad distinction between 'genus and species', *prayers* (*proseuchē*) being a generic word for every kind of prayer, while *requests* (*deēsis*), and *intercession* (*enteuxis*) are specific. Some modern commentators are prepared to go a bit further, suggesting that *deēsis* expresses profound personal need, while *enteuxis* came to mean 'to enter into a king's presence and to submit a petition to him'.[5] Perhaps G. W. Knight offers the most succinct statement to the effect that all four terms should delineate our prayers: '*deēseis*, making requests for specific needs; *proseuchas*, bringing those in view before God; *enteuxeis*, appealing boldly on their behalf; and *eucharistias*, thankfulness for them'.[6]

Although Paul uses this cluster of four words, they all focus on a single theme, namely that they should *be made for everyone* (1). This immediately rebukes the narrow parochialism of many churches' prayers. Some years ago I attended public worship in a certain church. The pastor was absent on holiday, and a lay elder led the pastoral prayer. He prayed that the pastor might enjoy a good vacation (which was fine), and that two lady members of the congregation might be healed (which was also fine; we should pray for the sick). But that was all. The intercession can hardly have lasted thirty seconds. I came away saddened, sensing that this church worshipped a little village god of their own devising. There was no recognition of the needs of the world, and no attempt to embrace the world in prayer.

The Grand Rapids Report (1982), by contrast, which summarized the findings of the Consultation on the Relationship between Evangelism and Social Responsibility, included this commitment:

We resolve ourselves, and call upon our churches, to take much more seriously the period of intercession in public worship; to think in terms of ten or fifteen minutes rather than five; to invite lay people to share in leading, since they often have deep insight into the world's needs; and to focus our prayers both on the evangelization of the world (closed lands, resistant peoples, missionaries, national churches etc.) and on the quest for peace and justice in the world (places of tension and conflict, deliverance from the nuclear horror, rulers and governments, the poor and needy etc.). We long to see every Christian congregation bowing down in humble and expectant faith before our sovereign Lord.[7]

[4] Calvin, p. 205.
[5] Barclay, p. 58. *Cf.* Lock, p. 24, Guthrie (1990), pp. 80–81, Hendriksen, pp. 91–93 and Barrett, p. 49.
[6] Knight (1992), p. 115.
[7] *Evangelism and Social Responsibility: An Evangelical Commitment*, Lausanne Occasional Paper 21 (Paternoster, 1982), p. 49.

I sometimes wonder whether the comparatively slow progress towards peace and justice in the world, and towards world evangelization, is due more than anything else to the prayerlessness of the people of God. When President Marcos was toppled in 1986, Filipino Christians attributed his downfall 'not to people power but to prayer power'. What might not happen if God's people throughout the world learned to wait upon him in believing, persevering prayer?

In particular, Paul directed the churches to pray *for kings and all those in authority* (2a). This was a remarkable instruction, since at that time no Christian ruler existed anywhere in the world. *The Book of Common Prayer* (1662) is wrong therefore in its Communion Service to limit its intercession to Christian leaders, asking God 'to save and defend all Christian kings, princes and governors'. By contrast, when Paul told Timothy to pray for kings, the reigning emperor was Nero, whose vanity, cruelty and hostility to the Christian faith were widely known. The persecution of the church, spasmodic at first, was soon to become systematic, and Christians were understandably apprehensive. Yet they had recourse to prayer. Indeed, prayer for pagan countries and their leaders already had a precedent in the Old Testament. For Jeremiah told the exiles to pray for Babylon's peace and prosperity,[8] and the edict of Cyrus, which ordered the rebuilding of the Jerusalem temple, included a request to the Jews to 'pray for the well-being of the king and his sons'.[9]

It is hardly surprising to find the early church following this warrant from both Old and New Testaments. Thus Clement of Rome, towards the end of the first century, included a prayer in his first letter to the Corinthian church for rulers and governors: 'Grant them, Lord, health, peace, harmony and stability, so that they may give no offence in administering the government you have given them.'[10]

Tertullian too in his *Apology*, which is usually dated about AD 200, wrote: 'We pray also for the emperors, for their ministers and those in power, that their reign may continue, that the state may be at peace, and that the end of the world may be postponed.'[11]

Paul is quite specific in directing why the church should pray for national leaders. It is first and foremost *that we may live peaceful and quiet lives*. For the basic benefit of good government is peace, meaning freedom both from war and from civil strife. Paul had had

---

[8] Je. 29:7.   [9] Ezr. 6:10.
[10] *1 Clement*, translated by K. Lake, in *Apostolic Fathers* 1, Loeb Classical Library (Heinemann, 1912), 61.1.
[11] Tertullian, *Apology*, translated by T. R. Glover, Loeb Classical Library (Heinemann, 1931), 39.2.

many experiences of this blessing, when Roman officials had intervened on his behalf, not least in Ephesus itself when 'a great disturbance about the Way' had arisen, and the city clerk had succeeded in quelling it.[12] Prayer for peace is not to be dismissed as selfish. Its motivation can be altruistic, namely that only within an ordered society is the church free to fulfil its God-given responsibilities without hindrance. Two are mentioned, and a third is implied. Those mentioned are *godliness and holiness* (2b). 'Godliness' (*eusebeia*) is a favourite word in the Pastorals,[13] where it is used as a synonym for *theosebeia* (2:10) meaning the worship of God or religious devotion. 'Holiness' (*semnotēs*) seems in the context to mean 'moral earnestness'.[14] The NEB portrays these two blessings of peace as the 'full observance of religion and high standards of morality'.

The third positive benefit of peace is implied in verse 3. *This is good* (namely prayer that those in authority will maintain peace), *and pleases God our Saviour* (3), *who wants all men to be saved . . .* The logic of this seems to be that peaceful conditions facilitate the propagation of the gospel. Certainly the *pax romana* was a major factor in its early rapid spread. The ultimate object of our prayers for national leaders, then, is that in the context of the peace they preserve, religion and morality can flourish, and evangelism go forward without interruption.

Here is important apostolic teaching about church and state, and about the proper relations between them, even when the state is not Christian. It is the duty of the state to keep the peace, to protect its citizens from whatever would disturb it, to preserve law and order (using this expression without the oppressive overtones it often has today, referring to a clampdown on dissidents), and to punish evil and promote good (as Paul teaches in Rom. 13:4), so that within such a stable society the church may be free to worship God, obey his laws and spread his gospel. Conversely, it is the duty of the church to pray for the state, so that its leaders may administer justice and pursue peace, and to add to its intercession thanksgiving, especially for the blessings of good government as a gift of God's common grace. Thus church and state have reciprocal duties, the church to pray for the state (and be its conscience), the state to protect the church (so that it may be free to perform its duties). Each should acknowledge that the other also has a divine origin and purpose. Each should help the other to fulfil its God-given role.

[12] Acts 19:23ff.   [13] See 3:16; 4:7–8; 6:3, 5–6, 11; 2 Tim. 3:5; Tit. 1:1.
[14] Kelly, p. 61.

b. God's desire concerns all people (2:3–4)

The reason the church should reach out and embrace all people in its prayers is that this is the compass of God's desire. True, he is accurately named *God our Saviour* (3b), but we must not attempt to monopolize him, since he *wants* not only us but *all men to be saved* (4a). In affirming this, Paul may have had in mind those nationalistic Jews who believed themselves to be God's privileged favourites and forgot God's original promise to bless all earth's families through Abraham.[15] Alternatively, Paul may have been thinking of élitist Gnostics who reserved initiation into *gnosis* (knowledge) for a select few. In our day there are other versions of the monopoly spirit of which we need to repent, *e.g.* racism, nationalism, tribalism, classism and parochialism, together with the pride and prejudice which are the cause of these narrow horizons. The truth is that God loves the whole world, desires all people to be saved, and so commands us to preach the gospel to all the nations and to pray for their conversion.

Does this emphasis on 'all people' lead us out of élitism (only *some* will be saved) into its opposite extreme of universalism (*everybody* will be saved)? No. That Paul was not a universalist is evident, not only from his other letters but from this one too. If he was shown mercy because of his ignorant unbelief, presumably others who are defiant in their unbelief will not receive mercy (1:13). Some will 'fall under the same judgment as the devil' (3:6), and sooner or later all sin will be judged (5:24), while the covetous will fall into harmful desires 'that plunge men into ruin and destruction' (6:9).

How then can we avoid both opposite extremes of élitism and universalism? Besides, is not the doctrine of election itself a form of élitism? And is it not incompatible with Paul's statement here that God wants all people to be saved? We begin our response by stating that Scripture indubitably teaches divine election both in the Old Testament (*e.g.* 'he loved your forefathers and chose their descendants after them'),[16] and in the New Testament (*e.g.* 'you did not choose me, but I chose you'),[17] although different churches formulate the doctrine differently. Yet this truth must never be expressed in such a way as to deny the complementary truth that God wants all people to be saved. Election is usually introduced in Scripture to humble us (reminding us that the credit for our salvation belongs to God alone), or to reassure us (promising us that God's love will never let us go), or to stir us to mission (recalling that God chose Abraham and his family in order through him to bless all the families of the earth). Election is never introduced in order to contradict the universal offer of the gospel or to provide us with an

---

[15] Gn. 12:1ff. [16] Dt. 4:37; *cf.* 7:6–7; 13:2. [17] Jn. 15:16.

excuse for opting out of world evangelization. If some are excluded, it is because they exclude themselves by rejecting the gospel offer. As for God, he *wants all men to be saved.*

How then can we affirm simultaneously God's desire that all people be saved and God's election of some to salvation? Christians have struggled with this question in every generation, and have tried to reinterpret the three words which form the backbone of the sentence in verse 4 (namely 'wants', 'all' and 'saved') in such a way as to affirm election and avoid both élitism and universalism. Some have translated 'wants' (*thelei*) as either 'desires' (NRSV) or 'wishes', and have emphasized the distinction between a desire and a purpose, between wishing and willing. This seems consistent with the similar scriptural statements that God takes 'no pleasure in the death of the wicked'[18] and that he is patient, 'not wanting anyone to perish, but everyone to come to repentance'.[19] These three texts all declare that God's 'desire' or 'pleasure' for everybody is salvation, not judgment. The linguistic experts tell us, however, that there is no difference between the two verbs *thelō* and *boulomai*, since both can mean either to 'wish' or to 'will'. So all we can say is that the statement 'God wants all people to be saved' cannot be pressed into meaning that it is his fixed purpose and intention that everybody will be. For alas! it is possible to resist his will.[20]

Secondly, others suggest that the verb to 'be saved' means here to 'be preserved physically' rather than 'rescued spiritually and morally', since some think it has this meaning elsewhere (*e.g.* 2:11 and 4:10), and since the immediate context is that of governments protecting and preserving their citizens. This proposal has not found wide acceptance, however, since Paul goes on to write about the death of Christ for our sins, and since the vocabulary of salvation in the Pastorals usually refers to a deliverance from sin.[21]

Thirdly, a number of commentators insist that 'all men' cannot be taken in an absolute sense as signifying every single individual. Instead, 'the apostle's meaning here', writes Calvin, following Augustine, 'is simply that no nation of the earth and no rank of society is excluded from salvation, since God wills to offer the gospel to all without exception'. Paul is speaking rather of classes and not of individuals.[22] Hendriksen argues similarly that the 'all' means 'all men regardless of social, national and racial distinctions' and not 'one by one every member of the entire human race, past, present and future, including Judas and the antichrist'.[23] G. W. Knight points

[18] Ezk. 18:23; 33:11.   [19] 2 Pet. 3:9.
[20] See *e.g.* Mt. 23:37; Lk. 7:30; Jn. 5:40; Acts 7:51.
[21] *E.g.* 1 Tim. 1:15; 2 Tim. 1:9; 3:15; Tit. 2:11; 3:5.   [22] Calvin, pp. 208–209.
[23] Hendriksen, p. 100.

out in addition that this is the natural interpretation of verse 1, for it is possible to pray for 'all kinds of people' (*e.g.* the rulers as well as the ruled), but not possible to pray for absolutely everybody.[24] And in many other passages of Scripture 'all' is not absolute, but limited by the context. For example, when Jesus commissioned Paul to be his witness 'to all men', he meant not 'absolutely everybody in the world' but 'Gentiles as well as Jews'.[25]

This is an important insight which needs to be affirmed. Nevertheless, it does not altogether solve the problem. However we interpret the words 'want', 'saved' and 'all' in verse 4, we are still left with an antinomy[26] between the universal offer of the gospel and God's purpose of election, between the 'all' and the 'some'. Moreover, it is not a purely Pauline problem; we find it clearly within the teaching of Jesus himself. On the one hand he invited all to come to him;[27] on the other he said that his ministry was limited to those whom the Father had given him out of the world.[28] Again, on one occasion he said, 'You refuse to come to me', on another 'No-one can come to me unless the Father . . . draws him.'[29] So why is it that some people do not come to Christ? Is it that they will not or that they cannot? Jesus taught both.

Wherever we look in Scripture we see this antinomy: divine sovereignty and human responsibility, universal offer and electing purpose, the all and the some, the cannot and the will not. The right response to this phenomenon is neither to seek a superficial harmonization (by manipulating some part of the evidence), nor to declare that Jesus and Paul contradicted themselves, but to affirm both parts of the antinomy as true, while humbly confessing that at present our little minds are unable to resolve it.

The universality of the gospel invitation rests on a double foundation, namely the two truths that there is only one God and only one mediator. Paul states these facts about God and Christ with such an economy of words that some have wondered if he is quoting from an early credal statement. If so, he still endorses it with his own apostolic authority.

He begins: *For there is one God* (5a). The fundamental contrast in verses 4 and 5 is between the *all men* God wants to be saved and the *one God* who desires that they should be. The reason he wants *all* to be saved is that he is the *one* God, and there is no other.

Supposing there were not one God, but many, and that the truth about God were not monotheism but polytheism. Supposing there

---

[24] Knight (1992), p. 115.   [25] Acts 22:15, 21; 26:16–17.

[26] A paradox is an apparent contradiction which can be resolved; an antinomy is a logical contradiction which cannot.

[27] *E.g.* Mt. 11:28; Jn. 12:32.   [28] *E.g.* Jn. 17:6, 9.   [29] Jn. 5:40; 6:44.

were, as the Greeks believed, a pantheon of many gods, or even, as popular Hinduism holds, millions of deities. Then presumably these many gods would either share out the human race between them, by some amicable comity arrangement, or engage in a fierce, competitive struggle with each other for the allegiance of human beings, as was represented in the grotesque mythologies of ancient Greece and Rome. But if there were many gods, no single deity would presume to claim a monopoly of the world's worship – or not until he had defeated his rivals in some unseemly celestial battle!

Over against such ludicrous speculations Scripture insists on the unity of God. In the Old Testament the recited Shema began with the declaration, 'Hear, O Israel: The LORD our God, the LORD is one.'[30] It was the basis of his demand for his people's wholehearted and exclusive love.[31] This fundamental truth found further expression in Isaiah: 'I am the LORD, and there is no other; apart from me there is no God.'[32] Hence the so-called 'jealousy' of God. Jealousy is the resentment of rivals. Whether it is good or evil depends on whether the rivals have any legitimacy. God's rivals have not, because they are false gods, indeed 'no-gods'. It is in the context of idolatry that he says, 'I, the LORD your God, am a jealous God . . .'.[33] He is intolerant of rivals; he refuses to share with any other the worship which is due to him alone. 'I am the LORD; that is my name! I will not give my glory to another or my praise to idols.'[34] Hence too his invitation to the nations to believe in him: 'Turn to me and be saved, all you ends of the earth; for I am God, and there is no other.'[35] So it is already plain in the Old Testament that it is the uniqueness of Yahweh as the only God which justifies his 'jealousy' and so his universal mission, calling on every knee to bow to him and every tongue to swear by his name.[36]

Precisely the same reasoning is found in the New Testament. Indeed Paul keeps repeating it. 'There is but one God, the Father,' he writes, who is the creator and heir of all things.[37] Again, 'there is . . . one God and Father of all'.[38] And here in 1 Timothy, *there is one God* (2:5; *cf.* 1:17; 6:15). Further, it is because 'there is only one God' that he is not the God of Jews only but the God of Gentiles too.[39] Thus both Old and New Testaments affirm first that God is one and then that this monotheism is the fundamental basis of world mission. Our *exclusive* faith (*there is one God*, and no other) leads necessarily to our *inclusive* mission (the one God *wants all men to be saved*).

---

[30] Dt. 6:4.   [31] Dt. 6:5.   [32] Is. 45:5; *cf.* 44:6ff.; 45:14, 18ff.; 46:9.
[33] Ex. 20:5.   [34] Is. 42:8; *cf.* 48:11.   [35] Is. 45:22.   [36] Is. 45:23.
[37] 1 Cor. 8:6.   [38] Eph. 4:6.   [39] Rom. 3:29–30.

c. Christ's death concerns all people (2:5–6)

The apostle moves on from the *one God*, who desires all people to be saved, to the *one mediator* between God and human beings, who gave himself as a ransom for all people. This additional reference to the one mediator is indispensable to Paul's argument; it would not have been watertight otherwise. It is as if he anticipates our possible response to what he has written about monotheism. We might say: 'I grant that there is only one God. I am no idolatrous polytheist. But this does not prove the propriety, let alone the necessity, of the Christian mission. After all, Jews and Muslims are also fiercely monotheistic. Even some traditional religionists (or "animists", as they were previously called) look beyond the spirits to a Supreme Being. The unity of God is not really in dispute. Instead, the question may be put thus: why should not the one God, who wants all people to be saved, save them in different ways, some through Hinduism or Buddhism, others through Judaism or Islam, and yet others through New Age and other contemporary cults? Why should he insist that all people be saved in the same way and *come to a knowledge of the* (same) *truth?*'

Paul's answer is that there is not only one Saviour God, but also one mediator between him and us, and therefore only one way of salvation.

This question is being hotly debated in our day. The status of other religions, and the relationship of Jesus Christ to them, is a living issue. Three main positions are held.

First, the traditional view, held until recently by the great majority of Christians, is that Jesus Christ is the only Saviour and that salvation is by explicit faith in him. This is commonly called 'exclusivism', although it is an unfortunate term because it sounds negative and élitist, and because it says nothing about the inclusivism implicit in the universal offer of the gospel. The leading exponent of this view in this century has been Hendrik Kraemer in *The Christian Message in a Non-Christian World* (1938).

The second view is usually named 'inclusivism'. It also affirms that Jesus Christ is the Saviour, but adds that he saves different people in different ways, especially through their own religion. The best-known exponent of this position is probably Karl Rahner in his *Theological Investigations*, vol. V (1957).

The third view, which is gaining ground in our postmodern world of scepticism about truth, is called 'pluralism'. It not only tolerates the different religions, but actively affirms their independent saving validity, and therefore denies uniqueness and finality to Jesus. The best known contemporary representative of this position is John Hick, especially in *The Myth of Christian Uniqueness* (1987). A simple quotation expresses his view. It is acknowledged by pluralists, he writes, 'that Jews are being saved within and through the Jewish stream of religious life, Muslims within and through the Islamic stream, Hindus within and through the Hindu stream . . .' etc.[40]

We may affirm, however, without fear of contradiction, that in this classification Paul would have declared himself an 'exclusivist'. In his day there was an abundance of religions and ways of salvation, 'many "gods" and many "lords"'.[41] For example, there were the popular mystery religions from the East. Also the Gnostics postulated a whole succession of angelic emanations spanning the gulf between God and the world, of which Jesus was the greatest but not the only one. Paul insisted, however, that there is only one mediator. We need to be clear, therefore, that Christians do not claim uniqueness for 'Christianity' as a system in any of its varied formulations, or for the church as an institution in any of its cultural expressions, but only for Christ himself as a historical person and uniquely qualified mediator.

A mediator is an intermediary, the person in the middle, who effects a reconciliation between two rival parties. *Mesitēs* was used in the papyri both for an arbiter in legal disputes and for a negotiator of business deals. And between God and the human race, Paul writes, there is only one, Jesus 'the only go-between'.[42]

So wherein does his uniqueness lie, that we dare to say he has no competitors and no successors? His unique qualifications as mediator are to be found in his person and work, in who he is and what he has done.

First, the person of Jesus is unique. He is *the man Christ Jesus* (5b). Of course he is also God. In the previous chapter he was bracketed with the Father as the single source of grace, mercy and peace (1:2); he was three times designated 'our Lord' (1:2, 12, 14); and it was said that he 'came into the world to save sinners' (1:15), which assumes a pre-existent purpose and decision. What Paul now adds is that he became a human being. The juxtaposition of words in the Greek sentence is striking: ' . . . one mediator between God and men, man Christ Jesus'. An intermediary must be able to represent both sides equally. This was Job's longing: 'If only there were someone to arbitrate between us, to lay his hand upon us both.'[43] And in Jesus Christ 'Job's pathetic cry . . . has been answered . . .'[44] For he is both God and man, and therefore able to mediate between us. He is God from the beginning, deriving his divine being from his Father eternally, and he became human in the womb of his mother Mary, deriving his human being from her in time. Thus the New

[40] J. Hick, *The Myth of Christian Uniqueness* (SCM, 1987), p. 22.
[41] 1 Cor. 8:5. [42] Alford, p. 315. [43] Jb. 9:33. [44] Simpson, p. 42.

Testament bears witness to him as the unique God-man. There is no parallel anywhere else, even in the so-called 'avatars' ('descents') of Hinduism, whose historicity is extremely dubious, and whose plurality sets them apart from the incarnation of God in Jesus, which took place once and for all and for ever.

Secondly, the work of Jesus is unique, in particular what he did when he died on the cross. He *gave himself as a ransom for all men* (6a). We note the apostle's remarkable leap from the birth of Jesus (*the man Christ Jesus*) to his death (*who gave himself*). The one led to the other. He was born to die. Next, his death is portrayed as both a sacrifice and a ransom. He 'gave himself' means he 'sacrificed himself' (REB), offering himself deliberately and voluntarily as a sacrifice for sin. The phraseology goes back to Isaiah 53:12, where the suffering servant is said to have 'poured out his life unto death'. Jesus applied the concept to himself as the good shepherd, who would lay down his life for his sheep, freely of his own accord.[45]

Moreover, he gave himself *as a ransom*. This expression is a clear echo of Jesus' own statement that the Son of Man had come 'to give his life as a ransom for many'.[46] The implications are unambiguous. A ransom was the price paid for the release of slaves or captives. Still in our day hijackers hold people to ransom. The word implies that we were in bondage to sin and judgment, unable to save ourselves, and that the price paid for our deliverance was the death of Christ in our place. The Greek version of Jesus' statement was *lytron anti pollōn* ('a ransom instead of many'). Paul strengthened it by attaching the preposition to the noun as a prefix, and adding a second preposition: *antilytron hyper pantōn* ('a substitute-ransom on behalf of all'). The presence of both prepositions is significant. 'Christ is pictured as an "exchange-price" on behalf of and in the place of all, on the ground of which freedom may be granted.'[47]

Paul also changed *pollōn* ('many') into *pantōn* ('all'). It is doubtful, however, if he thereby changed the sense. Joachim Jeremias has argued that, although in Greek contexts *polloi* is 'exclusive', meaning 'many' as opposed to 'all', in Jewish contexts *polloi* is 'inclusive', meaning 'the many who cannot be counted', indeed 'all'.[48]

But did Christ die for all? There has been a long-standing debate in the church whether the atoning sacrifice of Jesus was 'limited' in its scope (he died for his own people) or 'universal' (he died for everybody). It is not difficult to quote texts supporting both positions. On the one hand, the good shepherd laid down his life for his sheep[49] and 'Christ loved the church and gave himself up for

---

[45] Jn. 10:11, 18; *cf.* Gal. 1:4; 2:20; Eph. 5:2; Tit. 2:14.   [46] Mk. 10:45.
[47] Guthrie (1990), p. 82.   [48] *TDNT* VI, pp. 536ff.   [49] Jn. 10:11, 18.

her'.[50] On the other, *he gave himself as a ransom for all* (6) and he is 'the Lamb of God, who takes away the sin of the world'.[51] Various attempts at harmonization have been made, and both sides have legitimate concerns. The concern of those who defend a 'limited' atonement is for the justice of God, that the penalty of sin should not be paid twice, first by Christ on the cross and then by those who reject him and are condemned. The concern of those who defend a 'universal' atonement is for the universality of the gospel offer.

As with the statement that God desires all people to be saved, so with the statement that Christ gave himself for all people, it is possible to argue that 'all' means 'all kinds and classes' and not 'absolutely everybody'. Yet it is probably wiser to concede that Scripture appears to affirm both positions in an antinomy which we are at present unable to resolve. Whatever we may decide about the scope of the atonement, we are absolutely forbidden to limit the scope of world mission. The gospel must be preached to all, and salvation must be offered to all.

Here, then, is the double uniqueness of Jesus Christ, which qualifies him to be the only mediator. First there is the uniqueness of his divine-human person, and secondly the uniqueness of his substitutionary, redeeming death. The *one mediator* is *the man Christ Jesus, who gave himself as a ransom*. We must keep these three nouns together, the man, the ransom and the mediator. Historically, they refer to the three major events in his saving career, his birth by which he became *man*, his death in which he gave himself as a *ransom*, and his exaltation (by resurrection and ascension) to the Father's right hand, where he acts as our *mediator* or advocate today. Theologically, they refer to the three great doctrines of salvation, namely the incarnation, the atonement and the heavenly mediation. And since in no other person but Jesus of Nazareth has God first become man (taking our humanity to himself) and then given himself as a ransom (taking our sin and guilt upon himself), therefore he is the only mediator. There is no other. No-one else possesses, or has ever possessed, the necessary qualifications to mediate between God and sinners.

What we do not know is exactly how much accurate and detailed information people need about the Man-Ransom-Mediator before they can call on God for salvation. What we do know is that all human beings are sinful, guilty and perishing; that no human being can save himself or herself by good works, religious observances, beliefs or sincerity; that Jesus Christ, being God, man and a ransom, is the only competent mediator through whom God saves; and that therefore it is urgent to proclaim the gospel in its fullness to as many people as possible.

[50] Eph. 5:25.   [51] Jn. 1:29.

d. The church's proclamation must concern all people (2:7)

Paul's statement at the end of verse 6 is so compressed as to be enigmatic: *the testimony given in its proper time.* Some commentators think that it is the death of Christ which, at the proper time, when it took place, is itself the divine witness to God's loving desire to save sinners. But since Paul goes on at once in verse 7 to the contemporary proclamation of the gospel, it seems more probable that this is the testimony to which he is referring. The birth and death of Jesus took place in the first century; now *in its proper time* testimony to him has to be borne. *And for this purpose* [*sc.* of witness] *I was appointed a herald and an apostle – I am telling the truth, I am not lying – and a teacher of the true faith to the Gentiles* (7).

How are we to understand the three nouns 'herald', 'apostle' and 'teacher'? Paul was all three, but nobody is all three today. As we noted when considering the first verse of this letter, the designation 'apostle', when used of the 'apostles of Christ' in distinction to the 'apostles of the churches', alluded primarily to the Twelve, to whom Paul and James were later added. They were eye-witnesses of the historic Jesus, especially of his resurrection, were promised the special inspiration of the Holy Spirit, and were given authority to teach in Christ's name. In addition, Paul was appointed the 'apostle to the Gentiles'. His strong ejaculation that he was telling the truth and not lying[52] was probably necessary because the false teachers were challenging his apostolic authority.

Although there are no 'apostles' of Christ today, who are comparable in inspiration and authority to the writers of the New Testament, there are certainly 'heralds' and 'teachers'. How shall we describe their responsibilities? It was the task of the apostles to formulate, defend and commend the gospel. It is the task of heralds to proclaim it, and of teachers to give systematic instruction in its doctrines and ethics.

What, then, do they proclaim and teach? Jesus Christ, the God-man, the ransom and the mediator, and all that is implied by those truths. To whom do they minister? *To the Gentiles*, all people of all nations. How do they do so? 'In faith and truth' (NRSV). The NIV and REB take these words as indicating the substance of the Christian message and so translate 'the true faith'. In the context it seems more likely that 'faith' and 'truth' describe the characteristics rather than the content of the teaching. That is, heralds preach and teachers instruct with conviction and sincerity. Or possibly 'truth' may be the objective truth of the gospel, while 'faith' is the subjective state of the

[52] *Cf.* Rom. 9:1; 2 Cor. 11:31; Gal. 1:20.

teacher.[53] There is an urgent need for such heralds and teachers today. It is not enough that the Son of God was born, died and was raised, or that he is the uniquely qualified God-man, ransom and mediator; this great good news must be made known, both heralded and taught, throughout the world.

In summary, the first half of this chapter begins and ends with a reference to the church's world-wide responsibility. The local church has a global mission. According to verse 1 the church is to pray for all people; according to verse 7 it is to proclaim the gospel to all people, all nations. But how can the church be expected to include the whole world in the embrace of its intercession and its witness? Is not this perspective arrogant, presumptuous, even imperialistic? No! Chrysostom at the end of the fourth century gave us the reason: 'Imitate God!' he cried.[54] That is, the universal concern of the church arises from the universal concern of God. It is because there is one God and one mediator that all people must be included in the church's prayers and proclamation. It is the unity of God and the uniqueness of Christ which demand the universality of the gospel. God's desire and Christ's death concern all people; therefore the church's duty concerns all people too, reaching out to them both in earnest prayer and in urgent witness.

2. Sexual roles in public worship (2:8–15)

The topic of public worship, which Paul began to address in the first half of this chapter, he continues in the second. But now he turns from the priority and scope of the local church's prayers to the respective roles and appropriate behaviour of men and women whenever the church assembles for worship. He outlines the duties of the men in relation to prayer (8) and the duties of the women in relation first to dress, hairstyle and jewellery (9, 10), and then in relation to men (11–15).

I want men everywhere to lift up holy hands in prayer, without anger or disputing.

[9]I also want women to dress modestly, with decency and propriety, not with braided hair or gold or pearls or expensive clothes, [10]but with good deeds, appropriate for women who profess to worship God.

[11]A woman should learn in quietness and full submission. [12]I do not permit a woman to teach or to have authority over a man; she must be silent. [13]For Adam was formed first, then Eve. [14]And Adam was not the one deceived; it was the woman who was deceived and

---

[53] Ellicott, p. 32.   [54] Chrysostom, p. 430.

became a sinner. [15] *But women will be saved through childbearing – if they continue in faith, love and holiness with propriety.*

These are probably the most controversial verses (especially verses 11–15) in the Pastoral Letters. They have been much studied and discussed, not least in the recent church debates about the ordination and ministry of women. Moreover, the conclusions we draw from this text will depend largely on the hermeneutical principles we bring to it. Before we look at the details of these verses, therefore, it is necessary to consider the two principles which seem to be of paramount importance.

a. Hermeneutical principles

The first may be called *the principle of harmony*. Those of us who believe the Bible to be the written Word of God also believe that when God spoke, he did not contradict himself. Therefore, although we gratefully acknowledge Scripture's rich diversity of both theological emphasis and literary style, we also expect it to possess an underlying consistency. This does not mean that we shall be guilty of artificial manipulation, but we shall seek a natural harmonization, interpreting each text within the total biblical context. So, as we approach these verses about the place of women in the church, we shall not isolate them from Scripture's fundamental assertion of the equal value and dignity of men and women by creation and redemption.[55] There is no difference between the sexes either in the divine image we bear or in our status as God's children through faith in Christ. Every idea of gender superiority or inferiority is ruled out from the start.

Secondly, we must seek to apply *the principle of history.* That is, God always spoke his word in particular historical and cultural settings, specially of the ancient Near East (the Old Testament), Palestinian Judaism (the Gospels) and the Graeco-Roman world (the rest of the New Testament). No word of God was spoken in a cultural vacuum; every word was spoken in a cultural context. It is, in fact, the glory of divine revelation that, in order to communicate with his people, God did not shout culture-free maxims at them from a distance. Instead, he stooped to their level, entered their history, assumed their culture and spoke their language. Yet this divine condescension also creates acute problems of interpretation for us. For Scripture is an amalgam of substance and form, of eternal truth which transcends culture and its transient cultural presentation. The former is universal and normative; the latter is local and

[55] Gn. 1:26ff.; Gal. 3:28.

74

changeable. But how shall we distinguish between them? More particularly, how are we to handle the cultural element in Scripture? Three main answers are given, and it seems to me that disagreement on this issue lies at the root of disagreement on the interpretation of the text before us.

First, there are some who *enthrone* the cultural form, and invest it with the same normative authority which they attribute to the truth it expresses. Because it belongs to the Word of God, they feel unable to tamper with it in any way. So they adopt a rigid literalism, and regard other approaches as evasions of 'what the Bible plainly teaches'. If they are consistent in interpreting 1 Timothy 2:8-15, they will then insist that men must always lift up their hands when they pray (8), that women must never plait their hair or wear jewellery (9), and that in no circumstances may women teach men (11–12).

Secondly, there are others who, while refusing (like the first group) to distinguish in Scripture between eternal truth and its cultural expression, then go to the opposite extreme. Far from enthroning both, they *dismiss* both. Instead of upgrading the cultural expression to the level of eternal truth, they downgrade the eternal truth to the level of its cultural expression. Instead of investing both with divine authority, authority is denied to both. Since God's Word is clothed in such ancient cultural dress, they argue, although it may have spoken to people long ago, it is now completely out of date and irrelevant. Consequently, Paul's entire instruction to Timothy about the men's prayers, and about the women's adornment and submission, must be jettisoned. There is virtually nothing worth salvaging, for nothing is 'eternal', everything is merely 'cultural'. For example, A. T. Hanson has written: 'Just as the first half of this chapter showed us the author at his best, so the second half seems to show him at his worst. Christians are under no obligation to accept his teaching on women.'[56] Similarly, although less stridently, William Barclay writes: 'All the things in this chapter are mere temporary regulations to meet a given situation.'[57]

It is understandable that liberal commentators, who lack respect for the supreme authority of canonical Scripture, should feel able to be so dismissive. It is worrying, however, when conservative scholars argue somewhat similarly. To be sure, they do not affirm that the cultural conditioning of Scripture altogether undermines its contemporary authority, but they say that certain passages are so culture-specific that they do not apply to us, and we may safely ignore them.

Even Dr Gordon Fee, whose judicious commentary on the Pastoral Letters in general I warmly recommend, seems to me to fall into this trap. Drawing attention both to the importance of

[56] Hanson (1966), p. 38. [57] Barclay, p. 68.

Ephesus as the centre of the cult of the goddess Diana/Artemis and her foul rites, and to the success which the false teachers were having among 'weak-willed women',[58] he adds that 'within that context' Paul's instructions on women 'can all be shown to make sense'. But Paul's statement in 1 Timothy 2:11–12 'is specifically related to the problem in Ephesus. He obviously did not take this position about women in general.'[59]

Richard Clark Kroeger and Catherine Clark Kroeger further develop this principle of specific local application in their remarkable book *I Suffer Not a Woman: Rethinking 1 Timothy 2:11–15 in Light of Ancient Evidence*. It is a *tour de force*, the fruit of much painstaking research into the ancient world. I share their concern that this text has been improperly and oppressively used to deny women legitimate ministries. For without doubt Scripture affirms the leadership of many intelligent and gifted women. How then do the Kroegers handle the text in more than a hundred pages? Describing Ephesus as 'a bastion of feminine supremacy',[60] dominated by the great goddess, 'Diana of the Ephesians',[61] and infiltrated by weird Jewish and Gnostic myths, the Kroegers re-interpret every phrase of verses 11–15 as applying exclusively to that context. 'Let a woman learn in quietness and full submission' (11) is an instruction to Christian women, in contrast to the 'babbling nonsense' of the Gnostic women, to be taught in, and be silently submissive to, the Word of God. 'I do not permit' (12a) refers to 'a specific and limited situation [*sc.* in Ephesus] rather than a universal one'.[62] The teaching which women are forbidden to give refers only to 'wrong doctrine'.[63] The 'authority over a man', which is equally prohibited, is not only a domineering one, but means that a woman must 'not

---

[58] 2 Tim. 3:6; *cf.* 1 Tim. 5:6, 11.

[59] Fee (1988), pp. 70, 77. After writing this chapter, my attention was drawn to Dr Fee's book *Gospel and Spirit: Issues in New Testament Hermeneutics* (1991), and specially to chapter 4 which takes 1 Timothy 2:8–15 as a test case. He argues that, because of the *ad hoc*, historically particular character of Paul's teaching here, he did not intend it 'as a rule in all churches at all times'. Gordon Fee distinguishes, in effect, between different *categories* of New Testament teaching. Some of it is intended by its author to be of general, eternal and universal application, while other parts are meant only to be particular, transient and local. Then, once we know which is which, we must accept the former, but are free to reject the latter. In my view, the better and right way is to distinguish between two *levels* of New Testament teaching, one being the profound, fundamental word of God, and the other its surface cultural expression. Then the former must be accepted as normative, while the latter is not to be rejected on the ground of its 'cultural relativity', but rather to be transposed into a contemporary cultural form. The discernment we need, then, is not *between* texts (some normative, others disposable), but *within* each text (the eternal substance and the cultural expression).

[60] Kroeger and Kroeger, p. 54.   [61] Acts 19:28, 34.

[62] Kroeger and Kroeger, p. 83.   [63] *Ibid.*, pp. 80–81.

proclaim' herself the 'author' or 'originator' of man.[64] The Gnostic myths that woman was responsible for both the creation and the enlightenment of man are contradicted by Paul's references to the priority of Adam (13) and the deception of Eve (14).[65] Nevertheless she will be 'saved', not condemned (15).

I acknowledge that this reconstruction is coherent and ingenious, and evidences great learning and profound reflection. By it each of the seven or more constituent parts of verses 11–15 has been re-interpreted in reference to the heretical ideas which were probably circulating at that time. When I had finished the book, however, I had a strong sense of 'overkill'. Does this text really have nothing normative to say about the relations between men and women? Have those words 'authority' and 'submission' (11–12) been evacuated of any contemporary significance? Surely, there is still something left in the complementarity of our created sexuality which God intends for the enrichment of our human experience? As Dr Dick France concedes, even though it runs against his main thesis, 'the New Testament reveals . . . a wide-ranging concept of "order" (*taxis*) which God has designed for human society at many levels', and which demands 'submission' (*hypotagē*), including that of a wife to her husband in marriage. 'To submit is to recognise your place within the God-given order of society, and to act appropriately to that place, by accepting the authority of those to whom God has entrusted it.'[66]

It is this which leads Dr J. I. Packer to express his continuing conviction 'that the man-woman relationship is intrinsically non-reversible . . . This is part of the reality of creation, a given fact that nothing will change. Certainly, redemption will not change it, for grace restores nature, not abolishes it.' He therefore supports the proposal that we should 'theologize reciprocity, spiritual equality, freedom for ministry, and mutual submission and respect between men and women – within this framework of non-reversibility . . . It is important that the cause of *not* imposing on women restrictions which Scripture does not impose should not be confused with the quite different goals of minimizing the distinctness of the sexes as created and of diminishing the male's inalienable responsibilities in man-woman relationships as such.'[67] I fully agree.

The danger of declaring any passage of Scripture to have only local (not universal), and only transient (not perpetual) validity is that it opens the door to a wholesale rejection of apostolic teaching, since virtually the whole of the New Testament was addressed to specific situations. Whenever we can show that an instruction related

[64] *Ibid.*, p. 103.   [65] *Ibid.*, pp. 117ff.   [66] France, pp. 33–35.
[67] J. I. Packer, *Women, Authority and the Bible* (IVP [USA], 1986), p. 299.

to a particular context, shall we then limit it to that context and declare it irrelevant to all others? For example, the command to be 'subject to rulers and authorities'[68] was addressed to Cretans whose rebellious spirit was proverbial;[69] does it therefore not apply to non-Cretans? We might similarly argue that what Paul wrote about homosexual practice, simplicity of lifestyle, the uniqueness of Christ, world evangelization and many other topics was fine for his day. But times have changed, we belong to different cultures, and (some would add) we know more about these things than he did. So what he wrote has no authority over us.

So far, I have suggested that we should reject the two opposite extremes in relation to the cultural element in the biblical revelation. We might call them 'literalism' (enthroning both) and 'liberalism' (dismissing both). The third and mediating position is 'cultural transposition'. For this we have to discern in Scripture between God's essential revelation (which is changeless) and its cultural expression (which is changeable). Then we are in a position to preserve the former as permanent and universal, and transpose the latter into contemporary cultural terms. Thus, in response to Jesus' command to us to wash one another's feet, we neither obey literally and go round washing people's feet, nor dismiss the passage as having no relevance to us, but discern what is intrinsic (no service will be too menial if we love one another) and then transpose it into the realities of today (we will gladly wash the dishes or clean the toilet).

It is my belief that the most helpful way to handle verses 8–15 is to apply to them this *principle of cultural transposition*, and to recognize its applicability to all three topics, namely men's prayers (8), women's adornment (9–10) and women's submission (11–15). In the case of the first two, the application is not difficult. Take verse 8. Always and everywhere the men are to pray in holiness and love. But their bodily posture as they do so (standing, kneeling, sitting, clapping hands or raising arms) may vary according to culture. Next, verses 9 and 10. Always and everywhere women must adorn themselves with modesty, decency, propriety and good deeds, but their clothing, hairstyle and jewellery may vary according to culture.

Would cultural transposition be appropriate in verses 11–15 also? We note that verses 11 and 12 contain two complementary instructions to or about women. Positively, *a woman should learn in quietness and full submission* (11). Negatively, she is not *to teach or to have authority over a man* (12). Further, the antithesis is double. On the one hand, she is to learn in quietness and not teach. On the other hand, she is to be submissive and not exercise authority

[68] Tit. 3:1.   [69] Tit. 1:12.

over a man. Or, to express the double antithesis more sharply, a woman's behaviour in public worship is to be characterized by quietness and/or silence, not teaching, and by submission, not authority.

This brings us to the key question: what is the relation between these two antitheses? Are they simply parallel and therefore equally normative? Is a woman both to be silent and not teach, and to be submissive and not wield authority, with no distinction between these instructions? This is what many commentators assume. But must submission always be expressed in silence, and 'not exercising authority' in 'not teaching'? Or could it be legitimate to see the submission–authority antithesis as permanent and universal (because grounded in creation, see verse 13), while seeing the silence–teaching antithesis as a first-century cultural expression of it, which is therefore not necessarily applicable to every culture, but open to transposition into each?

Some readers will doubtless respond that there is no indication of this distinction in the text itself. For verses 11 and 12 contain just two prohibitions (teaching and having authority) and two commands (silence and submission). This is true. But the same could be said about verses 8 and 9. There is nothing in the text of verse 8 which requires us to distinguish between the commands to lift up holy hands and to be rid of anger and argument. Nor is there anything in the text of verse 9 which requires us to distinguish between the commands to women to dress modestly and to avoid hair-plaiting and jewellery. Yet a Christian mind, schooled in the perspectives and presuppositions of the New Testament, knows that its ethical commands and their cultural expressions are not equally normative and must therefore be distinguished. So it recognizes in verse 8 that holiness and love are ethical, but hand-lifting is cultural, and in verses 9 and 10 that decency and modesty are ethical, while hairstyles and jewellery are cultural. Why then should we not anticipate that the same distinction between the ethical and the cultural is to be found in verses 11 and 12? The context (with its three regulations about prayers, adornment and submission) should at least make us open to this possibility.

We should begin by affirming, against what is fashionable and 'politically correct', that a woman's 'submission' to male 'authority' is in God's purpose normative. Paul develops this teaching most fully in 1 Corinthians 11:2ff. And here in verses 12 and 13 he supplies a biblical basis for it, especially that *Adam was formed first, then Eve* (12). Some scholars dismiss this as an example of Paul's 'tortuous Rabbinic exegesis', but I for one claim no liberty to disagree with the apostles of Christ. His argument for masculine 'headship' from the priority of Adam's creation is perfectly reasonable when seen in the light of primogeniture, the legal rights and privileges accorded to the firstborn. For Adam was God's firstborn. In addition to being created after Adam, Eve was created out of him and for him, to be a helper suitable for him and corresponding to him.[70]

Not that 'authority' is to be understood in terms of decision-making, let alone the wielding of unlimited power. In Ephesians 5:21ff., in the context of the reciprocal relations between husbands and wives, Paul interprets the husband's position as 'head' of his wife as modelled on Christ being 'head' of his church. And this is a caring not a crushing headship, a headship of self-sacrifice not self-assertion, of love not pride, intended to be liberating not enslaving. Nor is male headship incompatible with sexual equality, any more than the assertion that 'the head of Christ is God'[71] is incompatible with the unity of the Father and the Son in the Godhead.

If, however, the authority–submission antithesis is to be retained as creational, may not the teaching–silence antithesis be regarded as cultural? May not the requirement of silence, like the requirement of veils,[72] have been a first-century cultural symbol of masculine headship, which is not necessarily appropriate today? For silence is not an essential ingredient of submission; submission is expressed in different ways in different cultures. Similarly, women teaching men does not necessarily symbolize taking authority over them. Teaching can be given in different styles, with different meanings. Thus public prophesying by women was not regarded as an improper exercise of authority over men, presumably because it took place under the direct inspiration and authority of God.[73] Nor was Priscilla's teaching of Apollos inappropriate, because she gave him private instruction in the home, and Aquila was present, sharing in the instruction. [74]

What, then, about the second biblical basis for Paul's instruction? If his first argument was derived from the creation (*Adam was formed first, then Eve*, verse 13), his second was derived from the fall (*Adam was not the one deceived; it was the woman who was deceived and became a sinner*, verse 14). The popular explanation of this is that the woman was shown up in the fall as constitutionally prone to deception and that on this account she should not teach men. But there is a fatal objection to this. If women are by nature gullible, they ought to be disqualified from teaching anybody, not just men, whereas Paul refers to the special role of women in teaching both children[75] and younger women.[76] It

[70] Gn. 3:18.   [71] 1 Cor. 11:3.   [72] 1 Cor. 11:10.
[73] 1 Cor. 11:5; *cf.* Acts 2:17; 21:9.   [74] Acts 18:26.
[75] 1 Tim. 5:10; 2 Tim. 1:5; 3:15.   [76] Tit. 2:3ff.

is more probable, therefore, that the essence of Eve's part in the fall was not that she was deceived, but that she took an improper initiative, usurped Adam's authority and thus reversed their respective roles.[77]

In the end, our decision whether women may ever teach men, or be ordained to the pastorate, or exercise other leadership roles in the church, will depend on our understanding of the nature of pastoral leadership. If we belong to the Reformed tradition and see the local presbyter as essentially an authority figure, responsible both to teach the congregation and to exercise discipline (including excommunication), then we are likely to conclude that it is inappropriate for women to occupy such an authoritative position. Supposing, on the other hand, we begin our thinking about Christian pastoral leadership with the teaching of Jesus in Mark 10:35ff., where he drew a distinction between two human communities whose leaders operate on different principles. In the world, he said, 'officials exercise authority over them'. But, he added, 'Not so with you.' Instead, in his community greatness would be measured by service.

Why should it be thought inappropriate for women to exercise such servant-leadership? They have done so throughout biblical history. Besides, there are now no authority figures in the church, who can teach like the apostles in the name and with the authority of Christ. The New Testament is now complete, and all Christian teachers are called to teach humbly under its authority. If then a woman teaches others, including men, under the authority of Scripture (not claiming any authority of her own), in a meek and quiet spirit (not throwing her weight about), and as a member of a pastoral team whose leader is a man (as a contemporary cultural symbol of masculine headship), would it not be legitimate for her to exercise such a ministry, and be commissioned (ordained) to do so, because she would not be infringing the biblical principle of masculine headship? Our answer to this question is likely to depend on whether we consider it legitimate to apply the principle of cultural transposition to verses 10 and 11.

b. Three apostolic instructions

Following our excursus into the hermeneutical principles which we should apply to this passage (8–15), we are ready to attempt its more detailed exposition. It consists of three instructions which all relate, as the context makes clear, to the conduct of public worship: the men

---

[77] Gn. 3:6, 17.

and their prayers (8), the women and their adornment (9–10), and
the women and their relation to men (11–15).

i. Men and their prayers (2:8)

Everywhere (literally 'in every place', namely wherever public
prayer is offered) the men are *to lift up holy hands . . . without
anger or disputing* (8). Here are three universal characteristics of
public prayer, or, expressing them negatively, three hindrances to
prayer, namely sin, anger and quarrelling. The reference to 'holy
hands' reminds us of Psalm 24, in which those who wish to ascend
the hill of the Lord and stand in his holy place must have 'clean
hands and a pure heart'. Here too Paul uses 'the outward sign for the
inward reality, for our hands indicate a pure heart'.[78] So it is useless
to spread out our hands to God in prayer if they are defiled with
sin.[79] As for anger and quarrelling, it is obviously inappropriate to
approach God in prayer if we are harbouring resentment or
bitterness against him or other people. As Jesus himself insisted,
reconciliation must precede worship.[80]

So holiness, love and peace are indispensable to prayer. But
what about the lifting up of our hands – is this equally essential?
No, bodily postures and gestures in prayer are cultural, and a
wide range of variations occurs in Scripture. The normal posture
while worshipping was to stand, as when the Levites summoned
the people to 'stand up and praise the LORD your God'.[81] And
while standing before God, it seems to have been common either
to 'lift' the hands to him or to 'spread' them before him, as an
expression of dependence and faith. So we read: 'I lift my hands
towards your Most Holy Place', and 'Let us lift up our hearts
and our hands to God in heaven'.[82] Meanwhile, the eyes could
also be lifted up in expectation[83] or else be cast down in humble
penitence.[84]

But standing was not the only acceptable prayer posture. David
'sat before the LORD',[85] and many times we read of people,
especially in times of humiliation, anguish or confession, bowing
down or kneeling before God.[86] Sometimes it seemed natural to

---

[78] Calvin, p. 214.   [79] Is. 1:15; *cf.* 59:1ff.
[80] Mt. 5:23–24; *cf.* 6:12ff.; Mk. 11:25.
[81] Ne. 9:5; *cf.* Gn. 18:22; 1 Sa. 1:26; Mk. 11:25; Lk. 18.11, 13; Rev. 7:9.
[82] Ps. 28:2; La. 3:41; *cf.* Ex. 9:29; 17:11–12; 1 Ki. 8:22; Ne. 8:6; Pss. 63:4; 134:2;
143:6.
[83] *E.g.* Pss. 25:15; 121:1; 123:1–2.; 141:8; Jn. 11:41; 17:1.   [84] Lk. 18:13.
[85] 2 Sa. 7:18.
[86] *E.g.* Gn. 17:3; 24:26, 48; Ex. 12:27; 1 Ki. 8:54; 2 Ch. 29:30; Is. 45:23 = Phil. 2:9ff.;
Ezk. 9:5; Dn. 6:10; Mt. 2:11; Lk. 22:41; Acts 7:60; 9:40; 20:36; 21:5; Rom. 14:11; Eph.
3:14; contrast Mt. 4:9.

God's people to express their sense of awe in his presence by prostrating themselves, with their faces to the ground,[87] especially after a vision of the majesty of God.[88]

To sum up, although holiness, love and peace should always accompany our prayers, yet whether we stand, sit, bow down, kneel or fall on our faces, and whether our hands are lifted, spread, folded, clasped, clapping or waving are matters of little consequence, although we may be inclined to agree with William Hendriksen that 'the slouching position of the body, while one is supposed to be praying, is an abomination to the Lord'.[89] Otherwise, we need to make sure that our posture is both appropriate to our culture and genuinely expressive of our inward devotion. For Jesus warned us of the dangers of religious ostentation,[90] and our worship must never be allowed to degenerate into 'a piece of sacred pantomime'.[91]

ii. Women and their adornment (2:9–10)

The Greek sentence begins with the word 'Likewise . . .', so that commentators have naturally asked what similarity Paul has in mind. Some suggest that we should read: 'In the same way I want women to pray . . .' and certainly Paul did expect women to engage in public prayer.[92] But it is more simple and straightforward to read *I also want . . .*

The skeleton of the sentence in Greek is 'I want women . . . to adorn themselves', and it is important to note the apostle's positive desire before coming to his qualifications. When a woman adorns herself, she is seeking to enhance her beauty. So Paul recognizes both that women are beautiful and that they should increase and exhibit their beauty. There is no biblical warrant in these verses for women to neglect their appearance, conceal their beauty or become dowdy and frumpish. The question is *how* they should adorn themselves. There are three parts to Paul's instruction.

First, he tells women *to dress modestly, with decency and propriety* (9a). It is not possible to distinguish these words from one another in a clear-cut way. But the general impression is clear, that women are to be discreet and modest in their dress, and not to wear any garment which is deliberately suggestive or seductive. This establishes a universal principle.

Secondly, Paul tells women not to adorn themselves *with braided hair or gold or pearls or expensive clothes* (9b). Unlike the first part of the verse, this is surely not an absolute ban on all hairstyles in which

---

[87] E.g. Nu. 14:5; 16:4, 22, 45; Dt. 9:18, 25–26; Jos. 5:14; Jdg. 13:20; 1 Ki. 18:42; 1 Ch. 29:20; 2 Ch. 7:1ff.; Ne. 8:6; Mk. 14:35.
[88] E.g. Ezk. 1:28; 3:23; 9:8; Dn. 8:17; 10:9; Rev. 1:17; 11:16.
[89] Hendriksen, p. 103.   [90] Mt. 6:1ff.   [91] Fairbairn, p. 122.   [92] 1 Cor. 11:5.

PUBLIC WORSHIP

the hair is plaited, all jewellery which incorporates gold or pearls, and all clothing which is elegant (the word 'expensive' raises a different issue, which, although cost is a comparative matter, could well apply universally). If the glorified church is portrayed in the book of Revelation as 'prepared as a bride beautifully dressed for her husband',[93] it is evident that all material adornment is not forbidden to women. No, hairstyle, jewellery and clothing have different meanings in different cultures. Christian women in Ephesus, for example, would need to make sure that their attire in no way resembled that of the hundreds of prostitutes who were employed in the great goddess Diana's temple. Chrysostom grasped this. 'Imitate not therefore the courtesans', he cried, 'for by such a dress they allure their many lovers.'[94]

James B. Hurley explains this more fully: 'He [sc. Paul] refers . . . to the elaborate hair-styles which were then fashionable among the wealthy, and also to the styles worn by courtesans. The sculpture and literature of the period make it clear that women often wore their hair in enormously elaborate arrangements with braids and curls interwoven, or piled high like towers and decorated with gems and/or gold and/or pearls. The courtesans wore their hair in numerous small pendant braids with gold droplets or pearls or gems every inch or so, making a shimmering screen of their locks.'[95] Dr Hurley also supplies references for further information on hairstyle and clothing in the Roman Empire.

Such hair-do's were inappropriate for Christian women in first-century Asia Minor. But the same could not be said about some African tribes today. Their Christian women have preserved traditional hairstyles, which involve the most intricate plaiting, but are neither expensive, nor ostentatious, nor sexually significant. What Paul is emphasizing is that Christian women should adorn themselves with clothing, hairstyles and jewellery which *in their culture* are inexpensive not extravagant, modest not vain, and chaste not suggestive.

Thirdly, they are to adorn themselves *with good deeds, appropriate for women who profess to worship God* (10), literally 'who profess godliness'. Paul is reminding women that there are two kinds of feminine beauty, physical and moral, beauty of body and beauty of character. The church should be a veritable beauty parlour, because it encourages its women members to adorn themselves with good deeds. Women need to remember that if nature has made them plain, grace can make them beautiful, and if nature has made them beautiful, good deeds can add to their beauty. Moreover, men can facilitate this process by recognizing and applauding in women the

[93] Rev. 21:2. [94] Chrysostom, p. 433. [95] Hurley, p. 199; cf. pp. 257–259.

84

beauty of Christlikeness. The apostle Peter also contrasted 'braided hair and the wearing of gold, jewellery and fine clothes' with 'the unfading beauty of a gentle and quiet spirit which is of great worth in God's sight'.[96] If it is valuable to him, it should be valuable to us also.

iii. Women and their role (2:11–15)

Several unsuccessful attempts have been made, exegetical and linguistic, to soften the apparent harshness of these apostolic instructions, by limiting their application.

First, it is suggested that they express only Paul's personal opinion, not his authoritative command. That is, 'I want' (*boulomai*) in verse 8 is no more than a wish, and 'I do not permit' (*epitrepō*) in verse 12 means 'Personally, I don't allow' (JBP) and 'lacks any sense of universal imperative for all situations'.[97] Other scholars, however, regard this as special pleading. J. H. Houlden writes that '*boulomai* carries a sense of legislative enactment',[98] while Gottlob Schrenk says that in its three occurrences in the Pastoral Epistles it refers to 'ordering by apostolic authority'.[99] As for *epitrepō*, in the parallel passage in 1 Corinthians, Paul identifies his permission as both the teaching of 'the Law' and 'the Lord's command'.[100]

The second limiting proposal is that Paul's instructions apply only to wives, not to women in general. They are intended, therefore, to regulate the private relation of a wife to her husband in the home, and not the public role of a woman in the church. Luther seems to have held this view. And the references to Adam and Eve in verses 13 and 14, and to 'husbands' in 1 Corinthians 14:35, lend plausibility to it. Certainly, *gynē* (11, 12) can mean either 'woman' or 'wife', and *anēr* (12) can mean either 'man' or 'husband'. On the other hand, the whole chapter relates to public worship, with verses 8–15 defining gender roles in it, so that the reference seems to be wider than to married couples only.

The third limiting suggestion is that Paul's instructions are directed only against noisy disturbances and interruptions by women, not against a quiet and orderly exercise of their ministry. They are certainly honoured by their responsibility to learn (11), in contrast to the chauvinistic Rabbinical opinion expressed in the Jerusalem Talmud that it would be better for the words of Torah to be burned, than that they should be entrusted to a woman. If she may learn, then, may she not also teach, if she does it quietly? In the Corinthian parallel,[101] whose context is that of disorder in public worship, it does seem to be the women's unruly chatter which Paul is

---

[96] 1 Pet. 3:3–4.   [97] Fee (1988), p. 77.   [98] Houlden, p. 69.   [99] *TDNT* I, p. 632.
[100] 1 Cor. 14:34, 37.   [101] 1 Cor. 14:34–35.

opposing. But his requirement in both passages of 'submission' as well as 'silence' (or quietness) indicates in both passages that he is concerned about more than noise.

Fourthly, it is argued that Paul's instructions only forbid a woman to 'domineer' over a man. She must not start 'lecturing him in public worship',[102] teach in 'an imperious manner'[103] or play the 'autocrat'.[104] But the exact meaning of the verb *authenteō* is uncertain, as it occurs only here in the New Testament. From a study of its occurrences elsewhere Dr George Knight has concluded that its use 'shows no inherent negative sense of grasping or usurping authority or of exercising it in a harsh or authoritative way, but simply means "to have or exercise authority"'.[105] Dr Leland E. Wilshire challenged some of his findings,[106] and in a further computer-based article proposed the meaning 'instigating violence', by which perhaps Paul was forbidding women to resist the false teachers with anger.[107] Meanwhile, the Kroegers' investigation into *authenteō* ran to twenty pages and led them to a quite different suggestion already mentioned.[108] The debate continues.

These four attempts to limit Paul's instructions cannot be pronounced successful. It seems to me that the better and more biblical proposal, as suggested earlier, is that Paul's instructions cover only the universal principle of female submission to male 'headship', and not its changeable cultural expression.

We can now sum up this distinction as it has recurred three times in the second half of 1 Timothy 1. As men should pray in holiness, love and peace, but not necessarily lift up their hands while they do so; and as women should adorn themselves with modesty, decency and good works, but not necessarily abstain from all hair-plaiting, gold and pearls; so women should submit to the headship (caring responsibility) of men, and not try to reverse sexual roles, but not necessarily refrain from teaching them.

In verses 13 and 14, as the conjunction 'for' implies, Paul supplies a biblical basis for what he has written in verses 11 and 12. From the men and women of his own day he looks back to Adam and Eve, the original human pair.[109] His argument for male 'headship' rests on the facts of the creation and the fall. The priority of Adam's creation

---

[102] Hendriksen, p. 109.   [103] Fairbairn, p. 127.
[104] Ellicott, p. 127.   [105] Knight (1992), p. 141. See also Knight (1984).
[106] 'The TLG Computer and Further Reference to AUTHENTEO in 1 Tim. 2:12', *New Testament Studies* 34 (1988), pp. 120–134.
[107] '1 Tim. 2:12 Revisited: A Reply to Paul W. Barnett and Timothy J. Harris', *Evangelical Quarterly* 65:1 (1993), pp. 43–55.
[108] Kroeger and Kroeger, pp. 84–104.
[109] For a defence of the historicity of Adam, see my *The Message of Romans*, pp. 162–166.

established his headship (13), as we have seen, while Eve's folly in challenging it led to disaster (14).

Anticipating that some of what he has written may upset his readers, Paul 'modifies' it 'by adding a consolation':[110] *But women will be saved* (literally 'she will be saved' in the singular, but Paul is obviously generalizing) *through childbearing – if they continue in faith, love and holiness with propriety* (15) or 'modesty' (REB, NRSV), 'splendid maternal attitudes',[111] since persistence in these four basic qualities will give evidence of a work of grace in their hearts.

There are three main ways in which this rather ambiguous promise has been understood.

The first is that women 'will come safely through childbirth' (JBP). In this case the allusion will be to the pain and peril of childbirth which were part of God's judgment on Eve.[112] But 'salvation' language in the Pastorals always seems to refer to deliverance from sin, not from danger. Besides, such a promise is not true, since many godly women have died in childbirth.

The second interpretation is that women 'will be saved through motherhood' (NEB), or 'salvation for the woman will be in the bearing of children' (REB). This might have in mind those false teachers who were forbidding people to marry (4:3). But the way of salvation for women, according to Paul, was certainly not through accepting their vocation to bear children.

It seems to me that the third understanding is the most likely, namely that women 'will be saved through the Birth of the Child' (NEB mg.), referring to Christ. By this rendering, 'saved' has a spiritual connotation, 'through' is the means by which salvation comes, and the definite article before 'childbearing' in the Greek sentence is explained. Above all, this interpretation commends itself by 'its extreme appropriateness'.[113] Earlier in the chapter the 'one mediator between God and men' has been identified as 'the man Christ Jesus' (5), who of course became a human being by being 'born of a woman'.[114] Further, in the context of Paul's references to the creation and fall, recalling Genesis 2 and 3, a further reference to the coming redemption through the woman's seed, recalling Genesis 3:15, would be most apt. The serpent had deceived her; her posterity would defeat him.

So then, even if certain roles are not open to women, and even if they are tempted to resent their position, they and we must never forget what we owe to a woman. If Mary had not given birth to the Christ-child, there would have been no salvation for anybody. No

---

[110] Calvin, p. 218.   [111] Kroeger and Kroeger, p. 177.   [112] Gn. 3:16.
[113] Ellicott, p. 39. See also Liddon, p. 20, Lock, p. 33, Oden, p. 102 and Knight (1992), pp. 146–147.   [114] Gal. 4:4.

greater honour has ever been given to woman than in the calling of Mary to be the mother of the Saviour of the world.

Concluding questions

In developing the concept of cultural transposition, I am not claiming (as my readers might wish me to claim) that it provides a slick solution to all our questions about sexual roles, although I think it will save us from wrong solutions and will put us on the road towards right ones. But further theological reflection is needed, especially in relation to three questions.

The first is a question about complementarity. How should we define the created complementarity of the sexes (including the notions of 'headship' and 'submission'), not just physically and physiologically, certainly not culturally (in terms of popular gender stereotypes), but psychologically, and in particular biblically? What does Scripture teach about the essence (permanent and universal) of our created maleness and femaleness? This question must be at the top of our agenda for debate, since whatever creation has established culture can express but not destroy.

The second is a question about ministry. Once the complementarity of the sexes has been biblically defined, what are the roles and responsibilities which belong properly to men and not women, and to women and not men?

The third is a question about culture. What visible symbols in our particular culture would appropriately express the sexual complementarity which Scripture lays down as normative?

1 Timothy 3:1–16
3. Pastoral oversight

From the importance of apostolic doctrine (chapter 1) and the conduct of public worship (chapter 2), Paul turns to the pastoral oversight of the church and the necessary qualifications of pastors (chapter 3). This remains a vital topic in every place and generation. For the health of the church depends very largely on the quality, faithfulness and teaching of its ordained ministers.

Two introductory points need to be made.

First, God intends his church to have pastors. Even though church history has oscillated between the equally unbiblical extremes of 'clericalism' (the clergy domineering over the laity) and 'anti-clericalism' (the laity rebelling against the clergy), the basic conviction has persisted that some kind of pastoral oversight is God's will for his people. Thus, on their first missionary expedition Paul and Barnabas 'appointed elders . . . in each church'.[1] Moreover, this provision was not a purely human arrangement. It was the ascended Christ who gave some to his church 'to be pastors and teachers',[2] and it is the Holy Spirit who still assigns 'overseers' to God's flock.[3] The same divine-human policy is seen in Paul's instructions to Timothy and Titus. Titus was left in Crete to 'appoint elders in every town' (Tit. 1:5), and Timothy was told the traits which would qualify leaders for the oversight of the churches of Ephesus (1 Tim. 3).

Secondly, God has not specified the precise form which pastoral oversight should take. For example, this chapter lists the qualifications of 'overseers' (*episkopoi*) in verses 1–7 and of 'deacons' in verses 8–13, but throws little light on their duties. It is clear, however, that it would be an anachronism to translate *episkopos* 'bishop'. Even if Timothy and Titus may be considered embryonic bishops, in that they had to supervise a cluster of churches and appoint their pastors, yet they are not called 'bishops'. The

[1] Acts 14:23.   [2] Eph. 4:11.   [3] Acts 20:28.

development of the 'monarchical episcopate' (a single bishop presiding over a college of presbyters) cannot be dated earlier than Ignatius of Syrian Antioch, c. AD 110.

In New Testament times it is all but certain that *episkopos* ('overseer', 'bishop') and *presbyteros* ('presbyter', 'elder') were two titles for the same office. The evidence is compelling. First, Paul sent for the 'elders' of the Ephesian church, but in addressing them called them 'bishops'.[4] Secondly, in the same way Peter appealed to the 'elders' among his readers to serve as 'bishops' of God's flock.[5] Thirdly, Paul wrote to the Philippian church 'together with the bishops and deacons';[6] he must have omitted to mention the 'elders' only because they were the 'bishops'. Finally, Paul instructed Titus to appoint 'elders', adding that 'a bishop [NIV mg.] . . . must be blameless' (Tit. 1:5–7).

Why then were the same people given two titles? For two reasons at least. The word *presbyteros* ('elder') was Jewish in origin (every synagogue had its elders) and indicated the seniority of the pastor, whereas *episkopos* ('bishop') was Greek in origin (it was used of municipal officials, supervisors of subject cities, *etc.*) and indicated the superintending nature of the pastor's ministry. In sum, 'the title *episkopos* denotes the function, *presbyteros* the dignity, the former was borrowed from Greek institutions, the latter from the Jewish' (GT). Dr Alastair Campbell argues for a third difference, namely that the term 'elders' 'refers collectively to men who were individually overseers of the churches that met in their homes. Each person is an overseer, and together they are the seniors (*sc.* elders).'[7]

A degree of uncertainty also surrounds the origin of the 'deacons' and the nature of their ministry. The traditional view is as follows: in secular society the *diakonos* was one who gave lowly service, especially the waiter at table.[8] Moreover, 'in Greek eyes serving is not very dignified. Ruling not serving is proper to a man.'[9] But Jesus reversed this evaluation. 'For who is greater,' he asked, 'the one who is at the table or the one who serves? Is it not the one who is at the table? But I am among you as one who serves (*ho diakonōn*)'.[10] Again, 'even the Son of Man did not come to be served, but to serve . . .'[11] It was from this teaching and example of Jesus that the general calling of all his followers to humble service derived. From it too came the particular calling of some to serve as 'deacons'. The appointment of the Seven in Jerusalem was an early instance of it,

---

[4] Acts 20:17, 28, NIV mg.   [5] 1 Pet. 5:1–2, NIV mg.
[6] Phil. 1:1, NIV mg. J. B. Lightfoot's essay on presbyter-bishops has never been refuted. See his commentary on *The Letter to the Philippians* (1868), pp. 95–99.
[7] Campbell, p. 13.   [8] *E.g.* Jn. 2:5, 9.   [9] *TDNT* II, p. 82.
[10] Lk. 22:27; *cf.* Lk. 12:37; 17:7ff.   [11] Mk. 10:45.

since the expression 'to wait on tables' occurs in the story,[12] although the noun *diakonos* does not. It seems, then, that the 'deacons' were entrusted with practical administration, including the distribution of funds, food and clothing to the needy, although the requirement that they 'must keep hold of the deep truths of the faith with a clear conscience' (9) suggests that they would also assist the 'overseers' in their teaching ministry.

But this reconstruction has been challenged by Dr John Collins in his book *Diakonia* (1990), in which he makes an exhaustive survey of the *diakon-* word-group in both Christian and non-Christian ancient sources. His conclusion is that the *diakonos* was essentially a 'go-between', both in word (a courier or messenger) and in deed (an authorized agent). The emphasis, he insists, is not on the humble, menial character of the service rendered, but on its in-between, representative nature.[13] If this is correct, then it is right to see the deacons as the assistants of the overseers. Yet one wonders if the antithesis has not been drawn too sharply. After all, the *diakonos* who operates as an agent is still called to a lowly and subordinate role, however exalted the person he represents.

1. The overseers (3:1–7)

Here is a trustworthy saying: If anyone sets his heart on being an overseer, he desires a noble task. [2]*Now the overseer must be above reproach, the husband of but one wife, temperate, self-controlled, respectable, hospitable, able to teach,* [3]*not given to drunkenness, not violent but gentle, not quarrelsome, not a lover of money.* [4]*He must manage his own family well and see that his children obey him with proper respect.* [5]*(If anyone does not know how to manage his own family, how can he take care of God's church?)* [6]*He must not be a recent convert, or he may become conceited and fall under the same judgment as the devil.* [7]*He must also have a good reputation with outsiders, so that he will not fall into disgrace and into the devil's trap.*

Paul begins with another *trustworthy saying* (the first having occurred in 1:15), that is, a popular proverb which he now endorses as reliable. It is not always clear whether the maxim in question is what precedes or what follows. Since the other sayings relate in some way to the doctrine of salvation, some commentators suggest that this one (in 3:1a) looks back to 2:15 as 'a well-known Christian saying about the effect of the Incarnation on women'.[14] But virtually all English translations and most commentators relate the saying

---

[12] Acts 6:2.   [13] Collins, pp. 148, 194, 237.   [14] Lock, p. 33.

rather to what follows, namely: *If anyone sets his heart on being an overseer, he desires a noble task* (1).

Although *oregō* (*sets his heart on*) means literally to 'stretch oneself, reach out one's hand' for (BAGD) and so to 'aspire' to (REB, NRSV), Paul is not condoning a selfish ambition for the prestige and power which are associated with the ordained ministry. He is rather recognizing that the pastorate is *a noble task*, because it involves the care and nurture of the people of God, and that it is laudable to desire this privilege. But is not becoming a pastor a matter rather of divine call than of human aspiration? Yes, elsewhere Paul clearly affirms the call and appointment of God.[15] So what we call the 'selection' of candidates for the pastorate entails according to Paul three essentials: the call of God, the inner aspiration and conviction of the individuals concerned, and their conscientious screening by the church as to whether they meet the requirements which the apostle now goes on to list.

The first and general requirement is that *the overseer must be above reproach* (2a). This cannot mean 'faultless', or no child of Adam would ever qualify for a share in the oversight. It means rather 'of blameless reputation' (JBP) and 'has to do with irreproachable *observable* conduct'.[16] This provides biblical warrant for requiring references or testimonials, so that a candidate's public reputation may be ascertained.

Under Paul's direction, as he proceeds from the general to the particular, we are now able to compile a kind of questionnaire relating to a candidate for the pastorate. The following ten areas are to be investigated.

a. His fidelity in marriage

The requirement that he be *the husband of but one wife* (2) or 'married only once' (NRSV) has been the subject of long and anxious debate. Whom is Paul wishing to exclude from the pastorate by this expression? Five answers have been given to this question.

First, it is suggested that Paul is excluding those who have *never married*. Certainly he assumes that pastors will normally be married (as were the other apostles),[17] and without doubt the experience of marriage and family life greatly helps them in their ministry. Nevertheless, Paul is not intending to disqualify those of us who are single (or indeed married but childless, verse 5). Only the Eastern Orthodox churches have taught from this text that marriage is obligatory for parish clergy (while requiring their 'higher' clergy to be celibate monks). But Jesus and Paul both maintained that some

---

[15] *E.g.* Acts 20:28.   [16] Fee (1988), p. 80.   [17] 1 Cor. 9:5.

are called to remain single.[18] They also taught that others are called to
marriage, which makes the compulsory celibacy of the Roman
Catholic priesthood indefensible. The Second Vatican Council
conceded that celibacy 'is not demanded of the priesthood by its
nature' and referred to these verses in 1 Timothy as evidence. Yet it
argued that celibacy is 'in harmony with' priesthood (a) on the
pastoral ground that celibate priests are 'less encumbered in their
service', and (b) on the theological ground that they are 'a living sign
of that world to come' in which there will be no marriage. So the
Council exhorts priests 'to hold fast ... with courage and
enthusiasm' to their celibacy[19] – a sentiment which must be judged
incompatible with Paul's expectation in this text.

The second interpretation is that Paul excludes *polygamists*. His
phrase will of course exclude such, but are they his chief target? Some
have held this because polygamy, although technically forbidden by
Roman law, was still widely practised, and was also tolerated in
Jewish culture. For example, in his *Dialogue with Trypho, a Jew*, the
second-century Christian apologist Justin Martyr wrote of 'im-
prudent and blind' Jewish teachers 'who even till this time permit each
man to have four or five wives'.[20] Yet there seems no evidence that
Christians ever practised polygamy. Moreover, Paul's complementary
requirement that a widow must be 'the wife of one husband'[21] would
then have to be understood as referring to polyandry, whereas this
was unheard of even among pagans. Nevertheless, this apostolic ban
has proved relevant in contemporary polygamous societies (*e.g.* in
Africa), where churches tend to admit polygamists to membership by
baptism, but not to leadership by ordination.

Thirdly, Paul is thought by many to be excluding from the
pastorate those who have *divorced and remarried*. This seems a more
probable explanation than the previous one, since divorce and
remarriage were frequent in Graeco-Roman society and were not
unknown among Jews. They are also increasingly common in the
West today, so that anxious questions are being asked about this
dilemma. Do divorce and remarriage constitute an absolute ban on
ordination, although they seem to have been allowed by Jesus to the
innocent party when the other has been guilty of serious sexual sin,[22]
and by Paul in the case of a newly converted person whose spouse
remained unconverted and was unwilling to continue the marriage?[23]
Do these concessions not apply to clergy and prospective clergy,

[18] Mt. 19:10–11; 1 Cor. 7:7.
[19] 'The Life of Priests', para. 16, in A. Flannery (ed.), *Documents of Vatican II* (Costello, 1992).
[20] Justin Martyr, *Dialogue with Trypho*, translated by E. P. C. Hanson (Lutterworth, 1963), CXXXIV.
[21] 1 Tim. 5:9, literally. [22] Mt. 5:31–32; 19:9. [23] 1 Cor. 7:12ff.

then? If not, does this not erect a double standard? Yes it does, but is it not reasonable and right that a higher standard should be expected of pastors who are called to teach by example as well as by words?

Fourthly, some have argued that Paul is excluding those who are *widowed and remarried*, much as the Old Testament priests were not permitted to marry widows.[24] A number of early church fathers interpreted Paul's prohibition in this way. Tertullian was the most outspoken. He urged his wife, if he were to die first, 'to refrain from marrying and have done with sex for ever'.[25] The same applied to widowed men. 'For men who have been married twice are not allowed to preside in the Church.'[26] In his later treatises *An Exhortation to Chastity* and *Monogamy* his false asceticism became even more extreme. He argued that marriage is to be contracted only once; that those who re-marry are setting themselves against God's will by demanding what he has decided to take away; and that to have two wives successively is no better than to have two simultaneously. The argument against this view is, however, conclusive. The remarriage of widows and widowers is specifically permitted in the New Testament.[27] True, Paul expressed a preference that they remain single like himself,[28] but his reason was personal and practical, not moral, and he urged the younger widows to re-marry (5:14). So to forbid marriage to pastors whose first wife has died would be dangerously like the false teachers who were guilty of forbidding marriage altogether (4:3).

The fifth proposal is that Paul is excluding all those *guilty of married unfaithfulness*. Or better, he is making a general and positive stipulation that a candidate for the pastorate must be 'faithful to his one wife' (NEB), 'a man of unquestioned morality, one who is entirely true and faithful to his one and only wife',[29] or 'a man who having contracted a monogamous marriage is faithful to his marriage vows'.[30] This explanation seems to fit the context best. The accredited overseers of the church, who are called to teach doctrine and exercise discipline, must themselves have an unblemished reputation in the area of sex and marriage.

b. His self-mastery

Under this heading we may take the next three words together. *Temperate (nephalios)* means 'sober', which Hendriksen reminds us

---

[24] Lv. 21:14; *cf.* Ezk. 44:22.
[25] *To His Wife*, translated by W. P. Le Saint, Ancient Christian Writers 13 (Longmans, Green and Co., 1931), I.1.6.
[26] *Ibid.*, I.7.   [27] Rom. 7:1ff.; 1 Cor. 7:39.
[28] 1 Cor. 7:8ff., 25ff., 40.   [29] Hendriksen, p. 121.
[30] Knight (1994), pp. 158–159.

is not the same as 'sombre',[31] or 'clear-headed'. *Self-controlled* (*sōphrōn*) means 'sensible' or 'disciplined', while *respectable* translates *kosmios*, and 'what the *sōphrōn* is within, the *kosmios* is without'.[32] It is the outward expression of an inward self-control. This self-mastery is an indispensable quality of Christian leaders. As François Rabelais, the sixteenth-century French satirist, put it, 'how shall I be able to rule over others if I have not full power and command of myself?'[33] Leaders are often left for considerable periods unsupervised, so that they have to supervise themselves. To be sure, they are still people of flesh and blood, with the same emotions and passions as other human beings. But 'the fruit of the Spirit is . . . self-control'.[34]

c. His hospitality

Hospitable follows *self-controlled* naturally, since self-mastery makes self-giving possible. *Philoxenia*, literally a 'love for strangers', is urged in the New Testament on all Christians,[35] but specially on Christian leaders (*cf.* 5; Tit. 1:8). For in those days there were no hotels comparable to those we are familiar with, and roadside inns were scarce, dirty, unsafe and unsavoury. So Christian travellers, especially itinerant Christian preachers, needed to be accommodated by the pastor and his wife.[36] Even today, although there are plenty of hotels at least in cities, there are also lots of lonely people, like senior citizens, singles and overseas visitors, to whom Christian leaders can show hospitality, thereby perhaps entertaining angels without knowing it.[37]

d. His teaching ability

Suddenly, in the middle of a series of moral qualities, a single 'professional' qualification is mentioned: *able to teach* (*didaktikos*) or 'an apt teacher' (NRSV). It follows from this that pastors are essentially teachers. Indeed, what distinguishes Christian pastoral ministry is the pre-eminence in it of the Word of God. This also indicates that we should not draw a hard and fast line (as is often done) between an 'institutional' ministry appointed by the church and a 'charismatic' ministry appointed by God, or between office and gift. The fact that overseers must have a teaching gift shows that the church has no liberty to ordain any whom God has not called and gifted.

---

[31] Hendriksen, p. 122.   [32] Bengel, p. 257.
[33] *Works*, translated by D. M. Frame (University of California Press, 1991), ch. 52.
[34] Gal. 5:22–23.   [35] *E.g.* Rom. 12:13; 1 Pet. 4:9; 3 Jn. 5.
[36] See Phm. 22; 3 Jn. 5–8.   [37] Heb. 13:2.

e. His drinking habits

Alcohol is a depressant. It blunts and blurs our faculty of judgment. Those called to teach should take special warning. It is perhaps not an accident that *not given to drunkenness* should immediately follow 'an apt teacher'. Drinking and teaching do not go well together.

The Old Testament contains several solemn warnings to leaders about the damaging effect of alcohol. Priests were forbidden to drink while on duty, for this was evidently the cause of the presumption of Nadab and Abihu (Aaron's sons) in offering 'unauthorised fire before the LORD'.[38] Kings and other rulers were not to drink, or they would forget their country's laws and 'deprive the oppressed of their rights'.[39] Magistrates also, if 'heroes at drinking wine', would pervert justice, acquitting the guilty and punishing the innocent.[40] And prophets, when 'befuddled with wine', would find that they were unable to teach.[41]

Against this background, it is hardly surprising that Paul should issue a similar warning to Christian overseers. He did not require them to be total abstainers, since Jesus himself changed water into wine and made wine the emblem of his blood. Yet there are strong social arguments for total abstinence, since much reckless, violent and immoral behaviour is due to excessive drinking. What Paul requires, however, is moderation, as an example of the self-mastery already mentioned, not least because pastors are invited to many social functions at which wine flows freely.

f. His temper and temperament

The next two qualifications in verse 3 may be taken together: *not violent but gentle, not quarrelsome*. Unlike the false teachers, who were characterized by conceit, quarrelsomeness and strife (6:3ff.), true Christian teachers are above all to be gentle. *Epieikeia* means 'gentleness' or 'graciousness', and contains within it an element of yieldingness. Matthew Arnold coined the translation 'sweet reasonableness' (GT). This was an outstanding quality of our Lord Jesus, so that Paul could appeal to the Corinthians 'by the meekness and gentleness of Christ'.[42] Since gentleness is a fruit of the Spirit, it should characterize all the disciples of Jesus, but specially Christian leaders who are the servants of the Lord.[43]

Once this positive virtue has been cultivated, the two negative correlatives should take care of themselves. A gentle pastor will be

[38] Lv. 10:1ff.   [39] Pr. 31:4ff.; *cf.* 20:1; 23:19ff. and 29ff.   [40] Is. 5:22–23.
[41] Is. 28:7ff.   [42] 2 Cor. 10:1; *cf.* Mt. 11:29.   [43] Gal. 5:22–23; 2 Tim. 2:24–25.

neither *violent (plēktēs)*, a bully 'with the tongue or the hand',[44] nor *quarrelsome*. His patience may be sorely tried by demanding and aggravating people, but like his Master he will seek to be gentle, never crushing a bruised reed or snuffing out a wick that is burning low.[45]

g. His attitude to money

Towards the end of this letter Paul will call the love of money 'a root of all kinds of evil' (6:10). So it is understandable that a candidate for the pastorate must be *not a lover of money* (end of verse 3), which is what the false teachers were (6:5; 2 Tim. 3:2).

Yet throughout history bad men have tried to make money out of ministry. In the ancient world there were quacks who made a good living by posing as itinerant teachers. In the Old Testament Micah fulminated against Jerusalem because her judges took bribes, her priests taught for a price and her prophets told fortunes for cash.[46] In the New Testament Peter urged the pastors to be 'not greedy for money, but eager to serve',[47] while Paul renounced his right to support and earned his own living in order to demonstrate the sincerity of his motives.[48] In our day there are still some disreputable evangelists who make themselves wealthy by financial appeals, whereas wise Christian leaders publish audited accounts of their enterprise. As for pastors, although Paul requires them to be paid adequately (5:17f.), their salary in most countries is too low, in comparison with other professions, for them to be tempted to seek ordination for financial reasons.

Samuel was able at the end of his life to challenge Israel: 'Here I stand. Testify against me in the presence of the LORD and his anointed. Whose ox have I taken? . . . Whom have I cheated? . . . From whose hand have I accepted a bribe . . .?' 'You have not cheated or oppressed us,' the people replied.[49] Somewhat similarly, Paul was able to challenge the Ephesian elders: 'I have not coveted anyone's silver or gold or clothing. You yourselves know that these hands of mine have supplied my own needs and the needs of my companions.'[50] Would that all of us could make the same claim!

h. His domestic discipline

He must manage his own family well and see that his children obey him with proper respect. (If anyone does not know how to manage his

---

[44] Bengel, p. 258. [45] Is. 42:3 = Mt. 12:20. [46] Mi. 3:11.
[47] 1 Pet. 5:2. [48] *E.g.* 1 Cor. 9:4ff. [49] 1 Sa. 12:1ff.
[50] Acts 20:32ff.; *cf.* 1 Thes. 2:5ff.

own family, how can he take care of God's church?) (4–5). Paul draws an analogy between the pastor's family and God's church. Indeed, he uses the word *oikos* ('household') of both (4, 5, 15). So the married pastor is called to leadership in two families, his and God's, and the former is to be the training-ground for the latter. The argument is straightforward. If he cannot look after his own family, he cannot be expected to look after God's. Eli the priest remains a solemn warning to us in this area, for his sons were both immoral and greedy, but 'he failed to restrain them'.[51] The word *manage* (4, 5) translates *proïstamenos*, which is a word for 'leader', combining the concepts of 'rule' and 'care', and which Paul uses elsewhere of presbyters (5:17 and perhaps Rom. 12:8). It indicates that, although pastoral ministry is a servant ministry characterized by gentleness, a certain authority also attaches to it. One cannot expect discipline in the local church if pastors have not learned to exercise it in their home.

So those responsible for selecting candidates for the pastorate must investigate not only their personal qualities, but also their home and family life. Yet one often hears of instances in which a candidate's wife and children are not included in the interview or even in the enquiry. Paul insists, however, that if the candidate is a married man, assurances are needed that he has been 'faithful to his one wife' (2, NEB) and that his children are both 'submissive and respectful in every way' (4, NRSV) and Christian believers (Tit. 1:6).

i. His spiritual maturity

He must not be a recent convert (neophytos, 'neophyte', newly planted in Christ), *or he may become conceited and fall under the same judgment as the devil* (6). It goes without saying that candidates for the pastorate must be converted people, who give evidence of the genuineness of their conversion; what they must not be is recent converts. Doubtless pastors were first called 'elders' because that is what they were, senior in age and mature in faith. Although the modern western custom of ordaining people in their twenties straight from college has much to commend it, it also has its dangers, if they have had insufficient time since conversion to put down roots and to grow up in Christ. The main danger (apart from not being mature enough to bear responsibility) is pride (too much responsibility too soon). They *may become conceited. Typhoō* is a colourful verb meaning to 'becloud' (from *typhos,* 'cloud' or 'smoke'). It describes people like the false teachers (6:4) who live in 'cloud-cuckoo-land', a realm of self-centred fantasy. Such people

---

[51] 1 Sa. 3:13.

will *fall under the same judgment as the devil* (6). That is, the judgment passed on the devil for his pride will be passed on proud presbyters too. So humility is a necessary qualification for the pastorate, including humility before God in a life of personal devotion, faith and obedience.

j. His outside reputation

He must also have a good reputation with outsiders, so that he will not fall into disgrace and into the devil's trap (7). By *outsiders* Paul means 'the non-Christian public' (NEB). He wants the people of God to remember that the world is watching them, to be wise in their behaviour towards outsiders,[52] and to win their respect.[53] This is specially true of pastors. It has already been said that candidates must be 'above reproach' (2); now Paul emphasizes that they must have a good reputation outside as well as inside the church. He evidently thinks of the pastorate as a public office requiring public esteem. Otherwise they will suffer public *disgrace* and *fall . . . into the devil's trap*. We note this second reference to the devil. But whereas 'the devil's judgment' (6) was evidently an objective genitive (judgment falls on the devil), 'the devil's trap' is a subjective genitive (we fall into his trap, which is also mentioned in 6:9 and 2 Tim. 2:26). That is, in his malicious eagerness to discredit the gospel, the devil does his best to discredit the ministers of the gospel. It is an old trick with a long history. The devil has used it for centuries; it remains an effective stratagem today.

Although some commentators disparage these ten qualifications for the pastorate as pedestrian, and as suitable for secular leadership, they have far-reaching Christian implications, as we have seen. And if Paul's standards are regarded by some as comparatively low, we need to reflect that contemporary standards are lower still! For the selection procedure of many churches today does not include an examination of candidates in these ten areas. They constitute a necessary, comprehensive and challenging test.

2. The deacons (3:8-13)

Deacons, likewise, are to be men worthy of respect, sincere, not indulging in much wine, and not pursuing dishonest gain. [9]*They must*

---

[52] Col. 4:5.
[53] 1 Thes. 4:12. This missionary concern is a recurrent theme in these letters. See 1 Tim. 5:7-8, 14 (where 'the enemy' may refer to 'unfriendly, anti-Christian neighbours', JB mg.); 6:1; Tit. 2:5, 8.

99

keep hold of the deep truths of the faith with a clear conscience.
¹⁰*They must first be tested; and then if there is nothing against them,*
let them serve as deacons.
¹¹*In the same way, their wives are to be women worthy of respect,*
not malicious talkers but temperate and trustworthy in everything.
¹²*A deacon must be the husband of but one wife and must manage*
his children and his household well. ¹³*Those who have served well*
gain an excellent standing and great assurance in their faith in Christ
Jesus.

Since the *diakonos* was the waiter at table, and *diakonein* means to
engage in service of a social kind, as we have already noted, it is
understandable that the 'deacons' are thought to have specialized in
practical administration and ministry, even if Acts 6 was not the
historical origin of the diaconate. But the requirement of verse 9, that
the deacons have a strong and steadfast grasp of the revealed faith,
suggests that they were expected to teach it, which was the chief
responsibility of the overseers. So then, rather than distinguishing
deacons from overseers as social workers from teachers, it is perhaps
better to think of the deacons as assisting the overseers in their
ministry.

Since the qualifications for the diaconate overlap with those for
the presbyterate, it will not be necessary to study them all in detail.
But the following four areas are emphasized.

First, deacons must have self-mastery. Four words in verse 8 seem
to form a natural grouping – *men worthy of respect* ('men' is not in
the Greek sentence), *sincere (mē dilogos)*, literally 'not double-
tongued', 'not indulging in double-talk' (REB) or, as we might say,
'not speaking out of both sides of their mouth', *not indulging in
much wine, and not pursuing dishonest gain,* 'with no squalid greed
for money' (JB). Thus in these four areas, in their behaviour, speech,
use of alcohol and attitude to money, candidates for the diaconate are
to have control of themselves.

Secondly, deacons must have orthodox convictions. *They must
keep hold of the deep truths of the faith with a clear conscience* (9), or
be 'conscientious believers in the mystery of the faith' (JB). For *deep
truths* translates *to mysterion*, and this 'mystery' is the sum-total of
the revealed truths of the faith. These the deacons must hold fast.
And unlike the false teachers, who have rejected their conscience and
so shipwrecked their faith (1:19), and have even 'cauterized' their
conscience by constantly disregarding it (4:2), the deacons are to
maintain 'a clear conscience' (*cf.* 1:6), holding on to God's revelation
with sincere and strong conviction.

Thirdly, deacons must have been tested and approved. *They must
first be tested* or 'undergo a scrutiny' (NEB). In addition to the

selection procedure Paul has been outlining, there needs to be a period of probation, in which the congregation may assess the character, beliefs and gifts of the candidates for the diaconate. It is right that in this way the congregation is given a share in the testing of potential deacons. *And then if there is nothing against them, let them serve as deacons* (10). This shows that the concept of 'probationers' or 'postulants' is wise and biblical.

Fourthly, deacons must have an irreproachable home life. Verse 11 raises a problem. It begins *In the same way, their wives are to be women worthy of respect...* Literally it runs: 'Women likewise...' And commentators are not agreed whether these women are the deacons' wives (as in NIV) or deaconesses (NIV mg.), for the word could apply to either.

In favour of 'deaconesses', the 'likewise' of verse 11, like that of verse 8, leads one to expect a new category; it would be strange for deacons' wives to be mentioned when elders' wives are not; there is no definite article or possessive before 'women' which there would have to be if it meant 'their wives' (NIV has unwarrantably added 'their'); and we know from Phoebe[54] that there were women deacons or deaconesses at that time.

In favour of 'deacons' wives', on the other hand, these women are not called 'deacons' like Phoebe; the reference to them is sandwiched between two references to deacons, which would make an allusion to their wives quite natural; and the omission of a reference to the women's married faithfulness, corresponding to verses 2 and 12, would be explained if these women were the deacons' wives.

Commentators are still divided on this question. One or two suggest that it could be a reference to both, since wives and deaconesses could share in assisting the deacons in their ministry. In either case, these women are to be *worthy of respect* (*semnos*), like the deacons in verse 8, *not malicious talkers but*, having control of their tongue, *temperate* (*nephalios*), like the presbyters in verse 2, *and trustworthy in everything* (11).

Paul now reverts to the deacons. Whether or not verse 11 refers to their wives, *a deacon must be the husband of but one wife and must manage his children and his household well* (12), just like the candidate for the presbyterate (verses 2, 4 and 5). Then *those who have served well* in the diaconate (*diakonēsantes*) will gain two things. The first is *an excellent standing. Bathmos* (*standing*) can denote a step, stair, grade or rank. It might mean here that to serve well in the diaconate is a step to the presbyterate, but concepts of ecclesiastical 'preferment' or 'promotion' are surely an anachronism. In this case the 'standing' will be spiritual, either a position of

[54] Rom. 16:1.

honour in the esteem of God and the church, or even 'a "step" in the soul's journey heavenward' (BAGD). The second thing which faithful deacons gain is *great assurance in their faith in Christ Jesus* (13). *Assurance* is *parrēsia*, which is freedom of speech or boldness before God or human beings. Faithful service will increase their Christian confidence.

Looking back, it is clear that the qualifications for the presbyterate and the diaconate are very similar. There is a core of Christian qualities, which all Christian leaders should exhibit. Putting the two lists together, we note that there are five main areas to be investigated. In regard to himself the candidate must be self-controlled and mature, including the areas of drink, money, temper and tongue; in regard to his family, both faithful to his wife and able to discipline his children; in regard to his relationships, hospitable and gentle; in regard to outsiders, highly esteemed; and in regard to the faith, strong in his hold on its truth and gifted in teaching it.

The whole first half of this chapter is a good example of the balance of Scripture. For there is material here both to encourage the right people to offer for pastoral ministry and to discourage the wrong ones from doing so. The discouragement is that the required standards are high and the task is arduous. The responsibility of caring for 'God's church' (5) is calculated to daunt the best and the most gifted Christians. But the corresponding encouragement is that the pastorate is a noble task, a beautiful undertaking, a laudable ambition (1). It involves giving oneself to the service of others. Besides, the words *episkopos* and *diakonos* are both applied to the Lord Jesus in the New Testament. Peter called him 'the Shepherd and Overseer (*episkopos*) of your souls',[55] and he applied to himself the verb *diakonein*.[56] Could there be any greater honour than to follow in his footsteps and share in some of his *episkopē* and *diakonia* which he is willing to delegate to us?

3. The church (3:14–16)

From the qualifications for the pastorate Paul turns to the church in which pastors serve. For the nature of the ministry is determined by the nature of the church.

Although I hope to come to you soon, I am writing you these in-structions so that, [15]if I am delayed, you will know how people ought to conduct themselves in God's household, which is the church of the living God, the pillar and foundation of the truth. [16]Beyond all

[55] 1 Pet. 2:25.   [56] *E.g.* Mk. 10:45; Lk. 22:27.

question, the mystery of godliness is great:

> *He appeared in a body,*
> *was vindicated by the Spirit,*
> *was seen by angels,*
> *was preached among the nations,*
> *was believed on in the world,*
> *was taken up in glory.*

Here is Paul's self-conscious apostolic authority. He is planning to visit Timothy in Ephesus. He says so twice (3:14 and 4:13).[57] And when he comes he will personally regulate the affairs of the church. But he senses that he may be delayed. So he writes his instructions for the interim period. Thus by a deliberate providence of God the New Testament letters came to be written and have been preserved for the edification of the church in subsequent generations. If the apostles' directions regarding the doctrine, ethics, unity and mission of the church had been given only in oral form, the church would have been like a mapless traveller and a rudderless ship. But because the apostolic instructions were written down, we *know* what we would not otherwise have known, namely *how people ought to conduct themselves* in the church.

Paul uses three descriptive expressions of the church, each of which illustrates a different aspect of it, namely *God's household* or family, *the church of the living God*, and *the pillar and foundation of the truth* (15).

a. God's household

The word *oikos* can mean either a house (the building) or a household (the family that occupies the building). And Scripture tells us that the church is both God's house[58] and God's household.[59] The two concepts are sometimes brought together.[60] But since in this chapter

[57] *Cf.* 1 Cor. 11:34; 2 Cor. 13:10.   [58] *E.g.* 1 Cor. 3:16; 1 Pet. 2:5.
[59] *E.g.* Heb. 3:5–6; 1 Pet. 4:17.
[60] *E.g.* Eph. 2:19ff. Dr David C. Verner investigates and compares three households – those of the Roman, Greek and Jewish worlds, the Christian household and the household of God (the church). Although Paul clearly sees a parallel between the last two, arguing that a leader who has failed to manage the former will not be able to manage the latter, Dr Verner makes a big hermeneutical leap. He assumes that by calling the church God's household the author of the Pastorals wanted the dominant aristocratic household values to be reproduced in it (Verner, p. 182). He concludes: 'The purpose for which the author employs the image of the Household of God is . . . clear. He intends to bolster a hierarchical social structure in the church . . . In this way he hopes to suppress the forces that threaten it and the radical social values which they represent' (p. 186). The evidence for this is extremely flimsy.

oikos has already been used three times of a household (verses 4, 5, 12),[61] it seems likely that it has the same connotation in verse 15.

By new birth of the Spirit we become members of the family of God, related to him as our Father and to all fellow believers as our sisters and brothers. Although Paul does not here draw out the implications of our being God's household or family, he does elsewhere. He emphasizes that as God's children we have an equal dignity before him, irrespective of age, sex, race or culture;[62] and that as sisters and brothers we are called to love, forbear and support one another, enjoying in fact the rich 'one anotherness' or reciprocity of the Christian fellowship.[63]

b. The church of the living God

On a number of occasions in the Old Testament Yahweh is named 'the living God' in deliberate contrast to the lifeless idols of the heathen. Indeed, still today Christian conversion involves turning 'to God from idols to serve the living and true God'.[64] But where does the living God live? Joshua answered this question succinctly: 'The living God is among you.'[65] For this was the essence of God's covenant promise to Israel: 'I will dwell among you and be your God, and you shall be my people.'[66] Israel's consciousness that the living God lived among them profoundly affected their community life. Even an elementary lesson in personal hygiene was based on the fact that the LORD God walked among them and must not see anything indecent.[67] And they were incensed when the heathen presumed to 'defy', 'insult' or 'ridicule' the living God.[68]

An even more vivid consciousness of the presence of the living God should characterize the Christian church today. For we are 'the temple of the living God',[69] 'a dwelling in which God lives by his Spirit'.[70] When the members of the congregation are scattered during most of the week it is difficult to remain aware of this reality. But when we come together as *the church* (*ekklēsia*, 'assembly') *of the living God*, every aspect of our common life is enriched by the knowledge of his presence in our midst.[71] In our worship we bow down before the living God. Through the reading and exposition of his Word we hear his voice addressing us. We meet him at his table, when he makes himself known to us through the breaking of bread. In our fellowship we love each other as he has loved us. And our

---

[61] *Cf.* Tit. 1:11; 2 Tim. 1:16.   [62] *E.g.* Gal. 3:26ff.
[63] *E.g.* Heb. 10:2–3.; Gal. 6:2.   [64] 1 Thes. 1:9; *cf.* Acts 14:15.
[65] Jos. 3:10; *cf.* Dt. 6:15.
[66] *E.g.* Ex. 25:8; 29:45–46; Lv. 26:12; *cf.* Ps. 114:2; Ezk. 37:27; 2 Cor. 6:16.
[67] Dt. 23:12ff.; *cf.* Nu. 35:34; 1 Ki. 6:13.   [68] 1 Sa. 17:26, 36; 2 Ki. 19:4, 16.
[69] 2 Cor. 6:16; *cf.* 3:16.   [70] Eph. 2:22.   [71] Mt. 18:20.

witness becomes bolder and more urgent. Indeed, unbelievers coming in may confess that 'God is really among you'.[72]

c. The pillar and foundation of the truth

Having considered our duty to each other as the household of God, and to God as his dwelling-place, we come to our duty to the truth as its pillar and foundation.

The *hedraiōma* of a building is its mainstay. It may refer either to its foundation or to a buttress or bulwark which supports it. In either case the *hedraiōma* stabilizes the building. Just so, the church is responsible to hold the truth steady against the storms of heresy and unbelief.

The word *stylos*, however, means a pillar or column. The purpose of pillars is not only to hold the roof firm, but to thrust it high so that it can be clearly seen even from a distance. The inhabitants of Ephesus had a vivid illustration of this in their temple of Diana or Artemis. Regarded as one of the seven wonders of the world, it boasted 100 Ionic columns, each over 18 metres high, which together lifted its massive, shining, marble roof. Just so, the church holds the truth aloft, so that it is seen and admired by the world. Indeed, as pillars lift a building high while remaining themselves unseen, so the church's function is not to advertise itself but to advertise and display the truth.

Here then is the double responsibility of the church *vis-à-vis* the truth. First, as its foundation it is to hold it firm, so that it does not collapse under the weight of false teaching. Secondly, as its pillar it is to hold it high, so that it is not hidden from the world. To hold the truth firm is the defence and confirmation of the gospel; to hold it high is the proclamation of the gospel. The church is called to both these ministries.

Some Christians, however, are confused about the relation between the church and the truth. Is it really so that the church is the foundation of the truth? Is it not rather the case that the truth is the foundation of the church? It was probably this concern which led Chrysostom to make a slip of the tongue and say 'for the truth is the pillar and ground of the church'.[73] Besides, Paul himself had earlier described the church as 'built on the foundation of the apostles and prophets [*sc.* their teaching], with Jesus Christ himself as the chief cornerstone'.[74] So is the truth the foundation of the church, or is the church the foundation of the truth? The answer is 'Both'. When Paul taught that the truth is the foundation of the church,[75] he was referring to the church's life and health: the church

[72] 1 Cor. 14:25. [73] Chrysostom, p. 442. [74] Eph. 2:20. [75] Eph. 2:20.

rests on the truth, depends on it, cannot exist without it. But when he taught that the church is the foundation of the truth (3:15), he was referring to the church's mission: the church is called to serve the truth, to hold it fast and make it known. So then, the church and the truth need each other. The church depends on the truth for its existence; the truth depends on the church for its defence and proclamation.

What then is the truth which the church must both guard against every distortion and falsification, and proclaim without fear or compromise throughout the world? It concerns Jesus Christ, to whom Paul now bears witness by quoting from an early hymn or creed. He introduces it with the following words: *Beyond all question, the mystery of godliness is great* (16a). First, it is a 'mystery', a cluster of truths which are now known only because God has been pleased to reveal them. Secondly, it is a 'mystery of godliness' as he has previously called it a 'mystery of the faith' (9, JB). It is the latter because it stimulates faith and is faith's object. It is the former because it stimulates our worship, our humility and reverence before God, as all truth does.[76] Thirdly, this divine godliness-promoting revelation is 'great beyond all question' (REB) or 'by common consent',[77] 'undeniably' great (BAGD) or 'demonstrably' great.[78] And fourthly, it focuses on the person and work of Jesus Christ, since 'the mystery' is essentially 'the mystery of Christ'.[79]

Spicq sees these verses as the 'doctrinal climax' of the letter, even its 'heart', since they define the church 'by her relation to the glorious Christ'. He also sees the credal affirmation ('great . . . is the mystery of our religion', REB) as 'a solemn public confession in opposition to that of Diana's devotees' who shouted in unison for two hours, 'Great is Diana of the Ephesians!'[80]

The liturgical statement Paul goes on to quote consists of six lines which, stylistically speaking, closely resemble one another. For all six begin with a verb which ends in the letters -*thē*, and is in the aorist tense and the passive mood. All also end with a noun in the dative, and all but one use the preposition *en* to link the verb with the noun. Moving from style to substance, however, what do the six statements mean, and how do they relate to one another? Three suggestions are made.

First, the six affirmations may be read chronologically,[81] each

---

[76] Tit. 1:1.   [77] Kelly, p. 88.
[78] Hanson (1966), p. 46; (1982), p. 84.   [79] Col. 1:26–27; 2:2–3; 4:3.
[80] Acts 19:28, 34. See Spicq, pp. 464, 469, 475.
[81] *E.g.* Barrett, p. 66. The most thorough examination of the interpretation and theological background of this verse has been offered by Dr Robert H. Gundry in

denoting a fresh, consecutive event or stage in the career of Jesus, taking us from his first coming to his second, from his appearance in flesh to his welcome in glory. So *he appeared in a body* (literally, 'in flesh') refers to his incarnation, by which the pre-existent Son was born into the world, and lived and died in it. Next, he *was vindicated by the Spirit*. Although the body–spirit contrast has suggested to some commentators a reference to his human and divine natures, 'spirit' is more likely to refer to the Holy Spirit who vindicated Jesus first by his mighty works,[82] and then supremely by his resurrection.[83] He was *seen by angels*, and attended by them, throughout his life.[84] But the chronological sequence following his incarnation and resurrection would expect this third statement to refer to his ascension. And indeed angels were present at it[85] and watched the whole unfolding drama of salvation.[86] That he *was preached among the nations* is a clear reference to the church's world-wide mission in obedience to the great commission of the risen Lord,[87] while he *was believed on in the world* is an equally plain allusion to the success of the gospel as people responded to it. The final statement, that he *was taken up in glory*, sounds like another reference to the ascension. But if the sequence is chronological, it must be the parousia which is in mind, his ascension foreshadowing his final epiphany in power and great glory. This interpretation is the more probable because otherwise 'there is no hint of eschatology'[88] in this Christological hymn.

A second and more popular reconstruction[89] is to divide the hymn into two stanzas, each consisting of a triplet, the first alluding to the life of the historical incarnate Jesus on earth (he appeared, was vindicated and seen), and the second to the life of the exalted Lord (he was preached, believed on and glorified).

The third and best suggestion,[90] however, is that the hymn consists of three couplets, in each of which there is a deliberate antithesis: between flesh and spirit, between angels and nations, between world and glory. The first couplet speaks of the revelation of Christ (*he appeared in a body, was vindicated by the Spirit*). Here are the human and divine aspects of his earthly life and ministry in Palestine. The second couplet speaks of the witnesses of Christ (*was seen by angels, was preached among the nations*). For now the significance of Jesus Christ is seen to extend far beyond Palestine to all the inhabitants of heaven and earth, to angels as well as humans, to the

---

'The Form, Meaning and Background of the Hymn Quoted in I Timothy 3:16' in W. W. Gasque and R. P. Martin (eds.), *Apostolic History and the Gospel* (Paternoster, 1970), pp. 203–222.   [82] Mt. 12:28.   [83] Rom. 1:4; 8:11.
[84] *E.g.* Lk. 2:13; Mk. 1:13; Lk. 22:43; 24:23; Mt. 28:2ff.   [85] Acts 1:9ff.
[86] Eph. 3:10; 1 Pet. 1:12.   [87] 1 Tim. 2:7; Mt. 28:19ff.   [88] Houlden, p. 85.
[89] *E.g.* Lock, pp. 45–46; Fee (1988), pp. 92–95.   [90] *E.g.* Kelly, pp. 90–93.

nations as well as the Jews. Then the third couplet speaks of the reception which Christ was given (*was believed on in the world, was taken up in glory*). For heaven and earth did more than see and hear him; they joined in giving him recognition and acclaim.

Some years ago Joachim Jeremias, in his book *Jesus' Promise to the Nations*, argued that this Christological hymn was essentially a missionary statement, announcing the inclusion of the nations in consequence of the death and resurrection of Jesus. He also suggested that this credal fragment was 'couched in the form of a hymn of three distichs, after the style of a coronation hymn', indeed 'the ancient coronation ritual exemplified for us in the ancient Egyptian ritual'. It consisted of the Elevation (of the king to deity), the Presentation (of the deified king to the world) and the Enthronement. This, Jeremias proposed, corresponded to the three couplets of verse 16, namely 'the Justification by resurrection of him who has been manifested on earth, the Announcement to heaven and earth of his exaltation, and his Assumption of the kingdom on earth and in heaven'.[91] Commentators have been intrigued by Jeremias's suggestion, and have pronounced it 'ingenious and attractive',[92] but have not been persuaded by it, mainly on account of the inexact nature of the parallelism. Yet the missionary emphasis is surely right. The mystery of godliness which the church proclaims, the truth of which the church is the foundation and pillar, is the historic yet cosmic Christ.

In conclusion, Paul's perspective in this chapter is to view the presbyters and the deacons in the light of the church they are called to serve, and to view the church in the light of the truth it is called to confess. One of the surest roads to the reform and renewal of the church is to recover a grasp of its essential identity as *God's household, the church of the living God,* and *the pillar and foundation of the truth* (15).

[91] Joachim Jeremias, *Jesus' Promise to the Nations* (1956; Eng trans. SCM, 1958), p. 38. Jeremias also referred back to his earlier commentary on the Pastorals, *Die Briefe des Timotheus und Titus* (Göttingen, 1934, sixth edition 1953).
[92] Lock, p. 92.

1 Timothy 4:1 – 5:2
4. Local leadership

Chapter 3 ended with a reference to the church as 'the pillar and foundation of the truth' (15) and with a summary of that truth in relation to Christ (16). Chapter 4 opens with a reference to the false teachers and their lies (1–2). Thus Paul warns Timothy that the false teachers are denying what the church confesses. His preoccupation throughout this chapter is with these two sets of teachers in opposition to one another. On the one hand, some people are abandoning the faith and embracing falsehood. On the other, some are questioning the truth Timothy is teaching, on account of his comparative youthfulness. So here are the two topics which Paul develops: first, how false teaching may be detected and exposed, in spite of its plausibility (1–10); and secondly, how true teaching may be commended and endorsed, in spite of Timothy's youth (4:11 – 5:2). Both topics seem to come appropriately under the heading of 'Local leadership', because the local church is the main arena in which the unremitting struggle between truth and error is fought out. So local leaders need help both in detecting error and in commending truth. However uncongenial theological debate may be, especially as an increasing number of people summarily dismiss the very concept of objective truth, it cannot be avoided.

1. The detection of false teaching (4:1–10)

The Spirit clearly says that in later times some will abandon the faith and follow deceiving spirits and things taught by demons. ²Such teachings come through hypocritical liars, whose consciences have been seared as with a hot iron. ³They forbid people to marry and order them to abstain from certain foods, which God created to be received with thanksgiving by those who believe and who know the truth. ⁴For everything God created is good, and nothing is to be rejected if it is received with thanksgiving, ⁵because it is consecrated by the word of God and prayer.

[6]If you point these things out to the brothers, you will be a good minister of Christ Jesus, brought up in the truths of the faith and of the good teaching that you have followed. [7]Have nothing to do with godless myths and old wives' tales; rather, train yourself to be godly. [8]For physical training is of some value, but godliness has value for all things, holding promise for both the present life and the life to come.
[9]This is a trustworthy saying that deserves full acceptance [10](and for this we labour and strive), that we have put our hope in the living God, who is the Saviour of all men, and especially of those who believe.

The key statement in this paragraph is that, in spite of the church's role as the guardian of the truth, *some will abandon the faith* (1a). It is a strong Greek verb (*apostēsontai*, 'will apostatize'), which was frequently used in the LXX of Israel's unfaithfulness to Yahweh.

When will this Christian apostasy take place? *In later times*, Paul replies. But he quickly slips from the future tense into the present (3–6), indicating his belief that the 'later times' have already begun. It is the same in 2 Timothy 3:1ff., where he writes of 'the last days' and almost immediately divulges that they have arrived by telling Timothy to avoid the people he has been describing. So 'later times' and 'the last days' both denote the Christian era, which Jesus inaugurated at his first coming and will consummate at his second.[1]

The reason Paul knew about the apostasy is that *the Spirit clearly*, 'explicitly' (JB, REB) or 'specifically' (JBP), *says that* it will happen. Perhaps he is referring to the prediction of a falling away from the faith which Jesus made,[2] through which the Spirit is continuing to speak (see the refrain about listening to 'what the Spirit says to the churches' through Christ's seven letters to the Asian churches in Rev. 2 and 3). Alternatively, Paul could be alluding to his own earlier prophecy of false teachers, who like 'savage wolves' would invade the Ephesian church and 'draw away disciples after them'.[3] Or possibly he is claiming that even as he writes these words the Holy Spirit is inspiring him to make this prophecy.

Paul now outlines first the causes of error (1–2), how it arises and spreads in the church, and secondly its tests (3–10), the criteria by which it may be detected and found wanting.

---

[1] *Cf.* Acts 2:17; 1 Cor. 10:11; Heb. 1:2.
[2] *E.g.* Mt. 24:10–11; Mk. 13:22.   [3] Acts 20:29–30; *cf.* 2 Thes. 2:3ff.

a. The causes of error (4:1–2)

On the surface the situation is quite straightforward. Certain teachers begin to spread their erroneous views, and some gullible people listen to them, are taken in by them, and in consequence abandon the apostolic faith. But Paul looks beneath this surface appearance, and explains to Timothy the underlying spiritual dynamic. He refers to three successive stages.

The first cause of error is diabolical. Those who *abandon the faith* do so because they have been 'paying attention to' (NRSV) or *follow deceiving spirits and things taught by demons* (1). Thus in the same verse Paul refers both to the Holy Spirit and to evil spirits or demons. For behind the false teachers he sees the activity of demonic forces. Speaking himself under the infuence of the Spirit of truth he declares the false teachers to be under the influence of deceiving spirits.

We tend not to take this fact sufficiently seriously. Scripture portrays the devil not only as the tempter, enticing people into sin, but also as the deceiver, seducing people into error. Often he does both together, as when in the Garden of Eden he prevailed upon our first parents to doubt and then to disobey God's word. No wonder Jesus called him 'a liar and the father of lies'.[4] And the apostles regularly attributed human error to devilish deceit.[5] Is this not why intelligent and educated people can swallow the fantastic speculations of the cults and of New Age paganism, some of the far-fetched doctrines of the ethnic religions, and the barrenness of atheistic philosophies? It is because there is not only a Spirit of truth but also a spirit of falsehood, who is able to delude, drug, bewitch and even blind people.[6]

Secondly, error has a human cause. The devil does not usually deceive people direct. 'Demon-inspired doctrines' (REB) gain an entry into the world and the church through human agents. *Such teachings come through hypocritical liars* (2a), or literally 'by means of the hypocrisy of liars'. It is a terrible combination of words, since hypocrisy is a deliberate pretence and a lie a deliberate falsehood. So then false teachers, although seduced by deceiving spirits, are themselves intentional deceivers, however misleading their mask of learning and religion may be. They do not themselves believe what they are teaching.

The third and basic cause of error is moral. For the hypocritical lies of the false teachers are now traced back to the violation of their

---

[4] Jn. 8:44.
[5] *E.g.* 2 Cor. 2:11; Eph. 6:11; 2 Thes. 2:9ff.; 1 Jn. 2:18; 4:1ff.; Rev. 13:14.
[6] 1 Jn. 4:6; 2 Tim. 2:26; Gal. 3:1; 2 Cor. 4:4.

consciences, which have been *seared as with a hot iron* (2b). The verb *kaustēriazō,* which occurs only here in the New Testament, means to 'brand with a red-hot iron' (BAGD). It was used of the branding of cattle and slaves, in order to establish their ownership. Most commentators opt for this interpretation and suppose that somehow the false teachers have been branded as the property of Satan. But how can their conscience bear a mark of identification which is visible to others? It seems more probable that *kaustēriazō* is used here in its alternative, medical sense of to 'cauterize'. When skin, a nerve or a superficial tumour is cauterized, it is destroyed by burning and so rendered insensitive. Just so, a cauterized conscience has been 'anaesthetized',[7] even deadened. 'By constantly arguing with conscience, stifling its warnings and muffling its bell',[8] its voice is smothered and eventually silenced. In that state of moral insensibility[9] false teachers easily fall prey to error. Paul has already mentioned Hymenaeus and Alexander as examples. By rejecting their conscience they 'shipwrecked their faith' (1:19).

The grim sequence of events in the career of the false teachers has now been revealed. First, they turned a deaf ear to their conscience, until it became cauterized. Next, they felt no scruple in becoming hypocritical liars. Thirdly, they thus exposed themselves to the influence of deceiving spirits. Finally, they led their listeners to abandon the faith. It is a perilous downward path from the deaf ear and the cauterized conscience to the deliberate lie, the deception of demons and the ruination of others. It begins when we tamper with our conscience. Instead, we need to say with Paul: 'I strive always to keep my conscience clear before God and man.'[10]

b. The tests of error (4:3–10)

By now our curiosity has been aroused as to what the false teachers were propagating. In telling us, Paul also moves from the causes of error to its tests. He puts into Timothy's hands two important criteria which may be applied to all teaching. The rest of the first half of this chapter is devoted to the question how error may be detected.

It is clear that the false teaching in Ephesus consisted of a false asceticism: *They forbid people to marry and order them to abstain from certain foods* (3a). Marriage and food relate to the two most basic appetites of the human body, sex and hunger. They are natural appetites too, although both can be abused by degenerating into lust and greed. Yet from the beginning of church history some teachers have gone further, and have argued that sex and hunger are themselves unclean appetites, that the body itself is a nasty

---

[7] Hanson (1982), p. 87. [8] Hendriksen, p. 146. [9] Eph. 4:19. [10] Acts 24:16.

encumbrance (if not actually evil), and that the only way to holiness is abstinence, the voluntary renunciation of sex and marriage, and, since eating cannot be given up altogether, then at least the renunciation of meat.

One origin of these tendencies was Jewish. The Essenes of Qumran, for example, were said by Josephus to 'reject pleasures as an evil, but esteem continence ... to be virtue', and to 'neglect marriage'.[11] Later this Jewish aberration came to be mingled with the dualism of Greek philosophy, and especially with incipient Gnosticism which regarded matter as evil and despised the material creation. The Encratites, for example, are described by Irenaeus as having 'preached against marriage, thus setting aside the original creation of God, and indirectly blaming him who made them male and female for the propagation of the human race'. They also enjoined abstinence from animal food, 'thus proving themselves ungrateful to God who made all things'.[12] Some other church fathers, like Tertullian, were themselves tainted with an exaggerated asceticism, and regarded virginity as always higher and holier than marriage. In rejecting this, we do not forget that according to Jesus and Paul some people are called to remain single, or that fasting has a place in Christian discipleship, but these are special cases. The point is that celibacy and vegetarianism are not God's general will for everybody; to forbid marriage and meat-eating is to be guilty of serious error.

But why? Wherein lies the essence of the false teachers' error? And how can it be detected? Paul now supplies two fundamental tests, which are widely applicable. The first is a theological test, the doctrine of creation (3–5). The second is an ethical test, the priority of godliness (6–10).

i. A theological test: creation (4:3–5)
Marriage and certain foods, which the false teachers were forbidding, are gifts *which God created to be received with thanksgiving by those who believe and who know the truth* (3b). The principle is plain. How can anybody despise marriage, let alone forbid it, when God instituted it? How can anybody command abstention from certain foods, when God created them to be received with thanksgiving? What God has made and given us, we are to receive and thank him for. The reference may be to an inward spirit of thanksgiving, but probably also to the open expression of it in saying grace before meals, which had long been the custom in Jewish households.[13]

We need to note carefully the double consecration of God's

[11] Josephus, *Wars* II.8.2; *cf. Ant.* XVIII.1.5.   [12] Irenaeus, I.28.1.
[13] *Cf.* Rom. 14:6; 1 Cor. 10:30.

creation gifts, which Paul repeats three times for emphasis. The first statement, as we have seen, brings together the divine creation and the grateful human reception (3). Secondly, the principle is given a universal application: *For everything God created is good, and nothing is to be rejected if it is received with thanksgiving* (4). If everything was declared good by creation, then nothing is to be declared taboo. This is assuredly an allusion to the refrain of Genesis 1 that everything God made was good. Thirdly, Paul clinches the argument: *because it is consecrated by the word of God and prayer* (5).

Thus marriage and food, and all God's many other creation gifts, are consecrated twice over, first and foremost objectively in themselves, since God made or instituted them, gave them to us to enjoy, and has said so in Scripture. Then secondly they are consecrated to us subjectively when we recognize their divine origin and receive them from God with gratitude. If God made something, calling it into being by his word, and by the same word declared it to be good, and if, as a result of our knowledge of these things, we can thank God for it with a good conscience, then we have a double cause to receive it, enjoy it, and thankfully celebrate it. God's creative word and our grateful prayer have together sanctified it to our use. Thus Fairbairn wrote of 'God's word to man warranting him to use the creation gift, and man's word to God, acknowledging the gift, and asking his blessing on it'. So 'the sanctification is complete both ways – objectively by the word of God, subjectively by prayer'.[14]

Notice carefully, however, what Paul writes. It is not that 'everything is good', but that *everything created by God is good*. This is an indispensable qualification, since not everything that exists has come unsullied from the Creator's hand. For the creation was followed by the fall, which introduced evil into the world and spoiled much of God's good creation. Indeed the creation has been 'subjected to frustration' and is now 'groaning' in pain.[15] We therefore need discernment to know what in our human experience is attributable to the creation, and what to the fall. A flagrant current misuse of the creation argument is the claim that the practices of heterosexual and homosexual people are equally good because equally created. Homosexual Christians regularly say, 'I'm gay because God made me that way, and so I intend to celebrate my homosexuality.' But no, what God created was 'male and female', with heterosexual marriage as the intended consequence.[16] It is no more appropriate to celebrate homosexuality than other disordered human tendencies which are due to the fall, like our irrationality, covetousness or pride. So we must be careful not to confuse creation

[14] Fairbairn, pp. 176–177.   [15] Rom. 8:20, 22.   [16] See Gn. 1:27; 2:24; Mt. 19:4ff.

and fall, order and disorder, but rather to ensure that we celebrate only what God created, and thankfully receive only what he gives.

And more grateful celebration there should be among us, uninhibited by our lingering evangelical asceticism. For the truth is that a world-denying Gnosticism has not yet been altogether eradicated from our theology and practice. Instead, we pride ourselves on our super-spirituality, which is detached from the natural order, and we look forward to an ethereal heaven, forgetting the promise of a new earth. We tend to have a better doctrine of redemption than of creation, and so are more grateful for the blessings of grace than of nature and of art. Perhaps G. K. Chesterton can put us right:

> You say grace before meals.
> All right.
> But I say grace before the play and the opera,
> And grace before the concert and pantomime,
> And grace before I open a book,
> And grace before sketching, painting,
> Swimming, fencing, boxing, walking, playing, dancing;
> And grace before I dip the pen in the ink.[17]

We should determine, then, to recognize and acknowledge, appreciate and celebrate, all the gifts of the Creator: the glory of the heavens and of the earth, of mountain, river and sea, of forest and flowers, of birds, beasts and butterflies, and of the intricate balance of the natural environment; the unique privileges of our humanness (rational, moral, social and spiritual), as we were created in God's image and appointed his stewards; the joys of gender, marriage, sex, children, parenthood and family life, and of our extended family and friends; the rhythm of work and rest, of daily work as a means to cooperate with God and serve the common good, and of the Lord's day when we exchange work for worship; the blessings of peace, freedom, justice and good government, and of food and drink, clothing and shelter; and our human creativity expressed in music, literature, painting, sculpture and drama, and in the skills and strengths displayed in sport.

To reject these things is to *abandon the faith*, since it insults the Creator. To receive them thankfully and celebrate them joyfully is to glorify God, 'who richly provides us with everything for our enjoyment' (6:17).

---

[17] Quoted in Dudley Barker, *G. K. Chesterton, A Biography* (Constable, 1973), p. 65, from unpublished notebook jottings.

ii. An ethical test: godliness (4:6–10)
The doctrine of creation has wide ramifications, as we have seen. It is the secret of developing a positive, world-affirming, grateful attitude to life, and of having a strong conscience which liberates us to enjoy the good gifts of the good Creator. Timothy is to *point these things out to the brothers* (6a). For what Paul teaches Timothy, Timothy must teach others also.[18] Indeed, he is to 'put these instructions before the brothers and sisters' (NRSV), like a waiter serving guests at a table, like a merchant displaying merchandise to a customer. Or perhaps the verb *hypotithēmi* (literally, to 'lay under') likens Timothy to a builder, who lays down truths 'as a foundation for their faith'.[19]

Whatever picture Paul has in mind, he adds that if Timothy is a faithful teacher, he *will be a good minister of Christ Jesus* (6b; the noun is *diakonos*, but Paul is not here using it in its technical sense 'deacon' as in 3:8, 12). I have always loved this expression. Jesus Christ has ministers of all sorts – good, bad and indifferent – but I cannot imagine a nobler ambition than to be 'a good minister' of his. Moreover, Paul makes it plain that it is *the good teaching* (6c) which makes *the good minister,* and that in two ways, namely that he both instructs people in it and nourishes himself on it, *brought up* (REB 'nourished') *in the truths of the faith and of the good teaching that you have followed* (6). This seems to be a general rule. Behind the ministry of public teaching there lies the discipline of private study. All the best teachers have themselves remained students. They teach well because they learn well. So before we can effectively instruct others in the truth we must have 'really digested' it (JB) ourselves.

With verse 7 the metaphor changes from the nourishment of a child to the exercise of an athlete: *Train yourself to be godly* (7b), for *physical training is of some value* (8a). Paul uses the verb *gymnazō* and the noun *gymnasia,* and it requires no knowledge of Greek to recognize his reference to gymnastics and the gymnasium. As a young man Timothy knew the importance of taking exercise; he also knew that training was essential for athletes intending to compete in the games, which were very popular throughout the Graeco-Roman world at that time. In fact, combining Paul's two metaphors, disciplined eating and exercising are both indispensable for bodily health. It is the same in Christian discipleship. What our spiritual food is he has already clarified. It is 'the truths of the faith and of the good teaching' (6), in other words, the doctrine of the apostles. For this is nourishing. But we are to *have nothing to do with godless myths and old wives' tales* (7a), for they are spiritual junk food.

Turning to the metaphor of exercise, Paul tells Timothy: *train*

[18] 2 Tim. 2:2.   [19] Lock, p. 50.

yourself to be godly (7b), or, literally, 'exercise yourself unto godliness'. Of the fifteen occurrences of *eusebeia* ('godliness') and *eusebēs* ('godly') in the New Testament, thirteen are in the Pastoral Letters, nine of them in 1 Timothy. So clearly it is an important concept in this letter. Its basic meaning is 'respect' or 'reverence', and in secular Greek it was used of respect for rulers, magistrates and parents. In the New Testament, however, it is used exclusively as a synonym for *theosebeia*, meaning reverence for God (*e.g.* 2:10). Although sometimes *eusebeia* seems to mean 'religion' in a formal sense, it usually has a more personal connotation as 'that mingled fear and love which together constitute the piety of man toward God'.[20] Godly people are God-fearing people. They have experienced the Copernican revolution of Christian conversion from self-centredness to God-centredness. Previously it could be said of them that in all their thoughts 'there is no room for God'.[21] But now they say: 'I have set the LORD always before me.'[22] They have heard God's call to renounce ungodliness and to live a godly life,[23] and so to anticipate on earth the God-centred life of heaven, which is dominated by God's throne.[24]

How then are we to 'exercise ourselves unto godliness'? What spiritual gymnastics are we to undertake? Paul does not go into detail. But the context, and in particular the parallel between nourishment and exercise, together suggest that we are to exercise ourselves in the same way that we nourish ourselves, namely in the Word of God. Certainly it has been a long-standing Christian tradition, belonging to the wisdom of the ages, that disciplined meditation in Scripture is indispensable to Christian health, and indeed to growth in godliness. For in contrast to 'godless myths', Scripture is the most godly book that has ever been written. It is a book by God about God. It might even be termed the autobiography of God, since in it he talks to us about himself. Consequently, we cannot become familiar with this godly book without becoming godly ourselves. Nothing evokes the worship of God like the Word of God.

In verse 8 Paul emphasizes the importance of spiritual exercise by contrasting it with physical exercise: *physical training is of some value* (8a), since it contributes to our physical fitness in this life, *but godliness* (including, it is implied, the training which promotes it) *has value for all things* or 'is valuable in every way' (NRSV), *holding promise for both the present life and the life to come* (8b). In brief, it prepares us for eternity.

This statement of verse 8 about the profit of godliness must surely

---

[20] Trench, p. 167. [21] Ps. 10:4; *cf.* 36:1. [22] Ps. 16:8. [23] Tit. 2:12.
[24] Rev. 4:1–2.

be the *trustworthy saying that deserves full acceptance* (9), which Paul now endorses, rather than verse 10 which follows. For, although verse 10 could be described as 'more theologically weighty' than verse 8,[25] yet verse 8 is not without theological importance and is certainly more pithy, more like a proverb.[26] *For this we labour and strive*, Paul continues, that is, we 'exercise ourselves unto godliness', because *we have put our hope in the living God*, who is the author and giver of both life and life to come (8b), and is also *the Saviour of all men, and especially of those who believe* (10). The precise relation between 'all men' and 'those who believe' has perplexed all commentators. In what sense is God the Saviour of all and specially of believers? This is not universalism, since Paul was not a universalist. Nor can it express the difference between the potential (God's desire to save) and the actual (God saving), since the text says he *is* the Saviour of all, not just that he wants to be. Some therefore propose that God is the preserver of all, but exercises a special providence towards believers. But, as we have had occasion to mention before, salvation language in the Pastorals seems to refer to spiritual salvation, not physical preservation. Several scholars have drawn attention to some research by T. C. Skeat in 1979, in which he claims that the word *especially* (*malista*) should rather be translated 'to be precise' or 'in other words'. In this case, Paul 'is not saying that God saves believers more than he saves others; he is simply modifying his general statement that God is the Saviour of all men by adding the limitation that you cannot be saved unless you believe'.[27]

Looking back over the first half of this chapter, we can now bring together the two tests which Paul gave Timothy, and which can still be applied to doubtful teaching today. The theological test is the doctrine of creation: does this teaching honour God as the Creator and giver of all good things? The second test is ethical, and concerns the priority of godliness: does this teaching honour God by drawing out our worship? We need have no hesitations about any teaching which glorifies God the Creator and promotes godliness.

2. The commendation of true teaching (4:11 – 5:2)

Command and teach these things. [12]*Don't let anyone look down on you because you are young, but set an example for the believers in speech, in life, in love, in faith and in purity.* [13]*Until I come, devote*

---

[25] Guthrie (1992), p. 107.
[26] So Knight (1992), p. 198. Knight (1968, 1979), p. 79, quotes H. B. Swete: 'In the Christian at Ephesus Christ had taken the place of Artemis, and the Church that of the Artemision; and the self-control and self-sacrifice of the new life in Christ, which were good for both worlds, were the Christian substitute for the drill of the gymnasium, which was serviceable only for the life that now is.'
[27] Hanson (1982), p. 92.

118

yourself to the public reading of Scripture, to preaching and to teaching. [14]*Do not neglect your gift, which was given you through a prophetic message when the body of elders laid their hands on you.*
[15]*Be diligent in these matters; give yourself wholly to them, so that everyone may see your progress.* [16]*Watch your life and doctrine closely. Persevere in them, because if you do, you will save both yourself and your hearers.*
[5:1]*Do not rebuke an older man harshly, but exhort him as if he were your father. Treat younger men as brothers,* [2]*older women as mothers, and younger women as sisters, with absolute purity.*

This section begins with a dramatic contrast between verse 11 and verse 12, which sums up the problem Timothy faced as a young leader. On the one hand, he had been put into a position of considerable responsibility as the apostle Paul's representative in Ephesus. *Command and teach these things* (11), Paul wrote. 'These things' (*tauta*) is an expression which occurs eight times in this letter;[28] it sums up the instructions and orders which Paul had given Timothy and which he was to keep passing on (both verbs are present imperatives) to the churches of Ephesus. On the other hand, he was still a relatively young man, probably in his thirties, so that Paul had to add: *Don't let anyone look down on you because you are young* (12a). So then, putting verses 11 and 12 together, Timothy had been called to Christian leadership beyond his years. His responsibility to 'command and teach' was in danger of being undermined by his youthfulness, and by the signs that his ministry was being rejected. Paul is not concerned now with error (and how it could be detected and rejected) but with truth (and how it could be commended and so accepted).

Perhaps some people were jealous of Timothy; they resented his having been promoted over their heads. Others simply looked down their noses at this pretentious youth, much as Goliath despised young David.[29] It is a perennial problem. Older people have always found it difficult to accept young people as responsible adults in their own right, let alone as leaders. And young people are understandably irritated when their elders keep reminding them of their immaturity and inexperience, and treat them with contempt.

How then should young Christian leaders react in this situation, so that their youth is not despised and their ministry is not rejected? Not by boastful, assertive or aggressive behaviour. Not by throwing their weight about and trying to impose their will. *But* (notice the strong adversative *alla* in the middle of verse 12) by different means altogether. 'Don't let people look down on you because you are

[28] 1 Tim. 3:14; 4:6, 11, 15; 5:7, 21; 6:2, 17.   [29] 1 Sa. 17:42.

young; see that they look up to you because . . .' (JBP). The apostle goes on to give Timothy six ways in which he should commend his ministry and gain acceptance for it.

a. Timothy must watch his example

Paul was careful about the example he set. He was never shy of inviting his readers to imitate him.[30] Timothy must do the same. *Don't let anyone look down on you . . . but set an example for the believers in speech, in life, in love, in faith and in purity* (12b). People would not despise his youth if they could admire his example. The apostle Peter gave the same instruction to church elders, urging them to serve humbly, 'not lording it over those entrusted to you, but being examples to the flock'.[31] And in writing these things, Paul and Peter were only echoing the teaching of Jesus, who introduced into the world a new style of servant-leadership.

The great temptation, whenever our leadership is questioned, threatened or resisted, is to assert it all the more strongly and to become autocratic, even tyrannical. But leadership and lordship are two quite different concepts. The Christian leads by example, not force, and is to be a model who invites a following, not a boss who compels one. Moreover, Timothy's example was to be comprehensive, *in speech* and *in life*, that is, in word and deed, in the way he spoke and in the way he behaved. And in those two spheres he was to be a model of Christian virtue, especially *in love*, the pre-eminent Christian grace, to be shown to the neighbour and to all humankind; *in faith*, which could mean either trust in God and in Christ, or trustworthiness, a fundamental Christian fidelity, or both; and *in purity*, which is Christian self-control.

b. Timothy must identify his authority

Paul's next instruction is this: *Until I come, devote yourself to the public reading of Scripture, to preaching and to teaching* (13). A certain authority had been delegated to Timothy as Paul's representative in Ephesus, but his authority was of course subordinate to the apostle's in two respects. On the one hand, what he was to *command and teach* was *these things*; he was to teach only Paul's teaching, not his own. On the other hand, he would continue only until Paul arrived, when the apostle would take over. Meanwhile, Paul reminded Timothy that he had another authority in Old Testament Scripture.

[30] *E.g.* 1 Thes. 1:6; 2 Thes. 3:7, 9; 1 Cor. 4:6; 11:1; Phil. 3:17.
[31] 1 Pet. 5:3; *cf.* Heb. 13:7.

The four words *public reading of Scripture* render the single Greek noun *anagnōsis*, since it often referred to reading aloud in public. MM supply examples of its use in the reading of wills, petitions, dispatches and reports. But it was also used of the public reading of Scripture, as when the priests read from the law in Ezra's day,[32] Jesus read from Isaiah in the Nazareth synagogue,[33] and the Old Testament was regularly read in synagogue worship.[34] This reading of the Old Testament was taken over by Christians from synagogue to church.

In addition, the apostles directed that the churches should read their letters aloud in the Christian assembly. 'I charge you before the Lord', Paul wrote to the Thessalonians, 'to have this letter read to all the brothers.'[35] He gave a similar instruction to the Colossian church: 'After this letter has been read to you, see that it is also read in the church of the Laodiceans and that you in turn read the letter from Laodicea.'[36] The book of Revelation also opens with a similar command: 'Blessed is the one who reads the words of the prophecy . . .'[37] These are extraordinary instructions. They indicate that the apostles put their writings on a level with the Old Testament Scriptures. So each local church would begin to make its collection of the letters and memoirs of the apostles, so that on the Lord's day in the Lord's assembly there would be two public readings, first from the Old Testament Scriptures (from the law or the prophets or both) and then from the apostolic writings. And this practice continues in most churches today, in the first and the second lessons. Already by about the middle of the second century these readings were part of the accepted liturgy. Justin Martyr in his *First Apology* wrote:

On the day called Sunday, all who live in cities or in the country gather together to one place, and the memoirs of the apostles and the writings of the prophets are read, as long as time permits; then, when the reader has finished, the president speaks, instructing and exhorting the people to imitate these good things.[38]

'Instructing and exhorting' are exactly what Paul goes on to require, when he adds *preaching* (*paraklēsis*, exhortation) and *teaching* (*didaskalia*, instruction) to the Scripture reading. It was already customary in the synagogue for the reading of Scripture to be followed by an exposition,[39] and this practice was carried over

---

[32] Ne. 8:8, LXX.   [33] Lk. 4:16.   [34] *E.g.* Acts 13:15; 15:21.
[35] 1 Thes. 5:27.   [36] Col. 4:16.   [37] Rev. 1:3; *cf.* 22:18–19.
[38] Justin Martyr, *First Apology*, translated A. W. F. Blunt, Cambridge Patristic Texts (Cambridge University Press, 1911), I.67.
[39] *E.g.* Lk. 4:16ff.; Acts 13:16ff.

into the Christian assemblies, being the origin of the sermon in public worship. It was taken for granted from the beginning that Christian preaching would be expository preaching, that is, that all Christian instruction and exhortation would be drawn out of the passage which had been read.

We note, however, that the public reading of Scripture came first, identifying the authority. What followed was exposition and application, whether in the form of doctrinal instruction or of moral appeal, or both. Timothy's own authority was thus seen to be secondary, both to the Scripture and to the apostle. All Christian teachers occupy the same subordinate position as Timothy did. They will be wise, therefore, especially if they are young, to demonstrate both their submission to the authority of Scripture and their conscientious integrity in expounding it, so that their teaching is seen to be not theirs but the word of God.

c. Timothy must exercise his gift

Do not neglect your gift, which was given you through a prophetic message when the body of elders laid their hands on you (14). It would not be an anachronism to refer to this as Timothy's 'ordination'. Although we are not told when or where it took place, Paul does remind Timothy that it had three constituent parts. Indeed all three of them are referred to again elsewhere in Paul's two letters to Timothy. First mentioned is a gift (*charisma*) bestowed on him, which is later specifically called a 'gift of God'.[40] What it was we do not know because we are not told, although it evidently related to Timothy's ministry. Calvin wrote of 'the grace with which he has been endowed for the upbuilding of the church',[41] Alford of the gift of 'teaching and ruling the church',[42] and Hendriksen of 'that gift of discernment between the true and the false, and consequently of being able to exhort, teach and guide'.[43] Perhaps Timothy's gift was his teaching ministry, together with the authority and power to exercise it.

Secondly, Paul mentions a 'prophetic message', which had been uttered about him (1:18), and through which the gift was given. Presumably this identified or designated him as a person God had called, much as the Holy Spirit had singled out Paul and Barnabas in Syrian Antioch for their service.[44] Thirdly, 'the body of elders' (was this in Lystra?) had 'laid their hands' on him, including Paul,[45] in order to signify the church's confirmation of God's call and gift. Although the precise relationship between the prophetic message,

---

[40] 2 Tim. 1:6.   [41] Calvin, p. 247.   [42] Alford, p. 742.   [43] Hendriksen, p. 159.
[44] Acts 13:1ff.   [45] 2 Tim. 1:6.

the divine gift and the presbyters' action is not clear, these three belonged inextricably together.

Paul's purpose in recalling the circumstances of Timothy's ordination was to urge him not to 'neglect' his gift, but rather to 'fan' it 'into flame'.[46] From this we learn that a *charisma* is not a static or permanent endowment from God; its human recipient must use it and develop it. True, Timothy was young and inexperienced. But let him remember (and remind others) that God had called him (through the prophetic word), equipped him (through the heavenly gift) and commissioned him (through the presbyters' hands), and the people will not despise his youth or reject his teaching.

It is still important today for Christian leaders to discern, cultivate and exercise their gifts, and be helped to do so by others. For the people will be receptive to their ministry, once they are assured that God has called them and they have not appointed themselves.

d. Timothy must show his progress

Having referred to Timothy's example, to the biblical authority under which he must teach, and to his divine call, gift and commissioning, Paul goes on to Timothy's need for concentration and perseverance. *Be diligent in these matters; give yourself wholly to them* (15a). The second of these two exhortations means literally 'be in them', that is, immerse yourself in these matters, devote yourself to them with all your heart and soul. The REB catches the emphasis well: 'Make these matters your business, make them your absorbing interest.' And the purpose of this commitment is *so that everyone may see your progress* (15b). That is, in all three spheres so far mentioned (his example, teaching and gift), it is not only Timothy's devotion to duty which must be seen, but his 'constant growth'.[47]

The example which Christian leaders set, then, whether in their life or their ministry, should be dynamic and progressive. People should be able to observe not only what they are but what they are becoming, supplying evidence that they are growing into maturity in Christ. Some Christian leaders imagine that they have to appear perfect, with no visible flaws or blemishes. But there are at least two reasons why this is a mistake. First, it is hypocritical. Since none of us is a paragon of all virtues, it is dishonest to pretend to be. Secondly, the pretence discourages people, who then suppose that their leaders are altogether exceptional and even inhuman. Paul himself conceded that he had not arrived. 'Not that I have already obtained all this, or have already been made perfect, but I press on . . .'[48] In the same way we should not give the false impression that we have reached our

[46] 2 Tim. 1:6.   [47] Lock, p. 50.   [48] Phil. 3:12.

goal; on the contrary, we are still on the road, still pilgrims. Not that we should go to the opposite extreme, parade our failures, or make embarrassing public confessions. That helps nobody.

e. Timothy must mind his consistency

Watch your life and doctrine closely. Persevere in them (16a). Thus Timothy is to keep a close eye on two things equally. First, his *life*, literally 'himself', his character and his conduct. Secondly, he is to watch his *doctrine*, his teaching of other people. He is to be neither so engrossed in teaching others that he neglects himself, nor so concerned with the culture of his own soul that he neglects his ministry to others. Instead, he is to be consistent, applying himself with equal attention and perseverance to himself and to others. As Paul had said to the Ephesian elders: 'Keep watch over yourselves and all the flock . . .'[49] Then there will be no dichotomy between his public and his private life, or between his preaching and his practice. Instead, he will manifest that most necessary of all leadership qualities, personal authenticity.

Of the two possible inconsistencies mentioned above, the more common is surely the first. It is fatally easy to become so busy in the Lord's work that we leave no time for the Lord himself, to be so concerned for the welfare of others that we fail to keep a watchful eye on ourselves. It is only by careful discipline that Christian leaders achieve a balance, determined not to neglect either duty for the other.

If you do persevere in these duties, Paul concludes, *you will save both yourself and your hearers* (16b). At first sight this sentence contains two shocking statements, namely that Timothy could save himself, and that he could save his hearers as well. First, how could Timothy save himself? Is not self-salvation an impossibility? Did not Paul repeatedly insist that salvation is by grace alone in Christ alone through faith alone? Has he suddenly gone berserk and contradicted himself? Has he forgotten his own assertions about 'God our Saviour' (1:1; 2:3) and about Jesus Christ coming into the world 'to save sinners' (1:15)? No, of course not. Salvation always and everywhere originates not in us but only in the grace and mercy of God. Nevertheless, the reality of our salvation has to be demonstrated in good works of love. It is in this sense that Paul tells us to 'continue to work out' our salvation 'with fear and trembling'.[50] Only those who persevere to the end will be saved.[51] Perseverance is not the meritorious cause, but rather the ultimate evidence, of our salvation.[52]

---

[49] Acts 20:28. [50] Phil. 2:12. [51] *E.g.* Mk. 13:13; 1 Cor. 15:2; Col. 1:22–23.
[52] Heb. 3:14.

Secondly, how could Timothy save his hearers? Surely only God could save them through Christ? Yes, but the New Testament not infrequently attributes salvation to evangelists, since it is through the gospel they preach that God saves believers. So the ascended Christ could tell Paul that he was sending him to the Gentiles 'to open their eyes and turn them from darkness to light, and from the power of Satan to God'.[53] Similarly he became 'all things to all men', in order that by all possible means he 'might save some'.[54] Of course Paul could not and did not save anybody. Nor could Timothy. But this is dramatic language which ascribes to evangelists direct the salvation which God himself effects indirectly through the gospel which they proclaim.

f. Timothy must adjust his relationships

Paul's sixth word of advice to Timothy takes us into the first two verses of chapter 5: *Do not rebuke an older man harshly* (the word is *presbyteros*, but here Paul is not using it in its technical sense of a 'presbyter', but of an older man generally), *but exhort him as if he were your father. Treat younger men as brothers, older women as mothers, and younger women as sisters, with absolute purity* (5:1-2). Although a comparatively young man, Timothy found himself responsible for several congregations which were mixed both in sex (men and women) and in age (old and young). Paul now tells him that the sex and age of the people should determine his attitude to them.

Take the older folk first. It may be Timothy's duty to admonish somebody considerably older than himself. Paul seems to assume that it will be. In this case, he must perform his duty, but do it as an exhortation, not as a harsh rebuke. These last two words translate the verb *epiplēssō*, which seems to imply 'sharpness and severity'.[55] In other words, Timothy is to give to senior members of the church the respect which is due to age[56] and the affection which is due to parents. He must treat older men like *fathers* (1) and older women like *mothers* (2), which is what Paul himself did to the mother of Rufus in Rome, affirming that she 'has been a mother to me too'.[57] I find here good biblical warrant for a recognition in the congregation of the generation gap. True, we are all brothers and sisters in Christ. Yet it seems to me artificial in the West when students breeze up to me and hail me by my Christian name, even though I am old enough to be their great-grandfather! The Asian and African cultures are wiser, since they encourage young people to address the older generation as 'uncle' and 'auntie'.

[53] Acts 26:18. [54] 1 Cor. 9:22; *cf.* Rom. 11:14. [55] Ellicott, p. 67.
[56] Lv. 19:32. [57] Rom. 16:13.

125

Paul also advises Timothy about his attitude to people of his own generation. He is to treat younger men like *brothers*, loving them, and not condescending to them, and younger women like *sisters*, loving them too, although with sensible restraint and *absolute purity* (2).

In brief, the local church is rightly called 'the church family', in which there are fathers and mothers, and brothers and sisters, not to mention aunts and uncles, grandparents and children. Leaders should not be insensitive and treat everybody alike. No, they must behave towards their elders with respect, affection and gentleness, their own generation with equality, the opposite sex with self-control and purity, and all ages of both sexes with that love which binds together members of the same family.

There is much practical wisdom here for everybody called to Christian leadership, and especially for younger people given responsibility beyond their years. If they watch their example, becoming a model of Christ-likeness; if they identify their authority, submitting to Scripture and drawing all their teaching from it; if they exercise their gift, giving evidence of God's call and of the rightness of the church's commissioning; if they show their progress, letting it be seen that their Christian life and ministry are dynamic, not static; if they mind their consistency, by practising what they preach; and if they adjust their relationships, being sensitive to people's age and sex – then other people will not despise their youth, but gladly and gratefully receive their ministry.

1 Timothy 5:3 – 6:2
5. Social responsibilities

Having just mentioned the older and younger men and women in the Ephesian churches (5:1–2), and how Timothy should relate to them, Paul now takes up three more particular groupings – widows, presbyters and slaves – and indicates what Timothy's and the churches' responsibilities are towards them. In relation to widows he is concerned about their need for support and their qualifications for ministry (5:3–16); in relation to presbyters about their pay, their appointment and their discipline (5:17–25); and in relation to slaves about the quality of their service, whether their masters are believers or not (6:1–2).

In each case Paul writes something about their service, since all three groups are called to *diakonia* (ministry) of some kind, and in the first two cases he adds instructions about their support. Moreover these two concerns belong naturally together, service being what we give and support what we receive. The interplay between them is healthy, for the Christian community (like every family) is a fellowship of 'giving and receiving'.[1]

1. Widows (5:3–16)

Give proper recognition to those widows who are really in need. ⁴But if a widow has children or grandchildren, these should learn first of all to put their religion into practice by caring for their own family and so repaying their parents and grandparents, for this is pleasing to God. ⁵The widow who is really in need and left all alone puts her hope in God and continues night and day to pray and to ask God for help. ⁶But the widow who lives for pleasure is dead even while she lives. ⁷Give the people these instructions, too, so that no-one may be open to blame. ⁸If anyone does not provide for his relatives, and

---

[1] Phil. 4:15.

especially for his immediate family, he has denied the faith and is worse than an unbeliever.

⁹No widow may be put on the list of widows unless she is over sixty, has been faithful to her husband, ¹⁰and is well known for her good deeds, such as bringing up children, showing hospitality, washing the feet of the saints, helping those in trouble and devoting herself to all kinds of good deeds.

¹¹As for younger widows, do not put them on such a list. For when their sensual desires overcome their dedication to Christ, they want to marry. ¹²Thus they bring judgment on themselves, because they have broken their first pledge. ¹³Besides, they get into the habit of being idle and going about from house to house. And not only do they become idlers, but also gossips and busybodies, saying things they ought not to. ¹⁴So I counsel younger widows to marry, to have children, to manage their homes and to give the enemy no opportunity for slander. ¹⁵Some have in fact already turned away to follow Satan.

¹⁶If any woman who is a believer has widows in her family, she should help them and not let the church be burdened with them, so that the church can help those widows who are really in need.

Scripture has much to say about widows, and honours them in a way that most cultures do not. Too often a married woman is defined only in relation to her husband. Then, if he dies, she loses not only her spouse but her social significance as well. In Scripture, however, widows, orphans and aliens (people without husband, parents or home) are valued for who they are in themselves, and are said to deserve special honour, protection and care. Throughout the Bible justice and love are demanded for them. God is described as 'a father to the fatherless' and 'a defender of widows';[2] and it is written of him that 'he defends the cause of the fatherless and the widow'.[3] Because this is the kind of God he is, his people are to be the same. 'Do not take advantage of a widow or an orphan,' he says. 'If you do and they cry out to me, I will certainly hear their cry. My anger will be aroused . . .'[4] So magistrates who withheld justice from widows would come under God's judgment;[5] farmers were instructed to store a tithe of their produce for widows and orphans, and to leave them the gleanings of field and orchard as well;[6] and the prophets regularly complained that, instead of defending and providing for widows, the nation exploited and oppressed them.[7]

---

[2] Ps. 68:5.   [3] Dt. 10:18; cf. Ps. 146:9; Pr. 15:25.   [4] Ex. 22:22ff.
[5] Dt. 27:19; cf. 24:17.   [6] Dt. 14:28–29; 24:19ff.; 26:12–13.
[7] Is. 1:17, 23; Je. 7:5ff.; 22:3; Ezk. 22:7; Zc. 7:10; Mal. 3:5; cf. Ps. 94:1ff.

Our Lord Jesus was himself consistently compassionate towards widows. He restored to life the only son of the widow of Nain.[8] He commended both the importunity of the widow who badgered the unjust judge into action and the generosity of the poor widow who contributed her two small copper coins to the temple treasury.[9] He warned his disciples against the scribes who 'devoured widows' houses', while at the same time they were ostentatiously religious.[10] And from the cross he practised what he preached, and commended his widowed mother to the care of John.[11]

The early church learned this lesson from the teaching of the Old Testament and the example of Jesus, and continued to show the same concern. Seven gifted leaders were appointed to supervise the daily distribution to the widows in Jerusalem,[12] while James categorically defines religion which is 'pure and faultless' in God's sight as 'to look after orphans and widows in their distress'.[13]

Coming to 1 Timothy 5, we notice at once that the section on widows appears to be divided into two paragraphs, each of which is introduced by a different main verb. The widows in mind in verses 3–8 Timothy is to *give proper recognition to*, literally 'to honour, or rather support',[14] whereas those in mind in verses 9–16 he is to *put on the list of widows*, that is, 'register' or 'enrol' them. Commentators differ as to whether Paul is referring to the same group of widows in both paragraphs, or to two distinct groups. That different categories are in view is suggested not only by the different introductory verbs ('honour' and 'register'), but also by the different conditions for admission into the two groups. In the first case it is destitution and godliness, while in the second it is a combination of seniority, married faithfulness and a reputation for good works. I shall take it this way, understanding that the former group of widows is to receive financial support, and the latter opportunities for ministry, alongside the presbyters and deacons of chapter 3, although no hard and fast line is drawn between the two groups, and they will probably have overlapped.

a. Widows to be supported (5:3–8)

The context makes it clear that the 'honour' due to widows (their *proper recognition*, in fact) must go beyond personal respect and emotional support to financial provision (see 4, 8 and 16). The honour to parents required by the fifth commandment had already been shown by Jesus to include this,[15] and the honour due to

[8] Lk. 7:11–12. [9] Lk. 18:1ff.; Mk. 12:41–42. [10] Mk. 12:38.
[11] Jn. 19:26–27. [12] Acts 6:1ff; cf. 9:39, 44. [13] Jas. 1:27.
[14] Chrysostom, p. 450. [15] Mk. 7:10ff.

presbyters, which Paul will come to next, implies the same thing (17). So '"honouring" includes material provision as well'.[16]

But who is responsible for the financial care of widows? And which widows qualify for such support? These are the questions Paul addresses here, for evidently the local church was maintaining some widows whom their own family should be supporting.

Dr Bruce Winter has thrown light on this situation by drawing attention to the social background in the Graeco-Roman world, and in particular to the dowry system. He writes:

> The dowry, which was provided by the bride's father, always accompanied a woman to her marriage. It constituted an important legal aspect of marriage . . . In the event of a husband's death, the laws governing that dowry were clearly defined. A widow was cared for by the person in charge of that dowry. Two options were open to her. If she had children, she might remain in her deceased husband's home. There she would be maintained by the new 'lord' (*kyrios*) of the household, possibly her son. She could also return to her parents, taking her dowry back to her family.[17]

This legal provision gave a widow financial security. She would be maintained out of her dowry either by her son or by her father. Such a widow did not need the church's support, since her own family had both a moral and a legal obligation to look after her.

The church's financial support should be limited to widows *who are really in need* (3), or 'widows in the fullest sense' (REB). This expression occurs three times (3, 5 and 16) and means that such a widow is destitute, being unable to support herself and having no dowry or relatives to support her. For *if a widow has children or grandchildren, these should learn first of all to put their religion into practice (eusebein) by caring for their own family* (4a).

Two motives are now given why family members should do this. First, it will be a way of *repaying their parents and grandparents* who cared for them when they were young. Secondly, it is *pleasing to God* (4b), the God who in Scripture both commands us to honour our parents and declares his own concern for widows. In contrast to widows who can and should be supported by their own family, Paul reverts to *the widow who is really in need*. She is *left all alone*. In consequence, having no surviving relatives to succour her, she *puts her hope in God and continues night and day to pray* (either privately or in prayer gatherings) *and to ask God for help* (5), like Anna the prophetess and widow.[18]

Totally different from such a godly woman is *the widow who lives*

---

[16] *TDNT* VIII, p. 179.   [17] Winter, p. 64. *Cf.* Simpson, p. 73.   [18] Lk. 2:36–37.

for pleasure (6a), that is, for herself rather than for God. She *is dead even while she lives* (6b), 'separated from the life of God'.[19] For one kind of life (self-indulgence) is in reality spiritual death, while one kind of death (self-denial) is in reality spiritual life. Several commentators suggest that *lives for pleasure* may be a euphemism for a widow who, lacking dowry, relatives or profession, has no alternative to prostitution.

So there are both material and spiritual conditions of eligibility for the church's maintenance of widows. The material condition is destitution, and the spiritual godliness. *Give the people these instructions, too*, Paul continues (7a), for the care of destitute widows is to be a church responsibility, not a personal ministry of Timothy's. The church must therefore develop a practical programme for the care of widows, *so that no-one may be open to blame* (7b). Before Paul concludes this part of his instruction, however, he repeats with even stronger emphasis what he has already written about families shouldering their own responsibilities. In verse 4 he gave positive reasons, but now he adds the negative counterpart: *If anyone does not provide for his relatives, and especially for his immediate family*, he sinks below the level of pagans; *he has denied the faith and is worse than an unbeliever* (8). Strong language! But nature itself teaches that children should care for their parents, for many pagans by the light of nature (by the law 'written on their hearts'),[20] have done so, and, as we have seen, provision for widows had come to be incorporated in Roman law. Are we, then, who have the fuller light of objective revelation, to despise those whom even pagans honour?

If we add verse 16, where Paul points out that to provide for our relatives is to spare the church an unnecessary burden, he has deployed four arguments. To care adequately for our own elderly family members is to repay our parents (4), to please God (4), to express and not deny the faith (8), and to relieve the church (16).

Here is an issue of considerable contemporary importance. As the medical care of the elderly improves, particularly in the West, the average age of the population continues to rise. There are many more old folk than ever before. Geriatric wards, homes and hospitals are full. And it is fine that the church and the government should provide these. But not if it means that senior citizens are abandoned or neglected by their own relatives. African and Asian cultures, which have developed the extended in place of the nuclear family, are a standing rebuke to the West in this matter. Verse 8 tells us that it is a fundamental Christian duty to provide for our relatives. This is plain biblical warrant for a life assurance policy, which is only a self-imposed savings plan for the benefit of our dependants. It is not a

[19] Eph. 4:18.   [20] Rom. 2:14–15.

contradiction of Jesus who told us to 'take no thought' for the future,[21] since he was prohibiting worry, not prudence or forethought. Nor is Paul contradicting his own dictum that 'children should not have to save up for their parents, but parents for their children',[22] for this is obviously the right perspective when parents are in their prime. But when parents grow old and feeble, it is then that roles and responsibilities are reversed. Proverbs 6 sends us to the ants to learn wisdom. They set us a fine example both of industry and of providing for the future. What they do by instinct, human beings should do by deliberate decision.

b. Widows to be registered (5:9–16)

The focus in verses 3–8 has been on the financial maintenance of widows, which in the first instance is the duty of their relatives and only becomes the duty of the church if the widow has no relatives. This concern does not recur in this paragraph, except as a kind of appendix in verse 16. Instead, this paragraph introduces new concerns. We read now of a 'list', 'roll' or 'register' of widows (9a, 11), of a quite different set of qualifications (9b, 10), of a 'pledge' to remain single (12), apparently in order to give themselves to service, and of the non-eligibility of 'younger widows' (11–15). From this it seems that the register is not for widows needing support, but for widows capable of offering service.

There is some evidence that such an identifiable group existed in the early church. For example, Luke refers to 'all the widows' in Joppa as if they were a known and even registered group. It is possible that Dorcas was one of them; she was certainly 'full of good works and acts of charity'.[23] Writing to Timothy, Paul's references to a register, and to conditions for registration, certainly suggest the beginnings of a defined group, but it is an exaggeration to say that 'at Ephesus there is now an officially recognised order of widows'.[24] At the beginning of the second century Ignatius sent a greeting 'to the virgins who are called widows' in Smyrna,[25] and Polycarp wrote to the Philippians that 'the widows must think soberly about the faith of the Lord and pray unceasingly for everyone' and stay away from all evil.[26] It is not until the end of the second century, however, that Tertullian gives us unequivocal evidence that an order of widows existed. In his time and in the third century the registered widows

[21] Mt. 6:25ff., AV.   [22] 2 Cor. 12:14.   [23] Acts 9:36, 39, 41.
[24] Kelly, p. 112. See also Hanson (1982), p. 96.
[25] Ignatius, *Epistle to the Smyrnaeans*, translated by K. Lake, in *Apostolic Fathers* 1, Loeb Classical Library (Heinemann, 1912), 13.1.
[26] Polycarp, *Epistle to the Philippians*, translated by J. B. Lightfoot, in his *The Apostolic Fathers* (Macmillan, 1891), 4.3; 6.1.

gave themselves to prayer, nursed the sick, cared for the orphans, visited Christians in prison, evangelized pagan women, and taught female converts in preparation for their baptism.[27]

Although there may not have been an 'order' of widows in Paul's time, there certainly was a 'register' of them, and he lists the three qualifications for registration, namely seniority, married fidelity, and good works. The first concerned the widow's age. *No widow may be put on the list of widows unless she is over sixty* (9a) and is therefore unlikely to wish to re-marry. Secondly, she must have been *faithful to her husband* (9b) – see the corresponding expression 'the husband of but one wife' (3:2). As argued in the comment on that text, this cannot mean that she has not re-married, since in verse 14 Paul counsels the younger widows to re-marry, but rather that she has been faithful.

Thirdly, in order to be registered, a widow must be *well known for her good deeds*. As examples Paul mentions what Newport White calls 'commonplace duties', a selection which he regards as 'characteristic of the sanity of apostolic Christianity'.[28] The first is *bringing up children,* meaning to 'care for them physically and spiritually' (*teknotropheō,* BAGD), whether her own children or orphans. Secondly, *showing hospitality,* presumably to travellers, a quality specially necessary in presbyter-bishops and other leaders (3:2). Thirdly, *washing the feet of the saints,* a menial ministry usually reserved for slaves, but beautified by the example of Jesus.[29] Her fourth good work must be *helping those in trouble,* referring to any kind of affliction or distress, including persecution. After these four specifics Paul adds the more general expression *devoting herself to all kinds of good deeds* (10). Such an experience of humble, unselfish and costly service would qualify a registered widow to undertake similar ministries as an accredited church worker. It would also necessitate a decision to remain unmarried, indeed to take a 'pledge' to this effect, so as to be fully available for service.

Having laid down the conditions for the registration of widows, it is clear that younger widows would not qualify. So Paul gives Timothy a different set of instructions for them. *As for younger widows, do not put them on such a list* (11a). Why not? For two reasons. The first is because such younger women would become restive in their single state and would naturally want to re-marry. *For when their sensual desires,* their natural sexual impulses, *overcome their dedication to Christ,* that is, become stronger than their

---

[27] See 'Widows' in Everett Ferguson (ed.), *Encyclopedia of Early Christianity* (St James Press, 1990), and 'Assistance and Charity' in A. D. Berardino (ed.), *Encyclopedia of the Early Church* (James Clarke, 1992).
[28] White, p. 130.   [29] Jn. 13:4ff.; *cf.* Lk. 7:44.

133

commitment to stay single and serve the church, *they want to marry* (11), and if they do so, *they bring judgment on themselves, because they have broken their first pledge* (12).

The second reason for not registering younger widows seems to be the uncertainty whether they will be able to concentrate on responsible service. Instead, *they get into the habit of being idle and going about* ('gadding about', NRSV) *from house to house. And not only do they become idlers, but also gossips and busybodies, saying things they ought not to* (13). Dr Gordon Fee identifies these young widows with the 'weak-willed women' of 2 Timothy 3:6–7, whom the false teachers had won over. Their 'going about from house to house' and their 'saying things they ought not to' he then interprets as their disrupting the house churches with their heterodox views.[30] It is an ingenious reconstruction, but Paul gives no explicit indication that they are doing more than wasting their time in frivolous talk.

So I counsel younger widows to marry, Paul writes (14a). There is no need to read this as contradicting what he has written in 1 Corinthians.[31] True, the apostle expressed a personal preference for singleness.[32] At the same time, he acknowledged that each person has his or her own grace-gift from God, whether to marry or not to marry,[33] that it is necessary to be realistic about sexual desires,[34] and that single people are free to become engrossed in the affairs of the Lord, while married people tend to become preoccupied with the affairs of the world.[35] When the younger widows have re-married, they will of course have their hands full, and so be largely rid of the temptation to be idle gossips and gadabouts. For they will be able *to have children* and *to manage their homes*, and so *to give the enemy*, whether human or devilish, *no opportunity for slander* (14). And it is important not to give the enemies of the gospel any further such occasion, because *some* younger widows *have in fact already turned away*, that is, from Christ and their pledge to him, in order *to follow Satan* (15).

After this common-sense counsel to the younger widows, and to Timothy about them, Paul reverts briefly to the other category of widows. He insists for the third time (3–4, 8) that only the destitute are to be maintained by the church, and not those who have family to look after them. *If any woman who is a believer has widows in her family, she should help them and not let the church be burdened with them, so that the church can help those widows who are really in need* (16).

---

[30] Fee (1988), pp. 70, 114–115, 120–123. [31] 1 Cor. 7:8, 40.
[32] 1 Cor. 7:7a, 8, 40. [33] 1 Cor. 7:7b. [34] 1 Cor. 7:2, 9; cf. 1 Tim. 5:11.
[35] 1 Cor. 7:32–35.

Two lasting principles of social welfare seem to emerge from these apostolic instructions. The first is the principle of discrimination. There was to be no general handout to all widows, irrespective of their circumstances. Widowhood was not in itself a qualification for support by the church. No, the church's welfare provisions are to be limited to those in genuine need. If there are any alternative means of support, they should be used. In particular, the first call is on the widow's family. All of us must accept responsibility for our own relatives. The church's sense of social responsibility is not to encourage irresponsibility in others. And government welfare programmes should supplement but not replace either individual or family obligations.

Secondly, there is the principle of dignity. It is very interesting to note the two distinct categories of widow Paul mentions, the one needing support and the other offering service. Although we have considered them separately, they must have overlapped. Indeed ideally, health and strength permitting, the supported and the serving widows should be the same people. Widows (together with others in similar circumstances like single mothers, abused and divorced women) should have the opportunity both to receive according to their need and to give according to their ability, that is, both to be served and to serve. I was impressed some years ago to see this principle operating in the 'Refugee Industries' of Zerka in Jordan. The refugees not only received food, clothing and shelter, but also found self-respect through contributing their own skills to a variety of cottage industries. Christian relief should never demean its beneficiaries, but rather increase their sense of dignity.

2. Presbyters (5:17–25)

The apostle now turns from the care of widows to the treatment of presbyters. Having declared pastoral leadership to be 'a noble task' (3:1), and having supplied a list of necessary qualifications (3:2ff.), he moves on to questions of their remuneration, discipline and ordination. This paragraph contains practical instruction for bishops and other leaders who are responsible for the church's pastors.

The elders who direct the affairs of the church well are worthy of double honour, especially those whose work is preaching and teaching. [18]*For the Scripture says, 'Do not muzzle the ox while it is treading out the grain,' and 'The worker deserves his wages.'* [19]*Do not entertain an accusation against an elder unless it is brought by two or three witnesses.* [20]*Those who sin are to be rebuked publicly, so that the others may take warning.*

[21]*I charge you, in the sight of God and Christ Jesus and the elect*

angels, to keep these instructions without partiality, and to do nothing out of favouritism.
  ²²Do not be hasty in the laying on of hands, and do not share in the sins of others. Keep yourself pure.
  ²³Stop drinking only water, and use a little wine because of your stomach and your frequent illnesses.
  ²⁴The sins of some men are obvious, reaching the place of judgment ahead of them; the sins of others trail behind them. ²⁵In the same way, good deeds are obvious, and even those that are not cannot be hidden.

'From this passage', wrote Calvin, alluding in particular to verse 17, 'it may be inferred that there are two kinds of presbyter.'[36] He meant on the one hand those with general pastoral and administrative functions (those *who direct the affairs of the church*) and on the other those who have received the particular call to teach (*those whose work is preaching and teaching*). Verse 17 is thus the origin of the familiar distinction in the Reformed churches between 'ruling elders' and 'teaching elders'.

Not all commentators are persuaded, however, that Paul is specifying two different kinds of elder. It is 'certainly not expressly said, and has often been disputed'.[37] For, according to chapter 3, all presbyters had to be able both to teach (3:2) and to take care of God's church (3:5). It may be, therefore, that the purpose of the adverb *especially* (*malista*) is not to distinguish preachers from rulers, but to identify them or give them a further description. The verse should then be translated: 'the elders who direct the church, that is, those who preach . . .'[38]

Throughout this paragraph (17–25) Paul instructs Timothy how to treat presbyters in the three areas of payment, discipline and appointment. It may be helpful to identify the five principles which were to guide him, and which should guide us in our dealings with those for whom we are responsible.

a. Appreciation (5:17–18)

We sometimes say or think that Christian workers need the appreciation only of the Chief Shepherd, and not of human leaders. But Paul was of a different opinion. For human beings are prone to discouragement and need to be affirmed. So elders who do *well* in

---

[36] Calvin, p. 262.   [37] Fairbairn, p. 213.
[38] Hanson opts for this interpretation (1982, pp. 92, 101), following T. C. Skeat in 'Especially the Parchments: A Note on 2 Timothy 4:13', *Journal of Theological Studies* 30 (1979), pp. 173–177. So does Knight (1992), pp. 203, 232.

their work *are worthy of double honour* (17). What kind of honour does Paul have in mind? That it includes adequate remuneration seems clear from the quotations of the following verse (18), and BAGD gives an example where *timē* ('honour') was used of 'a physician's honorarium'. Yet it seems unlikely that Paul is referring only to pay, let alone requiring the payment of 'a double stipend' (REB). In any case, did he mean double that of a registered widow or of another kind of presbyter, or double what he had been receiving before? It is more likely that 'double' alludes to the double meaning of *timē*. Conscientious elders should receive both respect and remuneration, both honour and an honorarium.

Paul took it for granted that the pastorate was a stipendiary ministry. As in Old Testament days the priests were supported 'so that they could devote themselves to the Law of the LORD',[39] so in New Testament days pastors should be supported so that they can devote themselves to the work of the gospel. True, Paul insisted on earning his own living by tent-making, but he also explained that his was a special case for special reasons.[40] Elsewhere he strongly defended the right of teachers to receive financial support.[41]

Here, as in 1 Corinthians 9:9 and 14, the apostle provides biblical authority for what he is saying, by bringing together two quotations. The first is from Deuteronomy 25:4: *For the Scripture says, 'Do not muzzle the ox while it is treading out the grain'* (18a). The argument is *a fortiori:* if God is concerned that working animals are adequately fed, how much more concern must he have for church workers? Paul's second quotation follows: *and 'The worker deserves his wages'* (18b). Although he does not attribute these words to Jesus, they do in fact occur in Luke 10:7, where they form part of Jesus' mission charge to the Seventy. Commentators who find it difficult to believe that Paul could have quoted a saying of Jesus as 'Scripture', suggest that the formula *the Scripture says* applies only to the first of the two quotations. It is more natural, however, to read the formula as bracketing both. And it is not impossible that Luke's gospel, or at least an early draft of it, was published before 1 Timothy and regarded by Paul as Scripture.

Neither quotation is particularly flattering to presbyters, since in the first they are likened to threshing oxen, and in the second to farm labourers. But Paul's purpose in employing these models is not to depreciate the pastoral ministry, but rather to emphasize that it is

---

[39] 2 Ch. 31:4.   [40] *E.g.* 1 Cor. 9:4ff.
[41] *E.g.* Gal. 6:6. Andrew Kirk draws a distinction between itinerant and local ministers, and argues that the former 'had the right to expect support, certainly hospitality and probably a regular income from the church to which they were ministering', whereas local elders were rewarded on a much more informal basis.

hard work, and that hard work performed conscientiously deserves to be rewarded. True, a presbyter is not to be 'a lover of money' (3:3), and verses 17 and 18 are not intended to stimulate covetousness. But they do say that good work is to be appreciated, and that appreciation may quite properly take a tangible, pecuniary form.

b. Fairness (5:19–20)

Paul now turns from good pastors who deserve appreciation to bad ones who may deserve a rebuke. He addresses himself to what we call 'grievance procedures', for the situation envisaged is one in which a complaint or accusation is made to Timothy about an elder. Paul gives him two complementary directions, first when a presbyter is accused of something (19) and secondly when he is found guilty (20).

First, *Do not entertain an accusation against an elder unless it is brought by two or three witnesses* (19). That is, it must be substantiated by several people. In the Old Testament two or three witnesses were required to sustain a charge and secure a conviction,[42] especially in regard to a capital charge.[43] The same principle applies in New Testament times,[44] in particular when Christian leaders are being accused. Indeed, two or three witnesses are to be required not only before an accusation is sustained, but before it is entertained at all.

This practical regulation is necessary for the protection of pastoral leaders, who are vulnerable to slander. 'None are more exposed to slanders and insults', wrote Calvin, 'than godly teachers.' They may perform their duties correctly and conscientiously, yet 'they never avoid a thousand criticisms'.[45] For the enemies of the gospel often take vengeance on the ministers of the gospel. A smear campaign can completely ruin a leader's ministry. So Paul's first word to Timothy is that he must never listen to gossip about leaders, or even to a serious accusation if it is made by only one person. Every charge must be endorsed by several responsible people before it is even listened to. Adherence to this biblical principle would have silenced many a malicious talebearer and saved many pastors from unjust criticism and unnecessary suffering.

Secondly, if an accusation against an elder is not only confirmed by two or three witnesses, but is 'actually proved' (JBP), and if (it is implied) the presbyters concerned, though admonished privately, refuse to repent but 'persist in sin' (as RSV renders the present tense), then the sadness and the scandal of a public showdown cannot be

---

[42] Dt. 19:15.   [43] Dt. 17:6.   [44] *E.g.* 2 Cor. 13:1; *cf.* Mt. 18:16.
[45] Calvin, p. 263.

avoided. The offenders *are to be rebuked publicly, so that the others may take warning* (20). Such a public rebuke, though an effective deterrent, must be the last resort, however. It is a safe rule that private sins should be dealt with privately, and only public sins publicly. It is neither right nor necessary to make what is private public, until all other possibilities have been exhausted.[46]

Verses 19 and 20, then, belong together. Timothy must neither listen to frivolous accusations nor refuse to take serious situations seriously. In the area of discipline he must be scrupulously fair, 'cautious in accusing and bold in rebuking',[47] as the situation demands.

c. Impartiality (5:21)

Paul now issues a charge to Timothy couched in the most solemn possible terms. He backs up his own authority as an apostle (*I charge you*) with the combined authority of heaven, of those 'who will judge the living and the dead'.[48] He speaks *in the sight of God*, who 'does not show favouritism',[49] and of *Christ Jesus*, 'the future Judge of all earthly judges',[50] and of *the elect angels*, the faithful as opposed to the fallen.

And what is his charge? It is *to keep these instructions*, namely the principles governing the treatment of elders, which he has just outlined in verses 17–20, and to do so with absolute fairness and without any taint of injustice. Two negatives are emphasized. The first is *without partiality*, literally 'apart from pre-judgment' (*prokrima*), that is, without jumping to conclusions of either guilt or innocence. And the second negative injunction is *to do nothing out of favouritism* (21). In the work of a bishop, superintendent or other Christian leader one of the worst sins is favouritism, and one of the most vital virtues is impartiality. Yet church history has been stained by gross favouritism, as church dignitaries have granted special favours to their relatives (nepotism), to members of their own caste, class or tribe, to people they happen to like, irrespective of their gifts or godliness, or to those to whom for some reason or other (even bribery) they are indebted.

d. Caution (5:22–23)

It is a common human tendency to make premature and ill-considered decisions, to be hasty when we should rather be cautious. Although the opposite fault is to be indecisive, yet in leaders it is better to take time to form judgments and make

---

[46] *Cf.* Mt. 18:15ff.   [47] White, p. 134.   [48] 2 Tim. 4:1.
[49] Rom. 2:11.   [50] Liddon, p. 66.

decisions than to be precipitate and live to regret it. So Paul bids Timothy: *Do not be hasty in the laying on of hands* (22a). Or, in the familiar AV, 'Lay hands suddenly on no man.' To what is Paul referring? To 'lay hands suddenly' on somebody may sound at first hearing like the arrest of a criminal. But Christian leaders are not policemen! Nor is the reference to episcopal confirmation, since the imposition of hands after baptism, which occurs two or three times in the Acts, belonged to particular and unusual contexts; it had not become the norm. Some commentators think Paul is alluding to the public absolution of a penitent offender, leading to his restoration to the Christian community after the public rebuke of verse 20. So NEB mg. Newport White detects in these verses the outline of a 'whole procedure',[51] namely accusation (19), conviction and sentence (20), repentance and reconciliation (21). Certainly Eusebius mentions the re-admission of penitents by the laying on of hands as an 'old custom' of the church,[52] but there is no evidence for it in New Testament times. Gordon Fee, who sees the whole paragraph as referring to the disciplining of the false teachers, understands verse 22 as giving 'some guidelines . . . for their replacement'.[53]

It is much more likely, however, that Paul is referring to ordination, since the Pastorals contain two clear statements that this took place through the laying on of hands.[54] The imposition of hands both identifies the persons being prayed for and publicly commissions them to the ministry to which God has called them. This makes sense in the context. In verse 20 Paul has mentioned the possible need to rebuke a presbyter publicly. The best way to avoid such a scandal is to ensure the thorough screening of candidates before they are ordained. In chapter 3 the apostle has elaborated the conditions of eligibility, including the provision that a candidate 'must not be a recent convert' (6); now he urges Timothy to take time to apply these criteria, and not to be in a hurry. Otherwise, if through excessive haste a mistake is made, and a scandal arises, Timothy will *share in the sins of others*, or find himself 'implicated in other people's misdeeds' (REB). Instead, Paul continues, *keep yourself pure* (22).

Verse 23, in which the apostle exhorts Timothy to *stop drinking only water*, and to *use a little wine* on account of his *stomach and . . . frequent illnesses*, 'has fairly nonplussed the commentators',[55] for it has no obvious connection with what either precedes or follows. Some think that Paul's injunction 'keep yourself pure' reminded him to add 'keep yourself fit' as well. He was perhaps anxious that Timothy was not looking after himself properly, and that his delicate

---

[51] White, p. 137.   [52] *Ecclesiastical History*, 7.2.   [53] Fee (1988), p. 131.
[54] 1 Tim. 4:14; 2 Tim. 1:6; *cf.* Acts 6:1ff.   [55] Simpson, p. 80.

constitution would 'interfere with the efficient discharge of his high office'.[56]

Others guess that verse 23 is intended as a deliberate modification of verse 22: 'Keep yourself pure. But in order to do so, don't adopt the extreme asceticism of the false teachers' (4:3). Not of course that Timothy would go to the opposite extreme and become 'given to drunkenness' (3:3). But wine was widely recognized in the ancient world as having medicinal properties. Spicq refers to several medical authorities who 'prescribed wine as tonic, prophylactic and remedy', especially in relation to indigestion.[57]

e. Discernment (5:24–25)

Verses 24 and 25 develop Paul's emphasis on the need for caution, and give a further reason to avoid haste. It is that human beings are frequently different from what they appear at first sight. They may seem initially either better or worse than they really are, for both their good and their bad points may take a while to surface. Therefore time is needed in which to discover the truth about a candidate for the pastorate. *The sins of some men are obvious.* In fact, they are so conspicuous that they reach *the place of judgment ahead of them*, or 'precede them into court' (REB), whether the judgment in mind is divine or human. *The sins of others*, however, *trail behind them* (24), for they do not appear until later. *In the same way*, as with evil so with goodness, *good deeds are obvious*, or at least many of them are, because they are done in the open. And *even those that are not* conspicuous at the time *cannot be hidden* for ever (25).

So Timothy would need discernment. It is the iceberg principle, namely that nine-tenths of a person are hidden from view. This is why Timothy must give himself time in which to form an accurate assessment of people's character. Attractive personalities often have hidden weaknesses, whereas unprepossessing people often have hidden strengths. Timothy must learn to discern between the seen and the unseen, the surface and the depth, the appearance and the reality.

Here are five qualities which are needed by Christian leaders in their dealings with others for whom they are responsible: appreciation (affirming outstanding performance), fairness (not listening to unsubstantiated accusations), impartiality (avoiding all favouritism), caution (not reaching hasty decisions) and discernment (looking beyond the outward appearance to the heart). Whenever these principles are in operation, mistakes will be avoided, the church will

---

[56] Alford, p. 354; cf. Lock, p. 62.   [57] Spicq, p. 549.

be preserved in peace and love, and God's name will be protected from dishonour.

3. Slaves (6:1–2)

Having given Timothy instructions about the treatment of widows and elders, the apostle now broaches a third social relationship, namely the behaviour of slaves towards their masters.

All who are under the yoke of slavery should consider their masters worthy of full respect, so that God's name and our teaching may not be slandered. *²Those who have believing masters are not to show less respect for them because they are brothers. Instead, they are to serve them even better, because those who benefit from their service are believers, and dear to them. These are the things you are to teach and urge on them.*

Slavery has been described as a 'monster abomination'.[58] Not that there is anything demeaning about service, when it is given voluntarily. On the contrary, Jesus himself demonstrated its dignity by washing his disciples' feet. He called himself both servant[59] and slave,[60] and added that each of his followers must be 'the slave of all'.[61] What is degrading, and fundamentally destructive of a person's humanness, is when one human being is forcibly owned by another and is thus robbed of all freedom. Slaves have three defining characteristics. Their person is another's property, so that they may be bought and sold; their will is subject to another's authority; and their labour is obtained by another's coercion.[62]

Paul does more than hint at these things here by describing slaves as being *under the yoke of slavery* (1). For yokes are designed for animals, particularly for oxen. And when the yoke is used in Scripture to picture a human experience, it usually symbolizes an oppressive régime.[63] True, Jesus spoke of his teaching authority as a yoke, but he added at once that, unlike other yokes, his is 'easy' to wear.[64]

So slavery was a form of tyranny. Even though some slave-owners were kind to their slaves, since they saw them as a valuable investment, the institution itself was a denial of human personhood. It was also a 'gigantic cancer', which drained the political, economic and moral forces of the Roman Empire.[65]

---

[58] Plummer, p. 175. [59] Lk. 22:27. [60] *Cf* Phil. 2:7, literally.
[61] Mk. 10:44.
[62] This threefold definition of slavery comes from D. B. Davies, *The Problem of Slavery in Western Cultures* (Cornell University Press, 1966), p. 31.
[63] *E.g.* 2 Ch. 10:4; Is. 9:4. [64] Mt. 11:29–30. [65] Plummer, p. 181.

Why is it, then, that neither Jesus nor his apostles called for the complete and immediate abolition of this horror? Probably the main reason is that slavery was deeply embedded in the structures of Graeco-Roman society. All well-to-do people had slaves, and very wealthy people had several hundreds. They were regarded as essential, especially as domestic servants and farm labourers, but also as clerks, craftsmen, teachers, soldiers and managers. It is believed that there were more than fifty million of them in the Empire, including one third of the inhabitants of Rome. In consequence, to dismantle slavery all at once would have brought about the collapse of society. Any signs of a slave revolt were put down with ruthless brutality. The fact is that 'monstrous evils' like slavery 'are not, like giants in the old romances, to be slain at a blow'. They are so firmly rooted that any attempt to tear them up may pull up the foundations of society with them.[66]

At the same time Paul enunciated principles which undermined the very concept of slavery and led inexorably to its abolition, even though Christians are ashamed that it did not happen sooner. What are these principles? At the beginning of this letter he has declared 'slave traders' to be in breach of God's law (1:10); in his earlier letters to the Ephesians and the Colossians he has also shown slavery to be in breach of the gospel. He has implied the equality of slaves and slave owners by declaring that they have the same heavenly master, who shows no favouritism.[67] In consequence, he has told masters to provide their slaves with what is 'right and fair', although in those days there was no such thing as 'justice' for slaves.[68] Paul has also written of the radical transformation of relationships which the gospel effects, so that slave and slave owner become brothers.[69] Indeed, 'there is neither . . . slave nor free . . . for you are all one in Christ Jesus', equally God's children and heirs without any distinction between them.[70] Meanwhile, even while slaves remain in bondage outwardly, they can enjoy an inner freedom in Christ.[71]

In both verses 1 and 2 the slaves whom Timothy is to instruct are clearly Christians and church members. There is a difference between the verses, however. Whereas in verse 2 we are explicitly told that their slave owner is a believer, in verse 1 it seems likely that he is not. So Timothy is to adjust his teaching to the context.

First, slaves *should consider their masters*, even though they are unbelievers, to be *worthy of full respect*. That is, they will treat them with respect because they consider them worthy of respect, which they are as human beings, irrespective of their behaviour. Then there is another and missionary reason why slaves should respect their

[66] *Ibid.*, p. 185.   [67] Eph. 6:9.   [68] Col. 4:1.
[69] Phm. 16; 1 Tim. 6:2.   [70] Gal. 3:26ff.   [71] 1 Cor. 7:22.

masters. It is because the reputation of *God's name and our teaching* (literally 'the teaching', meaning that of the apostles) are at stake. If slaves show disrespect for their masters, they will bring discredit on God's name and the apostles' teaching; but these will *not be slandered*, but will rather be honoured, if they respect their masters (1).

Secondly, *those who have believing masters are not to show less respect for them* ('must not take liberties with them', REB) *because they are brothers*. Evidently some slaves were guilty of this twisted reasoning, and were taking advantage of their masters' Christian faith. Christian employees in Christian firms today sometimes make the same mistake. *Instead* ('Quite the contrary', JBP, REB) *they are to serve them even better, because those who benefit from their service are believers, and dear to them* (2a), or 'are one with them in faith and love' (REB, following JBP). The two 'because' (*hoti*) clauses are parallel. Because their masters are brothers, slaves must not show them less respect. Instead, because they are believers and beloved, they must serve them even better. The faith, love and brotherhood which unite them in Christ, far from being an excuse for neglect, should be a stimulus to service. *These are the things*, Paul writes to Timothy in conclusion, which *you are to teach and urge on them* (2b). He is to pass on to the church the instructions he has received from the apostle.

These instructions have concerned the church's social responsibilities, particularly in relation to widows, presbyters and slaves. These three groups are disparate in several ways. They are men and women, slaves and free, young and old, workers at home and in church, church leaders and church members. What unites them? It is the word 'honour'. The church is to 'honour' real widows and care for them (3). Presbyters who lead well are to be counted worthy of a twofold 'honour' (17). Slaves are to regard their masters as worthy of 'honour' (6:1). The same Greek word, as either a verb (*timaō*) or a noun (*timē*), occurs in each of these three verses. Indeed, the duty to honour people is much emphasized in Scripture. For example, 'Give due honour [NIV "Show proper respect"] to everyone.'[72] Again, 'Honour one another above yourselves,'[73] or 'Outdo one another in showing honour' (RSV). Every human being is worthy of honour, even pagan slave owners, because they have been made in the image of God. Once we perceive the intrinsic worth of human beings by creation, and therefore recognize them as worthy of honour, all our relationships are enriched and ennobled.

---

[72] 1 Pet. 2:17.   [73] Rom. 12:10.

1 Timothy 6:3–21
6. Material possessions

Money and property continue to be matters of conscientious concern to all committed Christian people. This is partly because of Jesus' challenging teaching on the subject, and partly because of the gross economic inequality between North and South, and between groups within each country and region. Approximately 1,000 million inhabitants of the world are destitute, lacking the basic necessities for survival, while a small minority of people live in contrasting luxury. What should be a Christian's attitude to material possessions?

Having given Timothy instructions about three groups in the church (widows, elders and slaves), Paul comes to a fourth (false teachers), whose baneful influence is at the back of his mind throughout this letter. In 1:3–7 he has noted their speculations about the law, and in 4:1–5 their denial of creation. Now in 6:3–5 he characterizes them as deviating from sound doctrine, dividing the church, and being motivated by avarice. It is this last characteristic of theirs which leads Paul to give vital instruction about covetousness and contentment (7–10), and wealth and generosity (17–19), and which imparts to this chapter its distinctive emphasis, namely the place in Christian discipleship of material possessions. The apostle issues a series of five charges: first, to or about the false teachers (3–5), secondly to the Christian poor (6–10), thirdly to the 'man of God' (11–16), fourthly to the Christian rich (17–19) and finally to Timothy himself (20–21).

The bridge between the previous section of the letter and this new section is the apostle's terse announcement: 'These are the things you are to teach and urge on them' (2b). Some translators (e.g. NIV) regard this sentence as concluding the former section, while others (e.g. RSV, REB) see it as introducing the new one. It surely does both. On the one hand it looks back to the whole of the letter thus far. 'These things' are what Paul has taught Timothy and what Timothy is to pass on to the churches. On the other hand, the connecting

145

sentence anticipates what Paul goes on immediately to write, namely that there are heretics teaching a different message. *If anyone teaches false doctrines* . . . (3a). Thus two kinds of teacher are seen in sharp antithesis to one another – the true and the false, the orthodox and the heterodox, Timothy teaching 'these' things (*tauta*), which the apostle had taught, and his opponents teaching 'other' or 'different' things (*hetera*), which deviated from the apostle's instruction.

1. A charge about false teachers (6:3–5)

If anyone teaches false doctrines and does not agree to the sound instruction of our Lord Jesus Christ and to godly teaching, [4]*he is conceited and understands nothing. He has an unhealthy interest in controversies and quarrels about words that result in envy, strife, malicious talk, evil suspicions* [5]*and constant friction between men of corrupt mind, who have been robbed of the truth and who think that godliness is a means to financial gain.*

The apostle evaluates the false teachers in relation to questions of truth, unity and motivation. His criticism of them is that they deviate from the faith, split the church, and love money. They are heterodox, divisive and covetous.

a. The false teachers are deviating from the faith

Once again Paul implies that there is a standard of Christian belief which in this chapter he calls the 'teaching' (1, 3b), 'sound instruction' (3), 'the truth' (5), 'the faith' (10, 12, 21), the 'command' (14) and 'what has been entrusted' (20). From this norm the false teachers have turned aside. Paul individualizes them for emphasis: *If anyone teaches false doctrines and does not agree to* ('does not loyally adhere to')[1] . . . *sound instruction* . . . The first of these verbs is *heterodidaskaleō* (as in 1:3), in which *heteros* means 'other', 'different' or 'some doctrinal novelty' (JBP). It is false because it deviates from apostolic teaching, which is *sound* (healthy) *instruction.* Paul characterizes his healthy teaching in two ways.

First, it consists of the sound words (literally) *of our Lord Jesus Christ.* Some think that this genitive is objective, meaning that the teaching is about Christ. But Paul's instruction did not focus exclusively on Christ. Others take the genitive as subjective and suppose that Paul is referring to words spoken by Christ, perhaps to an already published gospel or a collection of the sayings of Jesus.

[1] Lock, p. 67.

But Paul seldom quoted Jesus' words, 5:18 and Acts 20:35 being exceptional.

The third and most probable explanation is that Paul regarded his own words as the words of Christ. 'He who listens to you listens to me,' Jesus had said when he sent out the Seventy,[2] and Luke implied that the ascended Christ would continue to act and speak through the apostles.[3] This was certainly Paul's conviction. He could command and exhort in the name or with the authority of Christ.[4] He claimed that Christ was speaking through him,[5] and he even commended the Galatians for having welcomed him as if he were Jesus Christ.[6] As Chrysostom put it, 'Thus says Paul, or rather Christ by Paul.'[7]

The second characteristic of 'sound instruction' is that it is *godly teaching* (3b), literally, 'the teaching which accords with godliness'. A similar expression occurs in Titus 1:1, which the NIV translates 'the truth that leads to godliness'. Here then are two essential marks of sound teaching. It comes from Christ and it promotes godliness. Anybody who disagrees with it, therefore, *is conceited and understands nothing* (4a). Or, putting the two phrases together, he is 'a conceited idiot' (JBP) or 'a pompous ignoramus' (REB). This is strong language. But then the false teacher is guilty of a serious offence. For to disagree with Paul is to disagree with Christ. Indeed, in the end there are only two possible responses to the Word of God. One is to humble ourselves and tremble at it; the other is to harden our hearts, stiffen our necks and reject it.

b. The false teachers are dividing the church

In addition to being arrogant and ignorant, the false teacher is divisive. *He has an unhealthy interest in controversies and quarrels about words* (4a), or 'a morbid enthusiasm for mere speculations and quibbles' (REB). It is noteworthy that Paul portrays him as 'sick', whereas he has called apostolic teaching 'sound' or 'healthy'. The false teachers' relish for profitless argument is positively pathological.

Petty quibbles and quarrels of this kind lead to a complete breakdown in human relationships. Five results are listed: *envy* (the resentment of other people's gifts), *strife* (the spirit of competition and contention), *malicious talk* (abuse of 'rival teachers'),[8] *evil suspicions* (forgetting that fellowship is built on trust, not suspicion), *and constant friction* (the fruit of irritability). These evils characterize *men of corrupt mind, who have been robbed of the truth . . .* (5a).

---

[2] Lk. 10:16.   [3] Acts 1:1.   [4] *E.g.* 2 Thes. 3:6, 12.   [5] 2 Cor. 13:3.
[6] Gal. 4:14.   [7] Chrysostom, p. 469.   [8] Lock, pp. 67–68.

When people's minds are twisted, all their relationships become twisted too.

c. The false teachers are lovers of money

Another symptom of the false teachers' depraved mind and loss of truth is that they *think that godliness is a means to financial gain* (5b). They have no interest in godliness itself, but only if it proves to be financially profitable.

Precisely how the false teachers whom Timothy had to combat were exploiting godliness for gain is not divulged. But we do know that Ephesus enjoyed great opulence, inflated by the trade which the cult of Diana brought to the city. On Paul's second visit there it was a silversmith and his craftsmen who were his main opponents. Their sale of silver shrines of Diana had brought them 'no little business', but now their income was dwindling under Paul's polemic against idolatry.[9] So it is not surprising that in his letter to the Ephesians, Paul needed to warn them against greed.[10]

The history of the human race has regularly been stained by attempts to commercialize religion. It was when Simon Magus thought he could buy spiritual powers from the apostles that the term 'simony' was coined, to denote the purchase and sale of spiritual privilege or ecclesiastical office. Paul himself found it necessary to declare that, unlike many, he did not peddle the Word of God for profit,[11] that he had never coveted anybody's silver, gold or clothing,[12] and that he had never used religion as a cloak for greed.[13]

Yet the church was discredited during the Middle Ages on account of the disgraceful sale of indulgences; religious cults still charge exorbitant fees for personal tuition in their particular tenets; some evangelists appeal for 'love offerings' which are never publicly audited; and some television preachers promise their viewers personal prosperity on condition that they send in enough 'seed money'.

Looking back over verses 3–5 we note that Paul has given us three practical tests by which to evaluate all teaching. We might put them in the form of questions. Is it compatible with the apostolic faith, that is, the New Testament? Does it tend to unite or divide the church? And does it promote godliness with contentment, or covetousness?

---

[9] Acts 19:23ff.   [10] Eph. 5:3.   [11] 2 Cor. 2:17.   [12] Acts 20:33.
[13] 1 Thes. 2:5.

2. A charge to the Christian poor (6:6–10)

But godliness with contentment is great gain. ⁷*For we brought nothing into the world, and we can take nothing out of it.* ⁸*But if we have food and clothing, we will be content with that.* ⁹*People who want to get rich fall into temptation and a trap and into many foolish and harmful desires that plunge men into ruin and destruction.* ¹⁰*For the love of money is a root of all kinds of evil. Some people, eager for money, have wandered from the faith and pierced themselves with many griefs.*

The very notion that godliness could be a means to gain (5b) sounds preposterous. Yet Paul's way of undermining it is not to contradict it but to confirm it. 'In an elegant manner and with an ironical turn he quickly throws back at his opponents the same words with the opposite meaning.'[14] 'Godliness' (*eusebeia*) is 'gain' (*porismos*), even *great gain* (6a), providing you mean spiritual gain, not financial, and providing you add *contentment*. Paul is echoing his earlier statement that 'godliness has value for all things', bringing blessing for both this life and the next (4:8). The REB expresses well his play on words: 'They think religion should yield dividends; and of course religion does yield high dividends, but only to those who are content with what they have.'

Paul's word for *contentment* (*autarkeia*) is the regular term used by the Stoics for a self-sufficiency which is altogether independent of circumstances. Christian contentment also does not depend on external things. Thus 'I have learned the secret', Paul wrote, 'of being content (*autarkēs*) in any and every situation, whether well fed or hungry, whether living in plenty or in want.'[15] This Christian 'secret' is not to be found within ourselves, however, as Stoics taught and New Agers teach, but in Christ. 'I can do everything', Paul went on, 'through him who gives me strength.'[16] Thus genuine contentment is 'not *self*-sufficiency but *Christ*-sufficiency'.[17] This is why godliness plus contentment equals great spiritual gain.

Paul's equation prompts him to extol the virtue of contentment and expose the folly of covetousness. He contrasts two categories of Christian poor, the contented who have the necessities of life (7–8) and the covetous, who love money and want to get rich (9–10).

[14] Calvin, p. 274.   [15] Phil. 4:12.   [16] Phil. 4:13; *cf.* Heb. 13:5–6.
[17] Fee (1988), p. 143.

a. The contented poor (6:7-8)

The people Paul is describing are not the destitute, who lack the basic necessities for survival. Nobody can be content with destitution. Rather they *have food and clothing* and *are content with that* (8).

How then does the apostle argue the Christian case for contentment and against covetousness? He reminds us of a fundamental (though often ignored) fact of our human experience, relating to our birth and death. It is that *we brought nothing into the world* ('absolutely nothing', as JBP expresses the emphasis), *and we can take nothing out of it* (7, 'absolutely nothing', JBP repeats). It seems probable that Paul is alluding to a salutary truth on which Israel's wise men reflected. Here is Job's version of it: 'Naked I came from my mother's womb, and naked I shall depart.'[18] That is, we are born naked and penniless, and when we die and are buried we are naked and penniless again. In respect of earthly possessions, our entry and our exit are identical. So our life on earth is a brief pilgrimage between two moments of nakedness. We brought nothing with us, and can take nothing away with us. As the officiating minister said at the funeral of a wealthy lady, when asked by the curious how much she had left, 'She left everything.' It is a perspective which should influence our economic lifestyle. For possessions are only the travelling luggage of time; they are not the stuff of eternity. It would be sensible therefore to travel light and, as Jesus himself commanded us, not to store up for ourselves (that is, to accumulate selfishly) treasures on earth.[19]

What, then, should be our attitude to material things? Paul replies: *But if we have food and clothing, we will be content with that* (8, or perhaps it is an exhortation, 'let us rest content', REB). He thus reverts to the topic of Christian contentment. Luxuries are not essential to it; but necessities are. These he calls *food and clothing*, the 'what to eat' and 'what to wear' which Jesus forbade us to worry about, because he promised that our heavenly Father would give them to us.[20] Paul's word for 'clothing' is *skepasma* (literally, a 'covering'), which means 'chiefly *clothing* ... but also *house*' (BAGD). So probably the couplet 'food and clothing' should be extended to include shelter, for these three are clearly essential for our journey.

Is this all? Probably not, for what Paul is defining is not the maximum that is permitted to the believer, but the minimum that is compatible with contentment. This is clear because he has already portrayed God as the good Creator, whose gifts we are to receive

---

[18] Jb. 1:21; *cf.* Ec. 5:15.   [19] Mt. 6:19ff.; Lk. 12:16ff.   [20] Mt. 6:25ff.; Lk. 12:22ff.

with thanksgiving (4:3ff.), and he will soon add that God 'richly provides us with everything for our enjoyment' (6:17). So he is not advocating austerity or asceticism, but contentment in place of materialism and covetousness.

This does not mean that we are free to go to the opposite extreme of extravagance. The Evangelical Commitment to Simple Lifestyle puts it well:

> We resolve to renounce waste and oppose extravagance in personal living, clothing and housing, travel and church buildings. We also accept the distinction between necessities and luxuries, creative hobbies and empty status symbols, modesty and vanity, occasional celebrations and normal routine, and between the service of God and slavery to fashion. Where to draw the line requires conscientious thought and decision by us, together with members of our family.[21]

b. The covetous poor (6:9-10)

Not until verse 17 does Paul give Timothy instructions for the rich. In verses 9 and 10 he is still describing the poor. It is not now the contented poor he has in mind, however, but the covetous poor, those who 'want to get rich' (9) and are motivated by 'the love of money' (10).

The Old Testament is full of admonitions against covetousness, especially the Wisdom literature. We are warned that money is addictive, since 'whoever loves money never has money enough'.[22] We are told not to be 'overawed' by the wealthy, but to remember that they will leave their wealth behind them.[23] It is also explicitly stated that 'one eager to get rich will not go unpunished'.[24] So we should pray to be given 'neither poverty [i.e. destitution] nor riches', but only our 'daily bread', i.e. the necessities of life.[25]

Jesus must have reflected on this strand of Old Testament wisdom. He certainly endorsed it, telling us to beware of greed, and reminding us that our life does not consist in the abundance of our possessions.[26]

Moreover, the warnings of Scripture are conveyed to us not only through verbal instruction and exhortation, but through cautionary tales as well. Adam and Eve, Achan, Judas, and Ananias and Sapphira all came to grief through some form of covetousness.[27]

---

[21] Para. 5, 'Personal Lifestyle', Evangelical Commitment to Simple Lifestyle (Lausanne Committee for World Evangelization, March 1980).
[22] Ec. 5:10.   [23] Ps. 49:10, 16ff.   [24] Pr. 28:20.   [25] Pr. 30:7ff.
[26] Lk. 12:15ff.   [27] Gn. 3:6; Jos. 7:20-21; Mt. 26:14ff. and Jn. 12:4ff.; Acts 5:1ff.

Paul now takes up the same theme and traces the downfall of the covetous. *People who want to get rich fall*. . .(9a). First, they *fall into temptation and a trap*. They thus do to themselves what they pray God will never do to them: they lead themselves into temptation, indeed into multiple temptations like dishonesty and theft. And the 'trap' they fall into is surely the devil's (as in 3:7 and 2 Tim. 2:26), for through their greed he ensnares them in materialism and moral compromise; they become ready 'to sacrifice duty and conscience to the pursuit of wealth'.[28]

Secondly, covetous people fall *into many foolish and harmful desires* (9b). Of course greed is itself a desire, selfish and even idolatrous,[29] but it breeds other desires. For money is a drug, and covetousness a drug addiction. The more you have, the more you want. Yet these further desires are *foolish* (they cannot be rationally defended) and *harmful* (they captivate and do not liberate the human spirit). As Schopenhauer said, 'gold is like sea water – the more one drinks of it, the thirstier one becomes'.[30]

As the third and final stage in the downfall of the covetous, their wrong desires *plunge* them *into ruin and destruction* (9c). The metaphor pictures them sinking and drowning, either in 'utter destruction' (BAGD) or, taking the two nouns separately, in disaster in this life and in the destruction of hell in the next. The irony is that those who set their hearts on gain end in total loss, the loss of their integrity and indeed of themselves. For, as Jesus asked, 'What good is it for a man to gain the whole world, yet forfeit his soul?'[31]

In order to enforce his solemn warning, Paul now quotes what seems to have been a current proverb: *For the love of money is a root of all kinds of evil* (10a). It has been found in varying forms in both Greek and Jewish literature. But in the contemporary western world it reminds us of the popular lyric by Joan Whitney and Alex Kramer, published in the USA in *Pickwick Music* (1946). It was entitled 'Money is the root of all evil' and had a thrice-uttered refrain, 'Take it away.' But the lyric is mistaken. There are three significant ways in which it differs from Paul's proverb. First, according to Paul the problem is not 'money' but 'the love of money'.[32] Secondly, it is not 'the' one and only root of evil, but only 'a' root. Although grammatically the Greek definite article is not essential to require the translation 'the', it would most naturally be expected. Thirdly, money or the love of it is not the root of 'all evil' in the singular, as a composite whole, but rather a root of 'all kinds of evil' in the plural.

---

[28] Liddon, p. 75.   [29] Eph. 5:5.
[30] Quoted by Bishop Otto Dibelius in his autobiography *In the Service of the Lord* (Holt, Rinehart and Winston, 1964), p. 31.
[31] Mk. 8:36.   [32] *Cf.* 2 Tim. 3:2.

What then are the evils of which the love of money is a major root or cause? A long list could be given. Avarice leads to selfishness, cheating, fraud, perjury and robbery, to envy, quarrelling and hatred, to violence and even murder. Greed lies behind marriages of convenience, perversions of justice, drug-pushing, pornography sales, blackmail, the exploitation of the weak, the neglect of good causes, and the betrayal of friends. But Paul concentrates on only two evils which spring from covetousness. First, *some people, eager for money, have wandered from the faith* (10b). It is not possible to pursue truth and money, God and mammon, simultaneously. People either renounce avarice in their commitment to the faith, or they make money their god and depart from the faith.

Secondly, they have *pierced themselves with many griefs* (10c), or 'have spiked themselves on many a painful thorn' (REB). What these 'griefs' or 'thorns' are Paul does not elaborate, but they could include worry and remorse, the pangs of a disregarded conscience, the discovery that materialism can never satisfy the human spirit, and final despair. Jay Gould, the nineteenth-century American financier, who died unlamented worth some $100 million, is said to have exclaimed with his dying breath, 'I'm the most miserable devil in the world.'

This whole passage (verses 6–10), which is the apostle's charge to the Christian poor, both the contented poor and the covetous poor, is calculated to make Christianity's critics explode with anger. 'This is precisely what Marx meant', they will say, 'when he called religion "the opium of the people". Christianity instils into the proletariat a false contentment with their lot. It encourages the poor to accept their poverty, and to acquiesce in the *status quo* (instead of rebelling against it), on the flimsy ground that they will be compensated in the next world.' How shall we reply? We have to concede that Marx was partly correct in his analysis. Christianity does teach contentment, and some Christians and churches have misused this Christian emphasis to defend the exploitation of the poor and to keep them in their oppression, while promising them freedom in heaven. But Paul is not guilty of this. Two clarifications of his teaching need to be made.

First, as we have already seen, the poverty he is writing about is not destitution, which is destructive of humanness, but a simplicity of lifestyle which is entirely compatible with human dignity. With the latter we should be content, but not with the former.

Secondly, the contentment Paul is writing about is not acquiescence in social injustice. On the contrary, we are called to combine personal contentment with the quest for justice, especially if it is justice for other people that we are fighting for.

The apostle's essential emphasis is clear, namely that covetousness is a self-destructive evil, whereas simplicity and contentment are beautiful and Christlike virtues. In a word, he is not for poverty against wealth, but for contentment against covetousness.

3. A charge to a man of God (6:11–16)

But you, man of God, flee from all this, and pursue righteousness, godliness, faith, love, endurance and gentleness. [12]*Fight the good fight of the faith. Take hold of the eternal life to which you were called when you made your good confession in the presence of many witnesses.* [13]*In the sight of God, who gives life to everything, and of Christ Jesus, who while testifying before Pontius Pilate made the good confession, I charge you* [14]*to keep this command without spot or blame until the appearing of our Lord Jesus Christ,* [15]*which God will bring about in his own time – God, the blessed and only Ruler, the King of kings and Lord of lords,* [16]*who alone is immortal and who lives in unapproachable light, whom no-one has seen or can see. To him be honour and might for ever. Amen.*

Paul couches his next appeal, which is to Timothy himself, in very poignant terms. He does not yet address him by name, as he will in verse 20 ('O Timothy', AV, RSV). Instead, he uses the honorific title 'man of God'. In the Old Testament it was a term reserved for the leaders of Israel. It was applied to Moses,[33] Samuel,[34] David,[35] the prophet Shemaiah,[36] Elijah,[37] Elisha,[38] Igdaliah the Rechabite[39] and three anonymous prophets.[40] In the only other use of the expression in the New Testament 'the man of God' appears to be any mature Christian who becomes 'thoroughly equipped for every good work'.[41]

As a man of God Timothy is deliberately contrasted with the false teachers who, being conceited, quarrelsome and covetous (4–10), are more men of the world than of God. *But you, man of God*, Paul writes (or, sharpening the antithesis, 'But as for you', RSV), you are to be radically different from them. Timothy must take his stand firmly against their ungodliness. And Paul goes on to develop a threefold appeal to him – ethical, doctrinal and experiential.

a. The ethical appeal (6:11)

As a man of God, Timothy must both *flee from all this* (*tauta*, 'these things') *and pursue* other things. He is to flee the love of money, and

---

[33] Dt. 33:1; Jos. 14:6; 1 Ch. 23:14; and the title of Ps. 90.   [34] 1 Sa. 9:6.
[35] Ne. 12:24, 36.   [36] 1 Ki. 12:22.   [37] 1 Ki. 17:18; 2 Ki. 1:9.   [38] 2 Ki. 4:7.
[39] Je. 35:4.   [40] 1 Sa. 2:27; 1 Ki. 13:1ff.; 2 Ch. 25:7ff.   [41] 2 Tim. 3:17.

all the many evils associated with it (9–10), together with 'the wayward passions of youth',[42] and everything else which is incompatible with the wholesome will of God. Instead, he is to pursue six qualities, which seem to be listed in pairs, and which are particularly appropriate as an alternative to covetousness. First, he must *pursue righteousness* (perhaps here meaning justice and fair dealing with people) and *godliness* (for God not mammon is the right object of human worship). Next, the man of God must pursue *faith* and *love*, a familiar couplet in Paul's letters. Perhaps in this context he means on the one hand faithfulness or 'integrity' (REB) and on the other the love of sacrifice and service which has no room for greed. Then Timothy's third goal is to be *endurance* (*hypomonē*), which is patience in difficult circumstances, *and gentleness*, which is patience with difficult people.

What is specially noteworthy is that this ethical appeal has both a negative and a positive aspect, which are complementary. Negatively, we are to 'flee' from evil, to take 'constant evasive action',[43] to run from it as far as we can and as fast as we can. Positively, we are to go in hot pursuit of goodness. This combination occurs frequently in the New Testament, although in different terms. We are to deny ourselves and follow Christ,[44] to say 'no' to ungodliness and 'yes' to godliness and self-control,[45] to take off the old clothing which belonged to our previous life and put on the new which belongs to our Christian life, and here to run away from evil and run after goodness.

Now we human beings are great runners. It is natural for us to run away from anything which threatens us. To run from a real danger is common sense, but to run from issues we dare not face or from responsibilities we dare not shoulder is escapism. Instead, we should concentrate on running away from evil. We also run after many things which attract us – pleasure, promotion, fame, wealth and power. Instead, we should concentrate on the pursuit of holiness.

There is no particular secret to learn, no formula to recite, no technique to master. The apostle gives us no teaching on 'holiness and how to attain it'. We are simply to run from evil as we run from danger, and to run after goodness as we run after success. That is, we have to give our mind, time and energy to both flight and pursuit. Once we see evil as the evil it is, we will want to flee from it, and once we see goodness as the good it is, we will want to pursue it.

b. The doctrinal appeal (6:12a)

Timothy's duty will involve fight as well as flight, standing as well as running. The AV translates Paul's second appeal as 'fight the good

---

[42] 2 Tim. 2:22, REB.   [43] Ward, p. 103.   [44] Mk. 8:34.   [45] Tit. 2:12.

fight of faith'. But the RSV and NIV are surely right to acknowledge the presence of the definite article and to render the sentence *fight the good fight of the faith* (12a). It is true that in the previous verse (11) 'faith' or 'faithfulness' is one of the qualities we are to pursue. But in verses 10 and 21 Paul describes the false teachers as having 'wandered from the faith', meaning the apostolic faith, the body of doctrine to which he alludes throughout the Pastoral Letters as 'the truth' (*e.g.* 2:4; 3:15; 4:3), 'the teaching' (*e.g.* 4:6; 6:1; Tit. 1:9; 2:1) or 'the deposit' (6:20; 2 Tim. 1:12, 14, literally). Since some have 'wandered' from it, it is all the more urgent that Timothy should 'fight' for it.

It is uncertain whether the model Paul has in mind is athletic (taken from the Olympic Games) or military (taken from warfare), and, if the former, whether he is thinking of a wrestling match or a race. The combination of the adjective 'good' with the noun *agōn* and the verb *agōnizomai* could be translated either 'fight the good fight' or 'run the good race'. And Paul will later bring the two metaphors together when he affirms that he has himself 'fought the good fight' and 'finished the race'.[46] Certainly a race and a fight both demand strenuous exertion. But the language of the similar exhortation to 'fight the good fight' in 1:18 definitely refers to a soldier's combat (*strateuō* and *strateia*).

It is striking that just as evil and goodness have been contrasted (11), so now are truth and error. For Timothy is both to 'turn away' from false teaching (20b) and to 'guard' (20a) and 'fight' for (12) truth. Thus in both Paul's appeals the negative and the positive are set in opposition. Ethically, we are to flee evil and pursue goodness. Doctrinally, we are to avoid error and contend for the truth.

Nobody enjoys a fight, unless of course the person concerned is pugnacious by temperament. Fighting is an unpleasant business – undignified, bloody, painful and dangerous. So is controversy, that is, fighting for truth and goodness. It should be distasteful to all sensitive spirits. There is something sick about those who relish it. Nevertheless, it is a 'good fight'; it has to be fought. For truth is precious, even sacred. Being truth from God, we cannot neglect it without affronting him. It is also essential for the health and growth of the church. So whenever truth is imperilled by false teachers, to defend it is a painful necessity. Even the 'gentleness' we are to pursue (the last word of verse 11) is not incompatible with fighting the good fight of the faith (12).

---

[46] 2 Tim. 4:7.

c. The experiential appeal (6:12b)

Paul's third appeal to Timothy advances beyond doctrine and ethics to experience: *Take hold of . . . eternal life . . .* (12a). Much misunderstanding surrounds the concept of 'eternal life', and many would accept the young girl's definition that 'God has given us life, so now we're stuck with it'. The emphasis is not on its duration, however, but on its quality. Eternal life means the life of the age to come, the new age which Jesus inaugurated. He defined its life in terms of knowing him and knowing the Father.[47] Consequently it is both a present possession and a future hope, as the Pastorals make clear. For the present possession see 1:16 and 2 Timothy 1:10, and for the future hope see Titus 1:2; 3:17. Those who think that in verses 12 and 19 the eternal life Timothy must grasp is future do so because they believe Paul is continuing his athletic metaphor and is alluding to the prize at the end of the race.

It seems more probable, however, that eternal life is here a present possession, because Paul describes it to Timothy as something *to which you were called when you made your good confession in the presence of many witnesses* (12b). The reference to 'many witnesses' has suggested to some that the occasion recalled is not Timothy's baptism but his ordination (*cf.* 4:14; 2 Tim. 2:2). But the combination of the calling (inward and private) and the confession (outward and public) more naturally refers to Timothy's conversion and baptism. Every convert was expected to make a solemn public affirmation of faith.[48]

It may seem strange, however, that a Christian leader of Timothy's stature should need to be exhorted to 'take hold of' eternal life. Had he not been a Christian for many years? Had he not therefore received eternal life long ago? Then why did Paul tell him to lay hold of what he already possessed? The probable answer is that it is possible to possess something without embracing and enjoying it. *Epilambanomai* means to 'take hold of, grasp . . . sometimes with violence' and to 'take hold of, in order to make one's own' (BAGD). The 'violence' is seen in Jesus catching Peter when he was beginning to sink,[49] in the soldiers seizing Simon of Cyrene,[50] in the crowd seizing Paul,[51] and in the tribune arresting him.[52] Just so, although Timothy had already received eternal life, Paul urged him to seize it, grasp it, lay hold of it, make it completely his own, enjoy it and live it to the full.

Here then is Paul's threefold charge to Timothy – ethical (to flee from evil and pursue goodness), doctrinal (to turn from error and

[47] Jn. 17:3.   [48] Rom. 10:9ff.   [49] Mt. 14:31.   [50] Lk. 23:26.
[51] Acts 21:30.   [52] Acts 21:33; *cf.* Phil. 3:12.

157

fight for the truth), and experiential (to lay hold of the life he has already received). It is good in our relativistic age to have truth, goodness and life set before us as absolute goals. They also constitute a healthy balance. Some fight for truth but neglect holiness. Others pursue holiness but have no comparable concern for truth. Yet others disregard both doctrine and ethics in their search for religious experience. The man or woman of God combines all three.

d. The grounds of the appeal (6:13–16)

Paul does more than appeal to Timothy, for he knows about human apathy and our consequent need for incentives. So he buttresses his appeal with strong arguments, namely the presence of God and the coming of Christ. First, it is impressive that Paul lived in the conscious presence of God, so that it was natural for him to write: *In the sight of God . . . and of Christ Jesus . . . I charge you* (13; cf. 2 Tim. 4:1). Moreover, he reminded himself and Timothy of an appropriate truth about each. God he describes as the one *who gives life to everything*.[53] As the giver and sustainer of the life of all living creatures, he is intimately involved in their affairs. Christ, on the other hand, is described as the one *who while testifying before Pontius Pilate made the good confession*, by acknowledging that he was indeed a king.[54] His disciples never forgot the historical precedent of bold testimony which he set. He was, beyond comparison, 'the faithful and true witness'.[55] The 'good confession' expected of us was first made by him (12, 13). It is in the sight of God the life-giver and of Christ the witness that Paul issues his charge.

I charge you, he writes, *to keep this command without spot or blame* (13b–14a). There is a difference of opinion whether *this command* refers to the threefold appeal which Paul has just made in verses 11 and 12, or to the ethical instruction of the whole letter, or – more widely still – to 'the whole law of Christ, the rule of faith and life enjoined by the gospel'.[56] Commentators also differ whether the words *without spot or blame* apply to Timothy or to the command. Perhaps the REB is best: 'I charge you to obey your orders without fault or failure.'

The second ground on which the apostle bases his charge is the second coming of Christ. Timothy is to keep the command without fault *until the appearing of our Lord Jesus Christ* (14b). It is evident that Paul is still as certain about the event as he is uncertain about its time.[57] Yet he knows that this too is in God's hands, since he *will*

---

[53] *Cf.* Acts 14:15; 17:28ff.   [54] Jn. 18:33–34; *cf.* Mk. 15:2.
[55] Rev. 3:14; *cf.* 1:5.   [56] Kelly, p. 144.   [57] *Cf.* Mk. 13:32; Acts 1:7; 1 Jn. 5:1.

bring it *about in his own time* (15a), or 'in his own good time' (REB). This assurance about the divine timetable is a notable feature of the Pastorals. Whether Paul is alluding to the first coming of Christ (past), the proclamation of the gospel (present) or his appearing (future), each event occurs in God's 'own', 'proper' or 'appointed' time (2:6; 6:15; Tit. 1:3).

Moreover, our confidence in God's perfect timing, and our consequent willingness to leave things in his hands, arise from the kind of God we know him to be. This Paul goes on to unfold, probably drawing on the words of an early Christian hymn, in a doxology similar to that in 1:17. He affirms four truths about God's sovereign power, four ways in which he is altogether beyond human control or manipulation.

First, God is invincible, beyond all interference by earthly powers; for he is *God, the blessed and only Ruler, the King of kings and Lord of lords* (15b). In the Old Testament Nebuchadnezzar of Babylon liked to be designated 'king of kings',[58] but Yahweh was acknowledged as 'God of gods and Lord of lords'.[59] In the New Testament Christ is given the combined title 'King of kings and Lord of lords',[60] in opposition no doubt to the blasphemies of the emperor cult. No human rule can challenge his authority.

Secondly, God is immortal, not subject to the changes caused by time, death or dissolution; he and he *alone is immortal*, literally 'possesses immortality' (16b, REB). True, human beings also are immortal, in the sense that we survive death. But only God 'has life in himself'.[61] 'Our immortality constitutes an endowment, not an innate property'.[62]

Thirdly, God is inaccessible, beyond the reach of sinful people, *dwelling in unapproachable light*. Darkness in any shape or form, whether falsehood or evil, cannot enter his presence, let alone overcome him.[63]

Fourthly, God is invisible, beyond human sight and so beyond human apprehension, for *no-one has seen or can see* him. All that human eyes have been allowed to behold is his 'glory',[64] his back not his face,[65] his appearing as a theophany,[66] or his image in his incarnate Son.[67] Being in himself invisible, we can come to know him only in so far as he has been pleased to make himself known. Otherwise, he is wholly beyond us.

To this great God, invincible, immortal, inaccessible and invisible,

---

[58] Ezk. 26:7; Dn. 2:37.   [59] Dt. 10:17; Ps. 136:2–3; *cf.* 2 Macc. 13:4.
[60] Rev. 17:14; 19:16.   [61] Jn. 5:26.   [62] Simpson, p. 89; *cf.* 2 Tim. 1:10.
[63] *E.g.* Jn. 1:5; 1 Jn. 1:5.   [64] *E.g.* Ex. 24:9ff.; Is. 6:1ff.; Ezk. 1:28.
[65] Ex. 33:18ff.   [66] *E.g.* Gn. 16:7ff.; 18:1ff; 32:24ff.
[67] Jn. 1:18; 14:6; Col. 1:15.

159

be honour and might for ever. Amen (16b). It is natural for Paul, when he is writing about God, to break into a doxology, whether he is praising God for his mercy (as in 1:17) or for his power (as here). It was in the presence of this God, and in anticipation of his bringing about Christ's appearing, that Paul has given Timothy his solemn charge. And in doing so, his mind has encompassed creation (God the life-giver, 13a), history (Christ before Pontius Pilate, 13b) and consummation (Christ's appearing, 14). Still today the presence of God and the appearing of Christ are two major incentives to faithfulness.

4. A charge to the Christian rich (6:17–19)

Command those who are rich in this present world not to be arrogant nor to put their hope in wealth, which is so uncertain, but to put their hope in God, who richly provides us with everything for our enjoyment. [18]*Command them to do good, to be rich in good deeds, and to be generous and willing to share.* [19]*In this way they will lay up treasure for themselves as a firm foundation for the coming age, so that they may take hold of the life that is truly life.*

It is obvious that this paragraph focuses on riches. Paul uses the adjective 'rich' (*plousios*, 17a), the noun 'riches' or 'wealth' (*ploutos*, 17b), the adverb 'richly' (*plousiōs*, 17c) and the verb 'to be rich' (*plouteō*, 18a). Thus after his digression (11–16), his charge to a man of God to flee from the evils of covetousness, Paul reverts to the topic of money. It is essential to note that 1 Timothy 6 contains two complementary paragraphs (6–10 and 17–19), which both handle the same theme of money, but are addressed to different groups in the church. In verses 6–10 Paul addresses the Christian poor, and in particular those among them 'who want to get rich' (8). In verses 17–19, however, Paul addresses the Christian rich, 'those who are rich in this present world' (17). Of course wealth and poverty are relative terms. Neither can be neatly defined. Among the poor some are poorer than others, and among the wealthy some are wealthier than others. Nevertheless, in every culture there is a recognized difference between them.

The first thing to notice about this paragraph (17–19) is that Paul does not direct the rich to divest themselves of their riches. Instead, he gives negative and positive instruction, first warning the rich of the dangers of wealth, and then laying down their obligations.

a. Negative instruction: the dangers of being rich (6:17)

The first danger to which the wealthy are exposed is pride. *Command those who are rich in this present world not to be arrogant* (17a). The Old Testament clearly warned people of this.[68] Wealth often gives birth to vanity. It tends to make people feel self-important, and so 'contemptuous of others' (JBP). Wealthy people frequently boast of their house, furniture, car, yacht or other possessions.

The second danger to which the rich are exposed is a false security. *Command those who are rich in this present world not . . . to put their hope in wealth* (17a). To do so is foolishly short-sighted. For one thing, wealth *is so uncertain*. Jesus warned us of the ravages of moth, rust and burglars,[69] and we would want to add fire and inflation as further hazards. Many people have gone to bed rich and woken up poor. For another thing, the proper object of our human trust is not a thing but a Person; not wealth but *God, who richly provides us with everything for our enjoyment* (17b).[70] This is an important addition. We are not to exchange materialism for asceticism. On the contrary, God is a generous Creator, who wants us to appreciate the good gifts of creation. If we consider it right to adopt an economic lifestyle lower than we could command, it will be out of solidarity with the poor, and not because we judge the possession of material things to be wrong in itself.

The two dangers, then, to which the rich are exposed are a false pride (looking down on people less fortunate than themselves) and a false security (trusting in the gift instead of in the Giver). In this way wealth can spoil life's two paramount relationships, causing us to forget God and despise our neighbour.

b. Positive instruction: the duties of being rich (6:18–19)

Timothy is not only to warn the rich of the perils they face, but also to alert them to the duties they have.

First, Timothy must seek to develop in the rich a sense of responsibility. The skeleton of verses 17 and 18 makes this clear: *Command those who are rich . . . to be rich . . .* More fully, command the *rich in this present world . . . to be rich in good deeds.* Let them add one kind of wealth to another. This is a necessary admonition. Wealth can make people lazy. Since they already have everything they want, they have no need to exert themselves or work for their living. It is not for nothing that some people refer to 'the idle rich'. So Timothy is to *command them to do good, to be rich in*

---

[68] *E.g.* Dt. 8:14; Ezk. 28:5.   [69] Mt. 6:19; *cf.* Pr. 23:5.   [70] *Cf.* Ps. 52:7; Je. 9:23.

good deeds, and to be generous and willing to share (18), using their wealth to relieve want and to promote good causes. In doing so, they will be imitating God. For he is rich, yet out of his riches he *richly provides us* with everything we need.[71]

Since God is such a generous giver, his people should be generous too, not only in imitation of his generosity, but also because of the colossal needs of the world around us. Many Christian enterprises are hampered for lack of funds. And all the time our conscience nags us as we remember the one fifth of the world's population who are destitute. If wealthy people are really and sacrificially generous, it goes without saying that they will no longer be as wealthy as they were. They may not become poor, but neither will they remain rich.

Secondly, Timothy must seek to develop in the rich a sense of proportion: *In this way they will lay up treasure for themselves as a firm foundation for the coming age, so that they may take hold of the life that is truly life* (19). This *treasure for themselves* which the wealthy lay up by their generosity is clearly not material treasure, for Jesus specifically told us not to do this.[72] It is rather spiritual treasure, which is (literally) 'a good foundation for the future', enabling the generous rich to lay hold of the authentic life which begins now and ends in heaven.[73] Perhaps the best commentary on this teaching is Jesus' parable of the unjust steward[74] or the shrewd manager (NIV). He used his influence in the present to secure his future, and Jesus commended him for his prudence, though not for his dishonesty. It is a question of perspective and of proportion. Which is the more valuable? Is it to be rich in this age (17) or in the age to come (19)? Is it to accumulate treasure on earth or in heaven? Is it to make a lot of money now, or to 'take hold of the life that is truly life'?

Bringing together Paul's negative and positive instructions to the wealthy, they are not to be proud and despise the poor, but to do good and be generous; they are not to fix their hopes on uncertain riches but on God the giver and on that most valuable of all his gifts, the treasure of eternal life.

Looking over both the paragraphs about money, the apostle's balanced wisdom becomes apparent. Against materialism (an obsession with material possessions) he sets simplicity of lifestyle. Against asceticism (the repudiation of the material order) he sets gratitude for God's creation. Against covetousness (the lust for more possessions) he sets contentment with what we have. Against selfishness (the accumulation of goods for ourselves) he sets generosity in imitation

---

[71] Cf. Eph. 1:7; Phil. 4:19.   [72] Mt. 6:19–20.
[73] Cf. Mk. 10:21; Lk. 12:33–34.   [74] Lk. 16:1ff.

of God. Simplicity, gratitude, contentment and generosity constitute a healthy quadrilateral of Christian living.

5. A charge to Timothy himself (6:20-21)

Timothy, guard what has been entrusted to your care. Turn away from godless chatter and the opposing ideas of what is falsely called knowledge, [21]*which some have professed and in so doing have wandered from the faith.*
Grace be with you.

In his final personal charge to Timothy ('O Timothy', RSV) Paul reverts to the false teachers, whose damaging activity has been the background of the whole letter. He contrasts two sets of teaching (his and theirs) and two possible attitudes to them (guarding the former and turning away from the latter). His own teaching he calls *what has been entrusted to your care* (20a), literally 'the deposit'. *Parathēkē* was a legal technical term (BAGD), which was used of money or valuables deposited with somebody for safe keeping. Here the valuable concerned is 'the faith' (21, *cf.* 2 Tim. 1:13f.), and Timothy is to *guard* it, preserving it and passing it on to others without dilution or distortion.

The false teaching, on the other hand, Paul urges Timothy to avoid: *Turn away from* ('Turn a deaf ear to', REB) *godless chatter, and the opposing ideas of what is falsely called knowledge* (20b). Because the word 'knowledge' translates *gnōsis* and 'opposing ideas' *antitheseis*, which was the title of a book by Marcion, the prominent heretic in mid-second-century Rome, some scholars have understandably thought they detected here a reference to Gnosticism and/or Marcionism. But even those who deny the Pauline authorship of the Pastorals do not suppose that they were written as late as the middle of the second century. All one can say is that what reached full flower in developed second-century Gnosticism appears in the Pastorals only in bud. Paul adds that those who *have professed* these notions *in so doing have wandered from the faith* (21a, *cf.* 1:6), that is, from the teaching of the apostles. The verb *astocheō* was used of missing the mark in archery, and so of swerving or deviating from truth.

In Paul's concluding prayer, *Grace be with you* (21b), the 'you' is plural. The REB captures this by rendering it, 'Grace be with you all.' It indicates that Paul is looking beyond Timothy, as he has done throughout the letter, to the congregations he is supervising. They would not be able in their own strength to reject error and fight for truth, to run from evil and pursue goodness, to renounce covetousness and cultivate contentment and generosity, and in these Christian

163

responsibilities to remain faithful to the end. Only divine grace could keep them. So at the letter's conclusion, as at its beginning (1:2), the apostle wishes for them above all else an experience of the transforming and sustaining grace of God.

B. The Message of Titus
Doctrine and duty

The letter's main themes

Paul's letter to Titus has always been a popular little New Testament document, especially among Christian leaders who hold responsibility in the church. For although the letter is directed to Titus as an individual, it also looks beyond him to the churches he supervised.

It does not require much imagination to sit down beside Titus and to read Paul's letter as if it were addressed to us. For the apostle's instructions to his trusted lieutenant have extraordinary contemporary relevance. We too need to hear Paul's exhortations: about the careful selection and appointment of church elders (1:5–9), about the damaging effects of false teaching (1:10–16), about the importance of helping different groups to relate duty to doctrine in the home (2:1–10), about the transforming power of the two appearings of Christ (2:11–15), about the civic and social responsibilities of the people of God (3:1–2), and about the implications for practical good works of God's salvation in its three tenses (3:3–8). Here are at least three major themes, namely Christian elders, in contrast to the false teachers (chapter 1), Christian homes, our duties to each other being enforced by confidence in the first and second comings of Christ (chapter 2), and Christian relationships in public life, which are the direct fruits of salvation (chapter 3).

But further reflection reveals that the three chapters of Titus relate to the three main contexts of Christian living, namely the church, the home and the world, while all three illustrate the vital nexus between doctrine and duty. So I will adopt the following analysis:

1. Doctrine and duty in the church (1:5–16)
2. Doctrine and duty in the home (2:1–15)
3. Doctrine and duty in the world (3:1–11)

Titus 1:1–4
Introduction

Paul, a servant of God and an apostle of Jesus Christ for the faith of God's elect and the knowledge of the truth that leads to godliness – ²a faith and knowledge resting on the hope of eternal life, which God, who does not lie, promised before the beginning of time, ³and at his appointed season he brought his word to light through the preaching entrusted to me by the command of God our Saviour,

⁴To Titus, my true son in our common faith:

Grace and peace from God the Father and Christ Jesus our Saviour.

Paul has significant things to say in his introduction about himself as the writer of the letter, about Titus as its recipient, and about the God whose grace unites them.

1. Paul introduces himself

He is both *a servant of God and an apostle of Jesus Christ.* It is the combination of these two epithets which we should notice. For 'servant' is properly 'slave', and 'slave of God' designated some Old Testament notables like Moses, Joshua, the prophets and the suffering servant.[1] Yet, like Paul's usual 'servant of Christ', it remains a title of great humility as one bought, owned and directed by God. 'Apostle of Jesus Christ', on the other hand, was a title of great authority, designating specially the Twelve and Paul, who had received a unique personal call, commission, authorization and equipment from Jesus Christ himself, to be his inspired messengers.

For what purpose had Paul become God's slave and Christ's apostle? This is what he now elaborates. His ministry is related to *God's elect,* that is, the New Testament people of God who enjoy a

---

[1] *E.g.* Jos. 1:2; 24:29; Je. 7:25; Is. 44:1.

168

direct continuity with Old Testament Israel (2:14).[2] But there is some uncertainty among commentators about the correct translation of the preposition *kata*, literally 'according to the faith of God's elect' (AV). What is the relationship between his apostleship and their faith? Is Paul the apostle 'marked as such' by their faith (REB), or was he appointed 'to further' it (RSV)? Does their faith characterize his apostleship, or does his apostleship promote their faith? It seems to me that in the context of defining his apostleship Paul is saying that its purpose is to serve their faith, possibly to bring it into being ('to bring those whom God has chosen to faith and to the knowledge of the truth', JB), but more probably to foster or nurture *the faith of God's elect and the knowledge of the truth that leads to godliness* (1).

Here then are two fundamental characteristics of the people of God: faith and knowledge. Far from being incompatible, faith and knowledge, or faith and reason, belong together. It is those who know God's name who put their trust in him.[3] Their knowledge of God's name or revealed character is the foundation of their faith in him. They trust him because they know that he is trustworthy.

Consider faith first, as Paul does. God's people are believers, 'the family of faith'.[4] Yet there are degrees of faith. Jesus spoke of people having either a 'little' or a 'great' faith. And Paul thanked God that the Thessalonians' faith was 'growing more and more'.[5] Our knowledge is also to grow, for it is part of Paul's apostleship to further or increase it. In particular, he has in mind our *knowledge of the truth*, which itself *leads to* (*kata* again) *godliness* or God-centredness (*eusebeia*). It is an essential feature of truth, and a good test of its authenticity, that since it comes from God it leads to God. Any doctrine which does not promote godliness is manifestly bogus.

The third characteristic of the people of God is *the hope of eternal life* (2a). Indeed, our Christian hope is such a firm foundation of our Christian life that our *faith and knowledge* (repeated in the NIV text, though not in the Greek) may be described as *resting on* it (the preposition *epi*). But how is it that our Christian hope, in contrast to all secular hopes, is so sure, so reliable? It is because its object is eternal life (here as in 3:7 meaning its future consummation in heaven), and because our eternal life has been given a threefold guarantee by God himself.

First, God . . . *promised* it *before the beginning of time*, because it is part of his eternal purpose for his people.[6] Secondly, the God who made this promise *does not lie*. We human beings lie, and the Cretans were notorious liars (12), but God never lies. Indeed he cannot,

---

[2] *Cf.* Rom. 8:33; Col. 3:22.   [3] Ps. 9:10.   [4] Gal. 6:10, NRSV.
[5] 2 Thes. 1:3.   [6] See 2 Tim. 1:9.

because 'he cannot disown himself', that is, contradict his own character.[7] Thirdly, this same trustworthy God who made the promise has *at his appointed season . . . brought his word* of promise *to light through the preaching (kerygma) entrusted to* Paul *by the command of God our Saviour* (3). Thus the promise, the character and the gospel of God combine to guarantee the certainty of eternal life. We may well marvel at Paul's grasp of time and eternity. For God made his initial promise before time began; he has revealed it to the world 'in his own good time' (REB) through the gospel; and he will fulfil it when time comes to an end. In this way the world-wide preaching of the gospel throughout the historical process is the bridge which spans the two eternities of past promise and future fulfilment.

Consider now, as we pause and reflect, Paul's account of his apostleship. Its purpose is to further or foster in the people of God a new triad of Christian graces – not now the familiar faith, hope and love, but faith, hope and knowledge (*pistis, elpis* and *gnōsis*). We too, although we are not apostles, yet if we are called to leadership in the church, should have the same vision and ambition, namely to cultivate in the people of God committed to our care *the faith* which lays hold of God and of his Christ, *the knowledge of the truth* which issues in *godliness,* and *the hope of eternal life* which, though still future, has been promised and guaranteed by God.

2. Paul addresses Titus

'Titus is the most enigmatic figure in early Christian history,' wrote Sir William Ramsay,[8] and went on to guess that his omission from Acts is best explained if he was Luke's relative, even his brother.[9] We know that he was a Greek by birth,[10] and that he became one of Paul's converts. In consequence, Paul could address his letter *To Titus, my true son* or 'my genuine child' *in our common faith* (4a), that is, 'common . . . to you a Gentile as much as to me a Jew', indeed 'common to all Christians', [11] being *the faith of God's elect* (1).

The first reference to Titus in the New Testament occurs in connection with the controversy over whether Gentile converts needed to be circumcised as well as baptized. The Judaizers were evidently bringing pressure to bear on Paul to circumcise Titus, whom he and Barnabas had brought with them to Jerusalem.[12] A little later Paul did circumcise Timothy, as a concession to the

---

[7] 2 Tim. 2:13; *cf.* Nu. 23:19; 1 Sa. 15:29; Heb. 6:18.
[8] *St Paul the Traveller and the Roman City* (Hodder, fifth edition, 1900), p. 284.
[9] *Ibid.,* p. 390.   [10] Gal. 2:3.   [11] Lock, p. 128.   [12] Gal. 2:1.

demands of the mission.[13] But the case with Titus was different. It was a question now of principle, not policy, since 'the truth of the gospel' was at stake. In consequence, 'we did not give in to them for a moment',[14] he wrote, and Titus was 'not . . . compelled to be circumcised'.[15]

After this it is likely that Titus accompanied Paul on his missionary journeys. He came into prominence in relation to the Corinthian church, so that in our 2 Corinthians he is mentioned nine times by name, always with affection and confidence. Paul entrusted him with a letter to the Corinthians, which seems to have been neither our 1 Corinthians nor our 2 Corinthians, but rather what scholars usually refer to as 'the severe letter', in which the apostle rebuked the Corinthians for rejecting his authority.

Having sent the letter with Titus, Paul waited on tenterhooks for news of its reception. He went to Troas to evangelize, and found there an open door. But he could not take advantage of it because he 'had no peace of mind'. As Titus had not come back, he left for Macedonia.[16] There he still had no rest,[17] until to his immense relief Titus arrived from Corinth. Thus God comforted him, he wrote, 'by the coming of Titus', not just by the pleasure of renewed fellowship with him, but also by the good news he brought of the Corinthians' change of heart, their sorrow over their previous disloyalty, and their rekindled love for Paul.[18] Titus too had been made happy and refreshed. Indeed, everything Paul had said to the Corinthians about Titus, and to Titus about the Corinthians, had come true. For Titus, who had not in any way exploited them,[19] loved them all on account of their obedience to the apostle and their respectful reception of him 'with fear and trembling'.[20] It was in response to all these events that our 2 Corinthians came to be written.

Then the apostle entrusted Titus with a second diplomatic mission in Corinth. This time it related to the collection which Paul was organizing among the Greek churches for the benefit of the poorer churches in Judea. Titus had already begun this work on his previous visit. Now, as he takes 2 Corinthians with him, Paul urges him to complete the task.[21] For God had 'put into the heart of Titus the same concern' that Paul had for them, so that Titus had welcomed the opportunity to return to Corinth. He was coming to them, Paul wrote, 'with much enthusiasm and on his own initiative'.[22] Paul commended Titus to them as his 'partner and fellow-worker', and urged them to receive him and his companions with love.[23]

Later, after Paul's presumed release from house arrest in Rome,

---

[13] Acts 16:1ff.   [14] Gal. 2:5.   [15] Gal. 2:3.   [16] 2 Cor. 2:12ff.
[17] 2 Cor. 7:5.   [18] 2 Cor. 7:6–7.   [19] 2 Cor. 12:18.   [20] 2 Cor. 7:13ff.
[21] 2 Cor. 8:6.   [22] 2 Cor. 8:16–17.   [23] 2 Cor. 8:23–24.

where Acts takes leave of him, he resumed his missionary travels. It must have been in the course of these that he left Titus in Crete (and Timothy in Ephesus), with instructions to complete what had been left incomplete, and in particular to appoint qualified elders in every town, to combat the false teachers (Tit. 1:5ff.), to teach the practical realities of Christian behaviour (chapter 2), and to remind God's people of their wider social responsibilities (3:1ff.). Then towards the end of his letter the apostle summoned Titus to join him at Nicopolis for the winter, near the Adriatic coast, once Artemas or Tychicus had arrived in Crete to replace him (3:11). It may have been from Nicopolis, or later from Rome, that Titus went (on a mission?) further north along the Adriatic to the coastal area of Dalmatia.[24]

There the New Testament loses sight of Titus, and later tradition is unreliable. But Eusebius wrote (c. AD 325) that Titus returned to Crete to become its first bishop, and that he died there in a ripe old age.[25]

3. Paul wishes Titus grace from God

Having introduced himself and Titus, and mentioned their 'common faith' (4a), Paul now alludes to the God who has united them. He sends Titus his customary, Christianized form of the conventional Greek and Hebrew greeting: *Grace* (the unmerited, unsolicited favour of God) *and peace* (the reconciliation with God and with the people of God, which only grace can effect). They come *from God the Father and Christ Jesus our Saviour* (4b). It is noteworthy that in verse 3 Paul alludes to *God our Saviour* and in verse 4 to *Christ Jesus our Saviour*. A. T. Hanson, who enjoys poking fun at the supposed pseudonymous author of the Pastorals, declares that 'this indiscriminate use of *sōtēr* ("saviour") undoubtedly implies a rather muddled soteriology' on his part.[26] But on the contrary, although the Father and the Son have different saving roles, both are engaged in the work of salvation and both together constitute the single source from which grace and peace flow forth. There is no muddle here.

[24] 2 Tim. 4:10.   [25] *Ecclesiastical History* 3.4.6.   [26] Hanson (1982), p. 171.

Titus 1:5–16
1. Doctrine and duty in the church

Paul gives two reasons why he had *left* Titus *in Crete*. The first was that he *might straighten out what was left unfinished*. Paul has mixed his metaphors, since one straightens out what is crooked, whereas what is unfinished needs rather to be completed. The English versions reflect this uncertainty. According to the RSV Titus was 'to amend what was defective', and according to the REB 'to deal with outstanding matters'. In particular, and secondly, because this was evidently the chief unfinished business, Paul had left Titus in Crete to *appoint elders in every town, as I*, writes Paul, using the *egō* of apostolic authority, *directed you* (5b). For the main way to regulate and consolidate the life of the church is to secure for it a gifted and conscientious pastoral oversight.

Verses 6–16 set in dramatic contrast the true elders Titus is to appoint (6–9) and the false teachers whom the elders are to silence (10–16). The apostle paints a graphic picture of each group.

1. The true elders (1:5–9)

The reason I left you in Crete was that you might straighten out what was left unfinished and appoint elders in every town, as I directed you. ⁶An elder must be blameless, the husband of but one wife, a man whose children believe and are not open to the charge of being wild and disobedient. ⁷Since an overseer is entrusted with God's work, he must be blameless – not overbearing, not quick-tempered, not given to drunkenness, not violent, not pursuing dishonest gain. ⁸Rather he must be hospitable, one who loves what is good, who is self-controlled, upright, holy and disciplined. ⁹He must hold firmly to the trustworthy message as it has been taught, so that he can encourage others by sound doctrine and refute those who oppose it.

Before we consider the qualifications for the presbyterate, on which the apostle concentrates, this paragraph allows us to make four statements relating to the pastoral oversight of the church. Both the qualifications and the statements overlap with 1 Timothy 3:1–13, and the reader is referred to the exposition of that passage.

First, the elder (*presbyteros*, 6) and the bishop (*episkopos*, 7) were the same person. They are not two distinct church officers, but the same people with distinct titles. The evidence for this is summarized above (p. 90). It is quite correct therefore (although it sounds odd) to call them 'presbyter-bishops'. 'Presbyter' or 'elder' draws attention to their seniority, and 'bishop' or 'overseer' to their task of pastoral oversight. They had deacons to assist them,[1] but the emergence of three orders of ordained ministry (bishops, presbyters and deacons) belongs to the beginning of the second century. It is not found in the New Testament, although Titus himself may be seen as an embryonic bishop in that he had jurisdiction over a number of churches on Crete, and chief responsibility for the selection and appointment of pastors.

Secondly, God intended each church to have a team of overseers. For Titus was told to appoint 'elders' in every town. This might mean a single elder in each house-church, assuming that there were several such churches in every town. But it could mean that there were several presbyters in each church. Within fifteen years of the resurrection there was already a plurality of elders in the Jerusalem church.[2] So the one-person pastorate (like the one-person band in which one musician plays all the instruments) is not a New Testament model of the local church. It is rather in a team ministry that room can be found for different people with different gifts and so with different specialities – ordained and lay, full-time and part-time, salaried and voluntary, elders and deacons, men and women.

Thirdly, the main function of presbyter-bishops was to care for God's people by teaching them. In verse 7 the overseer is called 'God's steward' (REB), dispensing food to the household,[3] and elsewhere a 'pastor' or 'shepherd', who leads the flock into good pasture. These are graphic metaphors of the ministry of the word of God, which will include both teaching truth and refuting error (9).

Fourthly, the selection of presbyter-bishops was a corporate responsibility. True, Paul told Titus to appoint the elders and laid down the conditions of their eligibility. But his emphasis on their need to have a blameless reputation indicates that the congregation will have a say in the selection process. We note that nothing is said here either about gifts and calling (we look to other parts of the New Testament for this) or about ordination (although we assume that, as

[1] 1 Tim. 3:8ff.; *cf.* Phil. 1:1.　　[2] Acts 11:30.　　[3] *Cf.* 1 Cor. 4:1–2.

in Timothy's case, this involved the laying on of hands by other presbyters).[4]

As we approach the question of eligibility for the pastorate, we are struck at once by the requirement of blamelessness, which is repeated. *An elder must be blameless* (6a); *an overseer . . . must be blameless* (7a). This does not of course mean that candidates must be flawless or faultless, or we would all be disqualified. The Greek word used is *anenklētos*, not *amōmos*. *Amōmos* means 'unblemished'. It occurs in the New Testament only in eschatological contexts; that is, it looks forward to our final perfection.[5] *Anenklētos*, however, means not 'without blemish' but 'without blame', 'unaccused'.[6] So candidates for the pastorate must be people of 'unquestioned integrity' (JBP), of 'unimpeachable' (REB) or 'irreproachable' (JB) character. Paraphrasing the word, they should be 'marred by no disgrace';[7] 'they should offer no loophole for criticism'.[8] All this recognizes that the pastorate is a public office, and that therefore the candidate's public reputation is important. Hence the requirement in many churches today both of individual references and testimonials and of a *si quis*, that is, a public statement by the candidate, followed by a public opportunity for the congregation to challenge it.

In seeking to establish the blameless reputation of a candidate for the pastorate, Paul specifies three spheres to be investigated. This passage and its exposition should be read alongside 1 Timothy 3:1–13.

a. Elders must be blameless in their marriage and family life (1:6)

'As in 1 Timothy,' Donald Guthrie writes, 'the home is regarded as the training ground for Christian leaders.'[9] Mention is made both of the spouse and of the children.

For the five possible interpretations of the expression *the husband of but one wife* the reader is referred to 1 Timothy 3:2 and its exposition above (pp. 92–94). The conclusion reached there is that it is not intended to exclude from the pastorate either those who have never married or remarried widowers, but rather the polygamous and those who have remarried after divorce. More generally and positively, ministerial candidates must have an unsullied reputation in the whole area of sex and marriage.

The elder must also be *a man whose children believe and are not*

---

[4] 1 Tim. 4:14.
[5] *E.g.* Eph. 1:4; 5:27; Phil. 2:15–16; Col. 1:22; 2 Pet. 3:14; Jude 14; Rev. 14:5.
[6] Ellicott, p. 184.   [7] Calvin, p. 358.   [8] Kelly, p. 231.
[9] Guthrie (1990), p. 195.

open to the charge of being wild and disobedient (6). 'Being wild' renders *asōtia*, which literally means 'incorrigibility' (BAGD). It 'combines the spendthrift and the rake, as in the picture of the prodigal son'.[10] It is a solemn thought that parents are held responsible for the belief and the behaviour of their children. And Christian parents whose children go astray in faith or morals experience acute pain. Yet the logic is plain. Parents cannot be expected to manage God's family if they have failed to manage their own. This principle is made explicit in 1 Timothy 3:4–5, and is also implicit in verse 7 here where the elder is said to be 'God's steward' (NRSV). An extension of the same principle may be that presbyter-bishops can hardly be expected to win strangers to Christ if they have failed to win those who are most exposed to their influence, their own children. It is legitimate to ask for how long the faith and conduct of children remain their parents' responsibility. The text suggests that Paul has childhood in mind. For, although *tekna* ('children') could be used of posterity in general[11] and occasionally of grown adults,[12] it usually refers to youngsters who are still in their minority (which of course varies in different cultures) and are therefore regarded as being still under their parents' authority.[13]

A further application of this principle may be envisaged, especially in cases where candidates are unmarried or childless. Before being accepted for a wider ministry, they should have proved themselves in a narrower one, for example in Sunday School or youth club.

b. Elders must be blameless in their character and conduct (1:7–8)

In describing the blamelessness expected of a presbyter-bishop who *is entrusted with God's work* or is 'God's steward' (NRSV), Paul employs eleven terms, five negative and six positive, all of which in Greek are single words. The leading thought, which applies to them all, and which occurs twice in verse 8, is that the pastor must be 'master of himself' (RSV), which the NIV translates *self-controlled (sōphrōn)* and *disciplined (enkratēs)*, the latter being also the final fruit of the Spirit.[14] So candidates for the pastorate must give visible evidence in their behaviour that they have been regenerated by the Holy Spirit, that their new birth has led to a new life, that their fallen passions are under control, and that the ninefold fruit of the Spirit has at least begun to appear and to ripen in their lives.

Paul lists the five negatives first. They relate to five areas of strong temptation, namely pride, temper, drink, power and money.

---

[10] Simpson, p. 97; *cf.* Lk. 15:13.   [11] *E.g.* Acts 2:39.   [12] *E.g.* Mk. 2:5.
[13] *E.g.* Eph. 6:1, 4; Col. 3:20–21.
[14] Gal. 5:23. For an Old Testament emphasis on self-control see Pr. 25:28; 29:11.

Exposure to them is an occupational hazard attached to Christian leadership. All five challenge us to self-mastery. The principle now is not that ministerial candidates cannot manage the church if they cannot manage their family, but that they cannot control the church if they cannot control themselves.

Not overbearing means not 'self-willed, stubborn, arrogant' (BAGD). Leadership roles bring prestige and power, and leaders are tempted to misuse these in order to get their own way and pander to their own vanity. Then they do not readily listen to either criticism or advice. Instead, they tend to lord it over other people, and to become headstrong and autocratic.

Not quick-tempered. Orgilos means 'choleric, peppery'.[15] Pastors are often obliged to minister to difficult and demanding people. Their temptation is to become irritable and impatient.

The third negative is *not given to drunkenness.* Pastors have to attend social functions at which wine is served. Not all are total abstainers; but all are called to temperance and moderation.

Not violent (to which 1 Timothy 3:3 adds the counterpart 'but gentle') is a necessary addition. A gift for leadership usually includes a forceful disposition. But pastors who have learned their leadership style from Jesus Christ will never ride rough-shod over other people's sensitivities. They will lead by example not by force, and by humble service not by self-assertion.

Paul's fifth and last warning is *not pursuing dishonest gain* (7). What he is here prohibiting is not so much dishonesty of practice as greed of motive. It is right for Christian teachers to be supported by those they teach,[16] but wrong for them to exploit this situation from love of money.[17] Pastors should be motivated by service, not by greed.[18]

After the vices come the virtues, after the five negatives the six positives, which are largely self-explanatory. A presbyter-bishop must be *hospitable*, welcoming into his home, and entertaining, both church members and visitors; *one who loves what is good*, a person of large charity and a supporter of all good causes; *self-controlled*, having both a sober, sensible judgment (*sōphrōn*) and a disciplined lifestyle; *upright* (*dikaios*) in his dealings with people, and *holy* or devout (*hosios*) in his attitude to God; *and disciplined* (8). This reference to self-control (*enkrateia*) comes last in this list of Christian virtues, as it does in the fruit of the Spirit, self-mastery being an appropriate climax, covering everything which has preceded it.

---

[15] Simpson, p. 98.   [16] *E.g.* Gal. 6:6.   [17] *Cf.* 1 Tim. 6:5.   [18] 1 Pet. 5:2.

c. Elders must be blameless in their doctrinal orthodoxy (1:9)

With verse 9 the apostle moves on, in regard to qualifications for the pastorate, from their home and family, and their character and conduct, to their necessary grasp of the truth. Presbyters *must hold firmly to the trustworthy message as it has been taught* . . . (9a). This message (*logos*, being a word from God) is characterized in two ways. First, it is reliable (*pistos*). It is *trustworthy* because it is true, and it is true because it is the word of the God who never lies (2). Secondly, it is (literally) 'according to the *didachē*', that is, consonant with 'the teaching', namely that of the apostles.[19] This was already an identifiable body of instruction, which in Romans Paul called both 'the form of teaching to which you were entrusted'[20] and 'the teaching you have learned',[21] and which in the Pastorals is termed interchangeably the teaching (*cf.* 9, 2:1),[22] 'the faith' (13),[23] 'the truth' (14),[24] and 'the deposit'.[25] It has now been bequeathed to us in the New Testament.

This reliable, apostolic teaching candidates for the pastorate are to *hold firmly* and never let go.[26] Why so? Because they will need it in their teaching ministry. And what form will their teaching take? It will have two complementary aspects, namely to *encourage others by* (RSV 'give instruction in') *sound doctrine and refute those who oppose it* (9b). To 'refute' people is not just to contradict them, but actually to overthrow them in argument. But neither of these ministries (instructing and refuting) will be possible unless the pastors concerned maintain their firm hold on the sure word of the apostles.

It is clear from this that presbyter-bishops are called essentially to a teaching ministry, which necessitates both a gift for teaching (*didaktikos*)[27] and loyalty to 'the teaching', that is, of the apostles (the *didachē*, 9). Only if they are *didaktikos* in communicating the *didachē* will they be able both to instruct and exhort people in the truth and to expose, contradict and confound error. The negative aspect of this teaching ministry is particularly unfashionable today. But if our Lord Jesus and his apostles did it, warning of false teachers and denouncing them, we must not draw back from it ourselves. Widespread failure to do it may well be a major cause of the doctrinal confusion which prevails in so many churches today.

Calvin clearly understood the double nature of our teaching ministry. Here is part of his comment on verse 9:

[19] *Cf.* Acts 2:42. For this double reliability (of both message and messenger) see also 2 Tim. 2:2.   [20] Rom. 6:17.   [21] Rom. 16:17.
[22] 1 Tim. 1:10; 2 Tim. 1:13; 2:2; 3:10.   [23] 1 Tim. 3:9; 4:1.
[24] 1 Tim. 2:4; 3:15; 4:3; 6:21.   [25] 1 Tim. 6:20; 2 Tim. 1:12, 14, literally.
[26] *Cf.* 2 Thes. 2:15.   [27] 1 Tim. 3:2.

A pastor needs two voices, one for gathering the sheep and the other for driving away wolves and thieves. The Scripture supplies him with the means for doing both, and he who has been rightly instructed in it will be able both to rule those who are teachable and to refute the enemies of the truth. Paul notes this double use of the Scripture when he says that he should be able *both to exhort and to convict* the gainsayers.[28]

Having given an ideal picture of true elders in their threefold blamelessness (5–9), Paul now by contrast describes the false teachers (10–16).

2. The false teachers (1:10–16)

The two paragraphs of chapter 1 (verses 5–9 and 10–16) are linked by the conjunction *gar*, 'for' or 'because'. The reason Titus is to appoint elders in every town and to ensure that they meet the standards Paul lays down is that there are many false teachers who are leading people astray. That is to say, when false teachers increase, the most appropriate long-term strategy is to multiply the number of true teachers, who are equipped to rebut and refute error. We need to be convinced that this is possible.

An example of how false teaching can be decisively overthrown by sound scholarship may be cited from the life of J. B. Lightfoot, who was a professor of divinity at Cambridge University from 1861, and Bishop of Durham from 1879. The publication of an anonymous book entitled *Supernatural Religion* upset many people by its vigorous attack on the credibility of the early church fathers. Praised by its reviewers, it quickly went into several editions. But Lightfoot, in a series of essays in the *Contemporary Review* between 1874 and 1877, so thoroughly exposed the book's many errors and demolished its arguments that, according to one bookseller, before the articles were finished 'the book was already a glut in the second-hand market'.[29] For 'under Lightfoot's searching criticism the foundation of the book had been destroyed'.[30] The articles reveal Lightfoot's best qualities – 'his patient investigation of facts, his scrupulous fairness, his generosity to an opponent, and above all his absorbing motive of loyalty to Christ'.[31] God give us scholars of his calibre in our day!

---

[28] Calvin, p. 361.
[29] George R. Eden and F. C. Macdonald (eds.), *Lightfoot of Durham: Memories and Appreciations* (Cambridge University Press, 1932), p. 10.
[30] *Ibid.*, p. 155.   [31] *Ibid.*

For there are many rebellious people, mere talkers and deceivers,
especially those of the circumcision group. [11]*They must be silenced,*
because they are ruining whole households by teaching things they
ought not to teach – and that for the sake of dishonest gain. [12]*Even*
one of their own prophets has said, 'Cretans are always liars, evil
brutes, lazy gluttons.' [13]*This testimony is true. Therefore, rebuke*
them sharply, so that they will be sound in the faith [14]*and will pay no*
attention to Jewish myths or to the commands of those who reject the
truth. [15]*To the pure, all things are pure, but to those who are*
corrupted and do not believe, nothing is pure. In fact, both their
minds and consciences are corrupted. [16]*They claim to know God, but*
by their actions they deny him. They are detestable, disobedient and
unfit for doing anything good.

In this paragraph Paul alerts Titus to the identity, influence, character
and errors of the false teachers.

a. Their identity (1:10)

Paul first describes them as *many rebellious people.* The adjective is
anypotaktos, meaning 'insubordinate'. Unlike the faithful presbyters
who are to 'hold firmly to the trustworthy message', the false teachers
refuse to submit to it. Next, they are *mere talkers (mataiologoi* as in 1
Tim. 1:6, purveyors of 'empty, fruitless talk', BAGD). Their teaching
lacks health-giving substance. Worse than that, they are *deceivers.*
Not only does their talk fail to edify; it actively leads people astray.
And *especially* Paul is referring to *those of the circumcision group.*[32] So
the false teachers were Jewish, not the Judaizers who argued that
circumcision was necessary to salvation,[33] but a Jewish group
obsessed with 'Jewish myths' (14) or 'myths and endless genealogies'.[34] There are other parallels between Titus 1:9–14 and 1 Timothy
1:4–10. Both passages call the false teachers 'liars' (12; 1 Tim. 1:10) and
'insubordinate' (10; 1 Tim. 1:9), and both say their teaching is 'futile'
(10; 1 Tim. 1:6) and deviates from apostolic truth (11; 1 Tim. 1:3).

b. Their influence (1:11)

They must be silenced, Paul writes, or 'muzzled' (REB). A policy of
laissez-faire will not do. The need to take action to stop them

---

[32] Recent commentators refer to research by T. C. Skeat (see above, p. 136, n. 38), in
which he argues that *malista* means not 'specially' but 'that is' or 'in other words'. See
Knight (1992), p. 297. Consequently in Tit. 1:10 it means not that among the deceivers
the Jewish group was predominant, but that the deceivers Paul was writing about are
the Jewish group. See Fee (1988), p. 183.
[33] *E.g.* Acts 15:1.   [34] 1 Tim. 1:4.

teaching (whether by argument or discipline is not divulged) is due to their growing influence. It is not only individuals who are being deceived; the errorists *are ruining whole households* (house churches?) *by teaching things they ought not to teach* (11a). In addition, despicable though this is, they have an ulterior motive, namely greed for *dishonest gain* (11b), the avarice from which all true teachers must be free (7).

c. Their character (1:12–14a)

This mention of 'sordid gain' (REB) leads Paul to enlarge on their character, or rather to draw attention to their reputation: *Even one of their own prophets has said, 'Cretans are always liars, evil brutes, lazy gluttons'* (12). Church fathers like Clement of Alexandria, Jerome, Chrysostom and Augustine all identified the author of this saying as the sixth-century BC Cretan teacher, Epimenides of Knossos, who was held in high honour by his compatriots as both a prophet and a miracle-worker. His threefold estimate of the Cretan character was decidedly unflattering, but there seems to have been some confirmation of it. As for their name for mendacity, the Greeks coined both the verb *krētizō* for to 'lie' or 'cheat', and the noun *krētismos* for a falsehood. As for being *evil beasts* or 'dangerous animals' (JB), Epimenides himself went further and joked that the absence of wild beasts on the island was supplied by its human inhabitants.[35] As for *lazy gluttons*, combining greed and sloth, their avarice was proverbial, so that Polybius could say: 'Greed and avarice are so native to the soil in Crete, that they are the only people in the world among whom no stigma attaches to any sort of gain whatever.'[36] Simpson thinks that Paul was writing 'with a twinkle in his eye' because he had the Cretans 'on the horns of a dilemma'. If they endorsed their prophet's statement, they condemned themselves; if they repudiated it, they made him the liar he said they were![37]

This testimony is true, Paul added (13a), thus acknowledging that 'all truth is of God',[38] whatever its source. But did Paul really accept this generalization about the Cretan character? The Christian conscience is very uncomfortable with ethnic stereotypes of this kind. We need, then, to remind ourselves that Paul believed in the power of the gospel to change people;[39] that some Cretans received the transforming Holy Spirit in Jerusalem on the day of Pentecost;[40] and that the elders Titus was to appoint (5–9) were themselves Cretans, who were certainly not liars, but teachers of the truth. It

---

[35] Oden, p. 61.   [36] Quoted in Barclay, p. 242.   [37] Simpson, p. 100.
[38] Calvin, p. 364.   [39] *Cf.* Rom. 1:16; 1 Cor. 6:11.   [40] Acts 2:11.

seems then that Paul was applying Epimenides' dictum to the false teachers, and their dupes, not to all Cretans indiscriminately.

Titus' responsibility *vis-a-vis* these errorists was to *rebuke them sharply, so that they will be sound in the faith* (13b) *and will pay no attention to Jewish myths or to the commands of those who reject the truth* (14). We note the positive purpose of all truly Christian rebuke. Paul's aim was not to humiliate the Cretans for being gullible, but to rescue them from error in order to establish them in the truth.

d. Their errors (1:14b–16)

In these final verses of chapter 1 Paul exposes the fundamental errors of the false teachers and their disciples.

First, they pay attention to 'commands of men' (14b, RSV). The NIV unaccountably omits the crucial words 'of men'. But the NEB indicates their importance by translating the phrase 'commands of merely human origin'. We can hardly fail to detect an echo of God's word to Jerusalem: 'their teachings are but rules taught by men'.[41] Jesus himself quoted this verse in his debate with the Pharisees, accusing them of letting go 'the commands of God' in order to hold on to 'the traditions of men'.[42] Paul also quoted it of the Colossians[43] as well as of the Cretans. The first and most basic error is to follow the commands of human beings *who reject the truth* of God, that is, to forsake divine revelation for human opinions.

Secondly, they have a false understanding of purity. Like the Pharisees, they prize external and ritual purity above the true purity which is internal and moral.[44] It is not only that inward and spiritual purity is paramount ('Blessed are the pure in heart').[45] But once we have been made clean inwardly, Jesus said, 'Everything will be clean for you.'[46] Just so, Paul writes here: *To the pure all things are pure* (15a), including of course the Creator's good gifts of marriage and food.[47] *But to those who are corrupted and do not believe, nothing is pure. In fact, both their minds* (what they believe) *and consciences* (what they feel able to do) *are corrupted* (15b).

Thirdly, *they claim to know God*, boasting of their *gnōsis, but by their actions they deny him* (16a). That is, there is a fundamental dichotomy between what they say and what they are, between their words and their deeds. Usually professions and denials are opposites, which exclude one another. We cannot profess what we deny, or deny what we profess. At least, to do so is the essence of hypocrisy, because then we profess God in word and deny him in

---

[41] Is. 29:13 mg., LXX.   [42] Mk. 7:7–8.   [43] Col. 2:22.   [44] Mk. 7:15.
[45] Mt. 5:8.   [46] Lk. 11:41.   [47] 1 Tim. 4:1ff.; Mk. 7:19; Rom. 14:20.

deed. This is ritual without reality, form without power,[48] claims without character, faith without works.

These three phenomena regarding the false teachers and their disciples provide us with three valid tests to apply to any and every system. We have to ask three questions about it. First, is its *origin* divine or human, revelation or tradition? Secondly, is its *essence* inward or outward, spiritual or ritual? Thirdly, is its *result* a transformed life or a merely formal creed? True religion is divine in its origin, spiritual in its essence and moral in its effect.

Finally, these false teachers and their disciples, whom Paul is delineating, *are detestable* (for their tenets provoke a certain disgust in the people of God), *disobedient* (dismissive of God's word) *and unfit for doing anything good* (16b). Of these three outspoken epithets perhaps the middle one is the most significant, for the theme of disobedience runs through the chapter. A pastor's children must not be disobedient or insubordinate (6) . But now the very same Greek word (*anypotaktos*) is used of the false teachers. 'Rebellious people' they are called in verse 10. A similar word describes the Cretan errorists (16). J. B. Phillips translates verse 16, 'there are many . . . who will not recognise authority'. They are disobedient, insubordinate, rebellious, Paul writes. It is strong language.

But in the final analysis this is the big question before the church. Is there such a thing as divine revelation? Do we concede that truth, having been revealed by God, *ipso facto* has authority over us? Are we ready to submit to it, that is, to him, in humble faith and obedience? Or are we brash enough to behave like unruly children and reject God's authority? An authoritative revelation, Harry Blamires has written, leaves us with only two alternative reactions: 'it is either the bowed head or the turned back'.[49]

Looking back over this chapter within the context of the contemporary church, there are two major lessons we need to learn.

First, *let us copy Paul's strategy.* He was profoundly disturbed by the prevalence of false teaching in the churches. He refers to it in all his letters. The Pastorals are full of allusions to deceivers, deviationists, empty talkers, speculators, divisive controversialists and hypocritical liars. The question is this: how did Paul react to this distressing situation? What was his strategy in the face of spreading error?

He refused to give in to it in a feeble spirit of defeat. He did not remain idle or silent on the ground that everybody has a right to his or her own opinion. He did not secede from the church in the belief that it was irredeemable. No, Paul was neither a defeatist, nor a pluralist, nor a secessionist. So what was his strategy in fighting the

[48] 2 Tim. 3:5.   [49] *The Christian Mind* (SPCK, 1963), p. 132.

183

good fight of the faith? It was this: when false teachers increase, we must multiply the number of true teachers. Titus was to appoint elders in every town (5), who would hold fast God's reliable word, teach it faithfully and refute those who contradicted it (9). Why? Because of the number of rebellious people or deceivers (10). So the more false teachers there are, the more true teachers are needed.

This is why the key institution in the church is the seminary or theological college. In every country the church is a reflection of its seminaries. All the church's future pastors and teachers pass through a seminary. It is there that they are either made or marred, either equipped and inspired or ruined. Therefore we should set ourselves to capture the seminaries of the world for evangelical faith, academic excellence and personal godliness. There is no better strategy for the reform and renewal of the church.

Secondly, *let us maintain Paul's standards.* When there is a shortage of pastors, the temptation is to lower the standards of eligibility, and accept and appoint everybody who applies, even if they are not blameless in home life, behaviour and doctrine. Virtually all churches have selection procedures. But they do not always maintain apostolic standards. Instead, in some churches today it is no barrier to ordination that a candidate has a public reputation for a lack of Christian integrity and consistency; is married, divorced and remarried, even more than once; is a practising homosexual; has children who are both unbelieving and undisciplined; has a serious flaw in character or conduct; or holds liberal theological views with little respect for the authority of Scripture. It is something of a scandal that, in defiance of the apostle's teaching, such persons are recommended and accepted for ordination.

So let us do what we can to copy Paul's strategy and maintain Paul's standards. The church would be in a far healthier condition if we did.

Titus 2:1–15
2. Doctrine and duty in the home

Being the rational people we are as human beings, since God has made us in his own image, we need to know not only how we ought to behave as Christians, but also why. We certainly need instructions about the kind of people we ought to be; but we also need incentives. So what is Christian behaviour? And what are its grounds? These questions belong to one another, and Titus 2 is an outstanding example of this double theme.

From the activities of the false teachers Paul turns to Titus' responsibilities as a true teacher. In fact, the opening words of the chapter, which the NIV fails to translate, are *sy de*, 'but as for you', emphasizing Titus' distinctive role in contrast to them. These words occur five times in the Pastoral Letters[1] and express the familiar call to the people of God to be different, to stand out from the prevailing culture.

In this case Titus is to behave in a way that is entirely unlike the false teachers. They professed to know God but denied him by their actions (1:16). They failed to practise what they preached. In Titus, however, there was to be no dichotomy in his teaching between belief and behaviour. 'But as for you,' Paul writes, *you must teach what is in accord with sound doctrine* (1). This compressed phrase indicates that two strands are to be interwoven in Titus' teaching. On the one hand there is 'the sound doctrine', the definite article once again implying that an identifiable body of teaching is in mind. On the other hand, there are 'the things which fit it', namely the ethical duties which the sound doctrine demands.

The word 'sound' translates *hygiainousēs*, the present participle of the verb *hygiainō*, 'to be healthy'. The cognate adjective *hygiēs* (which recalls our 'hygiene') also means 'healthy' or 'fit'. It is often used in the Gospels of people who, having been healed of some physical defect or disability, are now 'whole', with all their organs

[1] Tit. 2:1; 1 Tim. 6:11; 2 Tim. 3:10, 14; 4:5.

185

and faculties functioning normally. For example, the adjective occurs in this sense of the woman who suffered from internal bleeding, the invalid at the pool of Bethesda, and the congenital cripple outside the temple in Jerusalem, after they had been healed.[2]

In the Pastorals, however, the adjective is applied several times to Christian doctrine,[3] which is 'healthy' or 'wholesome' in contrast to the 'sick' teaching of the deceivers (*nosōn*).[4] Further, Christian doctrine is healthy in the same way as the human body is healthy. For Christian doctrine resembles the human body. It is a co-ordinated system consisting of different parts which relate to one another and together constitute a harmonious whole. If therefore our theology is maimed (with bits missing) or diseased (with bits distorted), it is not 'sound' or 'healthy'. What Paul means by 'the sound doctrine' is what he elsewhere called 'the whole purpose of God',[5] the fullness of divine revelation.

In addition to 'the sound doctrine', Titus is to teach 'the things which fit it', or are 'in accord with' it, that is, the practical duties which arise from it. For there is an indissoluble connection between Christian doctrine and Christian duty, between theology and ethics. Moreover, Paul immediately does what he has told Titus to do. First he outlines some detailed ethical instructions which Titus is to pass on to different groups in the Cretan churches (2–10), and secondly he unfolds the sound doctrines which undergird these duties, in particular the two comings of Christ (11–14).

Titus is not unique in having been given this double ministry. Still today Christian pastors and teachers are called first to teach both doctrine and ethics; secondly to teach them in relation to each other and show how they 'fit'; and thirdly to relate duty to doctrine, not in general principles only but in detailed applications.

This is what Paul goes on to tell Titus to do. He is not to be content with abstractions or generalizations. Instead, he is to lay down some concrete and particular duties. Paul mentions six categories of people according to age, sex and occupation, much as he has done in 1 Timothy 5:1–2, and selects for each category a few appropriate qualities. Many commentators refer to what follows as 'house tables' or 'domestic codes', because they parallel the rules for family groups which occurred in secular ethics. But Pauline teaching is far from a slavish imitation of them. He adapts them to his own purpose and christianizes them. Yet he does focus on Christian relationships in the home. Moreover, as with candidates for the

---

[2] Mk. 5:34; Jn. 5:9; Acts 4:10.
[3] *E.g.* 1 Tim. 1:10; 6:3; 2 Tim. 1:13; 4:3; Tit. 1:9; 2:1, 8.
[4] 1 Tim. 6:4; *cf.* 2 Tim. 2:17.   [5] Acts 20:27, REB.

pastorate (1:6ff.), so with these household groupings, the emphasis is on self-control (verses 2, 4, 5, 6, 12).

1. The ethical duties (2:1–10)

You must teach what is in accord with sound doctrine. ²*Teach the older men to be temperate, worthy of respect, self-controlled, and sound in faith, in love and in endurance.*

³*Likewise, teach the older women to be reverent in the way they live, not to be slanderers or addicted to much wine, but to teach what is good.* ⁴*Then they can train the younger women to love their husbands and children,* ⁵*to be self-controlled and pure, to be busy at home, to be kind, and to be subject to their husbands, so that no-one will malign the word of God.*

⁶*Similarly, encourage the young men to be self-controlled. In everything set them an example by doing what is good.* ⁷*In your teaching show integrity, seriousness* ⁸*and soundness of speech that cannot be condemned, so that those who oppose you may be ashamed because they have nothing bad to say about us.*

⁹*Teach slaves to be subject to their masters in everything, to try to please them, not to talk back to them,* ¹⁰*and not to steal from them, but to show that they can be fully trusted, so that in every way they will make the teaching about God our Saviour attractive.*

a. The older men (2:2)

Titus' first concern is to be for those Simpson calls 'the greybeards of the flock'.[6] They need special advice and encouragement. For, as Chrysostom puts it, 'there are some failings which age has, that youth has not. Some indeed it has in common with youth, but in addition it has a slowness, a timidity, a forgetfulness, an insensibility, and an irritability.'[7] The older men are to receive two main exhortations, which may be summed up in the words 'dignity' and 'maturity'. As for the first, *the older men* are *to be temperate, worthy of respect, self-controlled* (2a). That is, they are to exhibit a certain *gravitas*, which is both appropriate to their seniority and expressive of their inner self-control.

Secondly, one naturally expects older men to be *sound* or mature in every aspect of their character, not least in the three cardinal Christian virtues, namely *in faith* (trusting God), *in love* (serving others) *and in endurance* (waiting patiently for the fulfilment of their Christian hope).

---

[6] Simpson, p. 103.   [7] Chrysostom, p. 531.

b. The older women (2:3–4a)

Likewise, Paul continues, hinting at the closeness of the parallel, Titus is to *teach the older women*. Three areas of Christian conduct are singled out for them. First, they are *to be reverent in the way they live*. The Greek word for 'reverent' is *hieroprepēs*, which occurs only here in the New Testament. It can mean either 'befitting a holy person or thing' or more particularly 'like a priest(ess)' (BAGD). Lock may well be right to suggest that older women 'are to carry into daily life the demeanour of priestesses in a temple'.[8] Or, as we might say, they are to 'practise the presence of God' and to allow their sense of his presence to permeate their whole lives.

Secondly, the older women are strenuously to avoid two moral failures with which they have sometimes been associated. They are *not to be slanderers* (back-biters or scandal-mongers) *or* to be *addicted to much wine*.

Thirdly, and positively, instead of using their mouths for slander, they are to use them *to teach what is good* (3b). Whom are they to teach? Their own family no doubt (children and grandchildren), but also and specially *they can train the younger women . . .* (4a). It is noteworthy that, although Titus is himself to teach the older men and older women (2, 3), and later the young men (6), it is the older women who are given the task of teaching the younger women. This policy makes special sense when the presbyter-bishop is a bachelor, but may also be wise if he is married. There is a great need in every congregation for the ministry of mature women, whom *The Book of Common Prayer* calls 'holy and godly matrons'. They can share their wisdom and experience with the rising generation, prepare brides for their wedding, and later advise them about parenthood.

c. The younger women (2:4b–5)

The younger women are to be trained by the older women *to love their husbands and children* (4b). Since both Greek words include the term for 'love', this repetition should be preserved in the translation, *e.g.* 'how they should love their husbands and love their children' (JB). Thus love is the first and foremost basis of marriage, not so much the love of emotion and romance, still less of eroticism, but rather of sacrifice and service. The young wives are to be 'trained' in this, which implies that it can be brought under their control.

[8] Lock, p. 140.

The younger women are also to be trained *to be self-controlled and pure*, and *to be busy at home*. The AV expression 'keepers at home' is a mistake. It renders *oikouroi*, whereas the better reading is *oikourgoi* [9] which means 'working at home' (BAGD). It would not be legitimate to base on this word either a stay-at-home stereotype for all women, or a prohibition of wives being also professional women. What is rather affirmed is that if a woman accepts the vocation of marriage, and has a husband and children, she will love and not neglect them. J. B. Phillips' word 'home lovers' sums up well what Paul has in mind. What he is opposing is not a wife's pursuit of a profession, but 'the habit of being idle and going about from house to house'.[10]

Next, younger women are *to be kind*, perhaps in the context meaning 'hospitable', *and to be subject to their husbands . . .* This 'subjection' contains no notion of inferiority and no demand for obedience, but rather a recognition that, within the equal value of the sexes, God has established a created order which includes a masculine 'headship', not of authority, still less of autocracy, but of responsibility and loving care. And one of the reasons the younger women are to be encouraged to comply with this teaching is *so that no-one will malign the word of God* (5b). Christian marriages and Christian homes, which exhibit a combination of sexual equality and complementarity, beautifully commend the gospel; those which fall short of this ideal bring the gospel into disrepute.

d. The young men (2:6)

Similarly, Paul continues, perceiving a parallel between the younger men and the younger women in the self-control expected of both, *encourage the young men to be self-controlled* (6). Thus the young men are to be urged to develop one quality only, that of self-mastery. 'In this pregnant word', Bishop Ellicott comments, 'a young man's duty is simply but comprehensively enunciated.'[11] For doubtless Paul is thinking of the control of temper and tongue, of ambition and avarice, and especially of bodily appetites, including sexual urges, so that Christian young men remain committed to the unalterable Christian standard of chastity before marriage and fidelity after it.

Some valuable lessons can be learned from this verse. First, self-mastery is possible, even in young men, since there would be no point in exhorting them to an impossibility. Secondly, encouragement is an appropriate means to secure such self-control, especially if it is the sympathetic, supportive exhortation of one young man to another within the solidarity of the Christian brotherhood. Thirdly,

[9] Metzger, p. 654.   [10] 1 Tim. 5:13; Tit. 1:11.   [11] Ellicott, p. 195.

such an encouragement must be accompanied by a consistent example, which is exactly what Paul comes to next, namely the example which Titus must set.

e. Titus himself (2:7–8)

In everything set them an example ('a model', NRSV) *by doing what is good* (7a). We human beings seem to be imitative by nature. We need models; they give us direction, challenge and inspiration. Paul did not hesitate to offer himself, as an apostle, for the churches to imitate. 'Follow my example,' he wrote, 'as I follow the example of Christ.'[12] And Paul expected both Timothy (1 Tim. 4:12) and Titus (2:7) to provide a model which the churches could follow. The word he used was *typos*, a prototype or pattern. We are familiar with the idea that Old Testament characters are 'types' for us to learn from. What happened to them, we are told, 'occurred as examples',[13] and was recorded in Scripture as a warning or exhortation to us.[14] But God has not provided us with dead models only (whether patriarchs in the Old Testament or apostles in the New); he wants us to have living models as well. And chief among these should be the presbyter-bishops of the local church.

Titus was, however, to influence the young men of Crete not only by his example, but also by his teaching. Teaching and example, the verbal and the visual, always form a powerful combination. And his teaching was to have three characteristics, namely *integrity, seriousness and soundness of speech that cannot be condemned* (7b–8a). *Integrity* translates *aphthoria*, which literally means 'uncorruptness'. It may well allude to Titus' motives in ministry. *Seriousness*, on the other hand, clearly refers to his manner in teaching, while *soundness of speech* means that the matter of his instruction must be wholesome and true. Perhaps the most important emphasis here is that people will not take serious subjects seriously unless there is a due seriousness in the preacher's manner and delivery. As Richard Baxter put it, 'Whatever you do, let the people see that you are in good earnest . . . You cannot break men's hearts by jesting with them.'[15]

In this century Dr Martyn Lloyd-Jones made the same point. Having preached a sermon in Westminster Chapel on the wrath of God, and having called it 'a controlling conception' of Romans, where it occurs ten times, he said:

---

[12] 1 Cor. 11:1; *cf.* 4:16; Phil. 3:17; 2 Thes. 3:7, 9.
[13] 1 Cor. 10:6, *typoi.*   [14] 1 Cor. 10:11b.
[15] *The Reformed Pastor* (1656; Epworth, second edition 1950), p. 145.

I confess freely, I cannot understand a jocular evangelist . . . Go back and read the lives of the men whom God has used in the mightiest manner, and you will invariably find that they were serious men, sober men, men with the fear of the Lord in them.[16]

Titus, then, was to combine purity of motive, soundness of matter and seriousness of manner, *so that those who oppose you may be ashamed because they have nothing bad to say about us* (8b).

f. Slaves (2:9–10)

Teach slaves to be subject to their masters in everything (9a). For a discussion of the unacceptable essence of slavery, its prevalence in the Roman Empire, and why Paul did not call for its immediate and total abolition, see 1 Timothy 6:1f. and the exposition above (pp. 142–143).

The instructions Titus was to pass on to household slaves concern their work and their character. As for their work, they must *try to please* their masters by their conscientious service, and *not to talk back to them*, but to be polite and respectful (9b).

As for their character, slaves were to be honest, *and not to steal from* their masters, *nosphizō* being 'the regular term for petty larcenies, filching etc.'[17] Instead, they were to be dependable, *to show that they can be fully trusted* (10a). And the reason slaves were to be honest and reliable in both work and character was *so that in every way they will make the teaching about God our Saviour attractive* (10b), or 'adorn' it (RSV). For though forced labour is demeaning to human beings, voluntary service – even by slaves – is noble. So Paul chooses slaves as his example of how good behaviour can actually adorn the gospel. The verb *kosmeō* was used of arranging jewels in order to display their beauty. And the gospel is a jewel, while a consistent Christian life is like the setting in which the gospel-jewel is displayed; it can 'add lustre' to it (REB).

Three times in the course of these verses about the Christian behaviour of different groups, Paul has betrayed his concern about the effect of the Christian witness on the non-Christian world (5, 8, 10). In two of them he refers to Christian doctrine. Young wives are to be chaste and loving, in order that the word of God be not maligned or discredited (5). Household slaves are to be honest and reliable, in order that the gospel may be adorned or 'embellished'.[18] This is the alternative. Christian doctrine is salvation doctrine, a jewel called 'the teaching about God our Saviour' (10). So either we

---

[16] *Romans 1: The Gospel of God* (Banner of Truth, 1985), p. 332.
[17] Simpson, p. 106.   [18] Kelly, p. 243.

give no evidence of salvation, in which case the gospel-jewel is tarnished, or we give good evidence of salvation by living a manifestly saved life, in which case the gospel-jewel shines with extra lustre. Our lives can bring either adornment or discredit to the gospel.

2. The sound doctrine (2:11–14)

Paul now moves on from duty to doctrine, indeed from mundane duties to sublime doctrines. His usual method (as seen, for example, in Romans, Ephesians and Colossians) is to begin with doctrine and then with a mighty 'therefore' go on to its ethical implications. Here, however, the order is reversed. Paul begins with ethical duties, and now with a ringing 'because' he lays down their doctrinal foundation. Both approaches are legitimate, so long as the indissoluble link between doctrine and ethics is forged and maintained.

For the grace of God that brings salvation has appeared to all men. [12]*It teaches us to say 'No' to ungodliness and worldly passions, and to live self-controlled, upright and godly lives in this present age,* [13]*while we wait for the blessed hope – the glorious appearing of our great God and Saviour, Jesus Christ,* [14]*who gave himself for us to redeem us from all wickedness and to purify for himself a people that are his very own, eager to do what is good.*

The particular doctrine in Titus 2, on which Paul grounds his ethical appeal, is that of the two comings of Christ, which he here calls his two 'epiphanies' or appearings. Verse 11 says that *the grace of God . . . has appeared* (*epephanē*), and verse 13 says that *we wait for . . . the glorious appearing* (*epiphaneian*). Moreover, both Christ's appearings have a saving significance. For what has already appeared is *the grace of God that brings salvation* (11), while what we are waiting for is *the glorious appearing of our great God and Saviour* (13).

Now the noun *epiphaneia* means the visible appearance of something or someone hitherto invisible, a coming into view of what has been previously concealed. It was used in classical Greek of the dawn or daybreak, when the sun leaps over the horizon into view; of an enemy emerging out of an ambush; and of the supposed saving intervention of a god or gods in human affairs.

Luke gives us a good example of its meaning in the Acts. It is the only occasion in the New Testament when *epiphaneia* has a secular meaning and does not refer to Christ. Luke describes how the ship, in which Paul and his companions were travelling to Rome, was struck by a terrific north-easterly gale, and was now drifting helplessly in the Mediterranean. The sky was so overcast by day and night that for many days the sun and the stars 'made no epiphany'.[19] Of course the stars were still there, but they did not appear.

Apart from this one literal use of *epiphaneia*, the word occurs in the New Testament four times of Christ's first coming[20] and six times of his second coming.[21] Here at the end of Titus 2 the word is used of both Christ's comings (11, 14).

a. The epiphany of grace (2:11–12)

For the grace of God that brings salvation has appeared to all men (11). Of course grace did not come into existence when Christ came. God has always been gracious,[22] indeed 'the God of all grace'.[23] But grace appeared visibly in Jesus Christ. God's saving grace, given us before the beginning of time, 'has now been revealed through the appearing of our Saviour . . .'[24] It was brightly displayed in his lowly birth, in his gracious words and compassionate deeds, and above all in his atoning death. He was himself 'full of grace'.[25] His coming was moreover an epiphany of saving grace, of grace 'that brings salvation'. It *appeared to all men*, in the sense that it is now publicly offered to all, even slaves (10).

Now Paul personifies this grace of God. Grace the saviour becomes grace the teacher. *It teaches us* (12a), or maybe disciplines us. In 1880 a book was published in Britain entitled *The School of Grace*, and sub-titled *Expository Thoughts on Titus 2:11–14*. Its author was Canon Hay Aitken. He wrote: 'Grace not only saves, but undertakes our training.'[26] So all Christians become 'learners in the School of Grace'.[27] Further, 'Grace bases all her teaching upon the great facts in which her first grand revelation of herself was made, and finds all her teaching power in those mighty memories.'[28]

What then does grace teach? Two main lessons. First, and negatively, *it teaches us to say 'No' to ungodliness and worldly passions* (12a). Secondly, and positively, *it teaches us . . . to live self-controlled, upright and godly lives in this present age* (12b). Thus grace disciplines us to 'renounce' (REB) our old life and to live a new one, to turn from ungodliness to godliness, from self-centredness to self-control, from the world's devious ways to fair dealing with each other.

It seems clear that the second part of verse 12 was the biblical basis for a phrase, which occurs at the end of the Prayer Book's 'General

---

[19] Acts 27:20, literally.   [20] Lk. 1:78–79; 2 Tim. 1:10; Tit. 2:11; 3:4.
[21] Acts 2:20; 2 Thes. 2:8; 1 Tim. 6:14; 2 Tim. 4:1, 8; Tit. 2:13.   [22] Ex. 34:6.
[23] 1 Pet. 5:10.   [24] 2 Tim. 1:9–10.   [25] Jn. 1:14, 16–17.
[26] Aitken, p. 33.   [27] *Ibid.*, p. 216.   [28] *Ibid.*, p. 252.

Confession', in which we pray that in future we may 'live a godly, righteous and sober [that is, disciplined] life'. It was for this purpose that the epiphany of God's grace in Jesus Christ took place. It is not only that grace makes good works possible (enabling us to do them), but that grace makes them necessary (challenging us to live accordingly). The emphasis is on the necessity, not the mere possibility, of good works.

b. The epiphany of glory (2:13–14)

He who appeared briefly on the stage of history, and disappeared, will one day reappear. He appeared in grace; he will reappear in glory. In fact, this future epiphany of glory is the supreme object of our Christian hope, *while we wait for the blessed hope*, that is, the hope which brings blessing. How does Paul define it? He calls it *the glorious appearing of* (literally, 'the epiphany of the glory of') *our great God and Saviour, Jesus Christ* (13).

There has been a long and lively debate whether the future epiphany is of two persons, namely 'our great God (the Father)' and 'our Saviour Jesus Christ', in which case Jesus is designated only 'our Saviour', or of one person, whose full title is spelled out as 'our great God and Saviour', in which case this is perhaps the most unambiguous declaration in the New Testament of the deity of Jesus. Surprisingly the AV opts for the former, whereas the NIV, REB and NRSV all opt for the latter.

There are five main arguments in favour of this latter, longer version. First, there is no definite article before the noun 'Saviour', which suggests that the one article covers both nouns. In Greek 'nouns linked together by one article designate the same subject'.[29] Secondly, the majority of the ancient Greek fathers understood the phrase in this way, 'and they must have been able to appraise a Greek idiom'.[30] The third argument adds theology to grammar. All the ten New Testament references to the two epiphanies are to Christ; nowhere is there any reference to an epiphany of 'God'. Fourthly, the context most naturally requires the reference to be to Christ, since it goes on at once from his glory to his sufferings and death. Fifthly, the expression 'God and Saviour' was 'a stereotyped formula common in first-century religious terminology', normally referring to a single deity, and sometimes to the Roman Emperor.[31]

Bishop Ellicott writes that it is difficult to resist the conviction that 'our blessed Lord is here said to be our *megas Theos* [*sc.* "great God"], and that this text is a direct, definite, and even *studied*

[29] Simpson, p. 108.   [30] *Ibid.*
[31] M. J. Harris, quoted by Towner (1989), pp. 52, 272.

declaration of the divinity of the Eternal Son'.[32] It should be added, however, as Lock does,[33] that 'the question is not one of doctrinal importance'. For if the reference is to two persons, Jesus Christ 'is still placed on a level with the great God, as a manifestation of his glory, and as having effected Jehovah's work of salvation'.

Already at his first coming it could be said that 'we have seen his glory',[34] for he 'revealed his glory' in his signs,[35] and supremely in his death.[36] Nevertheless, his glory was veiled, and many did not perceive it, or even suspect it. So one day the veil will be lifted, his glory will make an epiphany, and 'we shall see him as he is'.[37]

Since this will be the epiphany of the glory of 'our great God and Saviour', who at his coming will perfect our salvation, Paul reverts naturally to his first epiphany when our salvation was begun. He *gave himself for us* on the cross. Why? Not just to secure our forgiveness (which the apostle does not mention here, though in 3:7 he refers to our justification), but also *to redeem us from all wickedness*, liberating us from its bondage, *and to purify for himself a people that are his very own, eager to do what is good* (14).

Paul deliberately chooses Old Testament words and images from the beginnings of Israel as a nation, so as to portray Christ's salvation as the fulfilment of these foreshadowings. Thus 'gave himself for us' ('sacrificed himself for us', REB) recalls the Passover sacrifice; 'to redeem us' the exodus redemption from Egyptian bondage; and 'a people that are his very own' the Sinaitic covenant by which Israel became Yahweh's 'treasured possession'. Paul uses the very expression *laos periousios* ('chosen people') which LXX uses.[38] Thus we enjoy a direct continuity with the Old Testament people of God, for we are his redeemed people and he is our Passover, our exodus and our Sinai.

This special people of God, whom Christ died to purchase for himself, is described as *eager to do what is good*, literally 'enthusiastic for good works'. This is not fanaticism. But it is enthusiasm, since 'grace trains us . . . to be enthusiasts',[39] so that we may live for him who died for us.

Thus the apostle, in this short paragraph of only four verses (11–14) brings together the two *termini* of the Christian era, that is, the first coming of Christ which inaugurated it and the second coming of Christ which will terminate it. He bids us look back to the one and on to the other. For we live 'in between times', suspended rather uncomfortably between the 'already' and the 'not yet'.

Of course the critics of Christianity seize on this with great

[32] Ellicott, p. 201.   [33] Lock, p. 145.   [34] Jn. 1:14.   [35] Jn. 2:11.
[36] *E.g.* Jn. 12:23–24; 17:1ff.   [37] 1 Jn. 3:2.
[38] Ex. 19:5; Dt. 7:6; 14:2; 26:18; *cf.* 1 Pet. 2:9.   [39] Aitken, p. 363.

indignation. 'You Christians are such hopelessly unpractical creatures,' they will say. 'All you do is to preoccupy yourselves with the
distant past and the remote future. Why can't you live in the present,
in the realities of the contemporary world?'

But that is exactly what the apostle Paul is summoning Titus, and
through him us, to do. Older men are to be dignified and mature.
Older women are to be reverent and teachers of the young. Younger
women are to be good wives and mothers. Young men are to control
themselves. Titus is to be a good teacher and model. Slaves are to be
conscientious and honest All of us are to renounce evil and to live
godly, righteous and disciplined lives *in this present age* (12b). Why?
On what does Paul base his appeal? What are the grounds of present
Christian behaviour?[40]

Paul's reply is straightforward, namely that in Jesus Christ there
has been an epiphany of God's grace, and there is going to be an
epiphany of his glory. That is, the best way to live now, in this
present age, is to learn to do spiritually what is impossible physically,
namely to look in opposite directions at the same time. We need both
to look back and remember the epiphany of grace (whose purpose
was to redeem us from all evil and to purify for God a people of his
own), and also to look forward and anticipate the epiphany of glory
(whose purpose will be to perfect at his second coming the salvation
he began at his first).

This deliberate orientation of ourselves, this looking back and
looking forward, this determination to live in the light of Christ's
two comings, to live today in the light of yesterday and tomorrow –
this should be an essential part of our daily discipline. We need to say
to ourselves regularly the great acclamation, 'Christ has died; Christ
is risen; Christ will come again.' For then our present duties in the
home will be inspired by the past and future epiphanies of Christ.

Canon Hay Aitken suggested that the two comings of Christ are
like 'two windows . . . in the School of Grace'. Through the western
window a solemn light streams from Mt. Calvary. Through the
eastern window shines the light of sunrising, the herald of a brighter
day. 'Thus the School of Grace is well lighted; but we cannot afford
to do without the light from either West or East.'[41]

The chapter ends as it began with the command to teach. Paul has
commissioned Titus to instruct the Cretan churches in both doctrine

---

[40] Towner (1986) emphasizes that in the Pastoral Letters the present age is the age of
salvation and 'the last days'; that it 'occupies a central position within the message of
the Pastoral Epistles' (p. 442); that salvation is best understood in the Pastorals as an
already/not yet phenomenon between the two epiphanies; and that, whereas *parousia*
refers to the fact of Christ's coming, *epiphaneia* focuses on it as his saving, helping
intervention.
[41] Aitken, pp. 253–254.

and ethics. *These, then, are the things you should teach*, or 'these are your themes' (REB), both the epiphany doctrines and the ethical duties. Moreover, Titus is not to communicate them objectively and diffidently as if they were mere cold facts. Paul goes on: *Encourage and rebuke with all authority. Do not let anyone despise you* (15).

Titus 3:1–8
3. Doctrine and duty in the world

Having given Titus directions about doctrine and duty in the church (chapter 1), and in the home (chapter 2), Paul now develops the same theme in regard to the world (chapter 3). He thus moves purposefully from the inner circles of home and church to the outer circle of secular society.

The pattern of this chapter is the same as that of chapter 2. The apostle begins with ethical instruction, in this case the need for submission to the authorities and for considerateness to everybody (1–2). He then immediately grounds Christian duty in Christian doctrine, giving us a magnificently full account of salvation (3–8). He reserves some final, more personal messages for his conclusion (9–15).

1. Christians in public life (3:1–2)

Remind the people to be subject to rulers and authorities, to be obedient, to be ready to do whatever is good, ²to slander no-one, to be peaceable and considerate, and to show true humility towards all men.

Remind the people (literally 'them'), he begins, for the teaching he is about to give is not new. The churches have heard it before. But there are many warnings in Scripture of the dangers of forgetfulness, and many promises to those who remember. A bad memory was one of the main reasons for Israel's downfall. 'They soon forgot', we read, and 'they did not remember'.[1] Jesus had to make the same complaint to the apostles: 'Don't you remember . . .?'[2] It is hardly surprising, therefore, that the leading apostles Paul, Peter and John in their New Testament letters all stress the importance of their reminding ministry.[3] So all conscientious Christian teachers, once

[1] Ps. 106: 13, 7.   [2] Mt. 16:9.
[3] *E.g.* Phil. 3:1; 2 Pet. 1:12–13; 3:11–12; 1 Jn. 2:21, 24.

they have been delivered from the unhealthy lust for originality, take pains to make old truths new and stale truths fresh.

What Titus is to remind the people about concerns their social relationships in the world, first to the authorities in particular (1) and then to everybody in general (2).

a. Christian relationships with rulers (3:1)

Remind the people to be subject to rulers and authorities, to be obedient (1a). 'Paul is possibly glancing at the notoriously turbulent character of the Cretans, of which Polybius tells us';[4] they were constantly involved in 'insurrections, murders and internecine wars'.[5] Crete had been subjugated by Rome in 67 BC, and since then had been continuously restive under the Roman colonial yoke. Paul has hinted at their 'insubordinate' spirit in 1:10 and 16. Now through Titus he tells them to be submissive to their rulers.

Paul has already written to Timothy about the need to pray for those in authority (1 Tim. 2:1ff.); now he writes to Titus about our Christian duty to obey them. Not that Christian citizens can ever give the state an unconditional allegiance. That would be to worship the state, as in the emperor worship of the first century, which Christians recognized as idolatry. How could they call Caesar 'Lord' when they had confessed Jesus as Lord? Nevertheless, Christian duty in principle is to submit to the state, because, as Paul has explained in Romans 13, the state's authority has been delegated to it by God. This means that our first loyalty is to him, whose authority it is; and if our duty to him comes into collision with our duty to the state, our duty to God takes precedence. As Peter said, 'We must obey God rather than men.'[6]

It is not enough, however, for Christians to be law-abiding (so far as our conscience permits us); we are to be public-spirited as well, *to be ready* (eager, not reluctant) *to do whatever is good* (1b), whenever we have the opportunity. According to both Paul and Peter, the state has the double duty to punish evil and to promote good.[7] So God's people should be ready to cooperate with it in both these areas. The emphasis on 'whatever is good' not only clarifies our responsibility but limits it. We cannot cooperate with the state if it reverses its God-given duty, promoting evil instead of punishing it, and opposing good instead of rewarding and furthering it.

---

[4] Kelly, p. 249.   [5] Quoted by Barclay, p. 258.
[6] Acts 5:29. For a further consideration of our duty to the state, and of civil disobedience as mandatory to Christians in certain situations, see my *The Message of Romans*, pp. 338–347.
[7] Rom. 13:4; 1 Pet. 2:14.

b. Christian relationships with everybody (3:2)

From our Christian responsibility towards the leaders of the community, Paul turns to our relationship with everybody in the community. He looks beyond the Christian fellowship to secular society. How are believers to relate to unbelievers? It is essential to see that this is Paul's concern, for he begins with a reference to 'no-one' and ends with a reference to 'all men', meaning everybody. He selects four Christian social attitudes which are to be universal in their application, two negative and two positive.

Negatively we are *to slander no-one* and *to be peaceable,* which in Greek is also negative, 'to avoid quarrels' (REB). So we must neither speak against, nor fight against, other people. We are to be neither offensive nor 'argumentative' (JBP) in either speech or behaviour.

Positively, we are *to be . . . considerate, and to show true humility towards all men* (2b). It is difficult to find appropriate English equivalents to these two lovely Greek words. The first (*epieikēs*) means to show 'clemency, gentleness, graciousness' (BAGD), and specially to be 'conciliatory'.[8] The second (*prautēs*) may be translated 'gentleness, humility, courtesy, considerateness, meekness' (BAGD). Both were characteristics of Jesus, so that Paul could appeal to the Corinthians 'by the meekness and gentleness of Christ'.[9] Moreover, we must not miss the totality of the apostle's requirement. Literally, he bids us show '*all* gentleness to *all* men'. There is to be no limit either to our humble courtesy or to the people to whom we are to show it.

Here then is a very brief delineation of Christian behaviour in public life. In relation to the authorities we are to be conscientious citizens (submissive, obedient and cooperative), and in relation to everybody, irrespective of their race or religion, we are to be conciliatory, courteous, humble and gentle.

2. Ingredients of salvation (3:3–8)

Paul now spells out the theological reason why we can expect Christians to have a social conscience and to behave responsibly in public life. The logic is seen in the pronouns: 'Remind *them* to be conscientious and considerate citizens, because [*gar* is unaccountably omitted by NIV] *we* were ourselves once anti-social, but *he* (God) saved and changed *us*.' That is, the only reason we dare instruct others in social ethics is that we know what we were once like ourselves, that God nevertheless saved us, and that he can therefore transform other people too. It is not enough to affirm that

[8] Kelly, p. 249.   [9] 2 Cor. 10:1.

the grace of God that brings salvation has appeared to all men (2:11); we must be able to say that he saved *us* (3:5), even he saved *me*. It is not just history which raises our expectations; it is experience. Without a personal experience of salvation we lack the right, the incentive and the confidence to teach social ethics to others.

So Paul now gives a condensed but comprehensive account of salvation. Verses 4–7 are a single long sentence, which he may have taken from an early Christian creed.

At one time we too were foolish, disobedient, deceived and enslaved by all kinds of passions and pleasures. We lived in malice and envy, being hated and hating one another. ⁴But when the kindness and love of God our Saviour appeared, ⁵he saved us, not because of righteous things we had done, but because of his mercy. He saved us through the washing of rebirth and renewal by the Holy Spirit, ⁶whom he poured out on us generously through Jesus Christ our Saviour, ⁷so that, having been justified by his grace, we might become heirs having the hope of eternal life. ⁸This is a trustworthy saying. And I want you to stress these things, so that those who have trusted in God may be careful to devote themselves to doing what is good. These things are excellent and profitable for everyone.

The whole sentence hinges upon the main verb *he saved us* (5). It is perhaps the fullest statement of salvation in the New Testament. Yet whenever the phraseology of salvation is dropped into a conversation today, people's reactions are predictable. They will either blush, frown, snigger, or even laugh, as if it were a huge joke. Thus the devil, whose ambition is to destroy, not to save, succeeds in trivializing the most serious question we could ever ask ourselves or put to anybody else. For Christianity is essentially a religion of salvation. To prove this, it is enough to quote two biblical assertions: 'the Father has sent his Son to be the Saviour of the world'[10] and 'the Son of man came to seek and to save what was lost'.[11]

So we have to come to terms with the concept of 'salvation', and one of the best ways is to study verses 3–8 of Titus 3. For here Paul isolates six ingredients of salvation – its need (why it is necessary), its source (where it originates), its ground (what it rests on), its means (how it comes to us), its goal (what it leads to) and its evidence (how it proves itself).

[10] 1 Jn. 4:14. [11] Lk. 19:10.

a. The need of salvation

In verse 3 the apostle supplies an unsavoury picture of the state and conduct of unregenerate people. In doing so, he discloses what we ourselves used to be like. Moreover, this is not an exaggeration, but 'the very exact image of human life without grace'.[12] It is perhaps best grasped as four couplets.

First, *at one time we too were foolish, disobedient.* In other words, we were both mentally and morally depraved. We lacked sense (*anoētos*) and sensibility (*apeithēs*). This is elaborated in the next pair.

Secondly, we were *deceived and enslaved by all kinds of passions and pleasures.* Both verbs are passive in form, and so indicate that we were the victims of evil forces we could not control. We were not 'foolish' only, but *deceived.* We were not 'disobedient' only, but *enslaved.* Doubtless Paul is alluding to the Evil One, that arch-deceiver who blinds people's minds[13] and that arch-tyrant who also takes people captive.[14] We were his dupes and his slaves.

Thirdly, *we lived in malice and envy,* which are very ugly twins. For malice is wishing people evil, while envy is resenting and coveting their good. Both disrupt human relationships.

Fourthly, we were *being hated and hating one another.* That is, the hostility which we experienced in our relationships was reciprocal.

Thus a deliberate antithesis seems to be developed between the kind of people Christians should be (1, 2) and the kind of people we once were (3). It is a contrast between submissiveness and foolishness, between obedience and disobedience, between a readiness to do good and an enslavement by evil, between kindness and peaceableness on the one hand and malice and envy on the other, between being humble and gentle and being hateful and hating.

How is it possible to get out of the one mindset and lifestyle into the other, and to exchange addiction for freedom? The answer is given in verse 5: *he saved us,* he rescued us from our former bondage and changed us into new people. The New Testament loves to dwell on this transformation, which salvation entails, by using the formula 'once we were . . . but now we are . . .'[15]

b. The source of salvation

If we were truly deceived and enslaved, one thing is obvious: we could not save ourselves. Yet the possibility of self-salvation is one of the major delusions of New Age philosophy. It teaches that salvation

[12] Bengel, p. 324.   [13] *E.g.* 2 Cor. 4:4.   [14] *E.g.* 2 Tim. 2:26.
[15] *E.g.* Rom 6:17ff.; 1 Cor. 6:11; Eph. 2:1ff.; Col. 3:7ff.

comes not from without (someone else coming to our rescue) but from within (as we discover ourselves and our own resources). So 'look into yourself', Shirley MacLaine urges us, 'explore yourself', for 'all the answers are within yourself'.[16] And in her subsequent book, which is revealingly entitled *Going Within*, she writes that 'the New Age is all about *self*-responsibility', *i.e.* taking responsibility for everything that happens, since 'the only source is ourselves'.[17]

But Paul teaches a different source of salvation. With verse 4 he turns from us in our depravity to 'God our Saviour' (1:3; 2:10; 3:4), from our hatred of one another to his amazing love for us. Paul traces our salvation right back to its source in the love of God. *But when the kindness and love of God our Saviour appeared* (4), that is, in the birth, life, death and resurrection of Jesus, *he saved us.* Then at the end of verse 5 Paul mentions God's 'mercy' and in verse 7 his justifying 'grace'. These are four tremendous words. God's 'kindness' (*chrēstotēs*) is shown even to 'the ungrateful and wicked';[18] his 'love' (*philanthrōpia*) is his concern for the whole human race; his 'mercy' (*eleos*) is extended to the helpless who cannot save themselves; and his 'grace' (*charis*) reaches out to the guilty and undeserving.

Thus salvation originated in the heart of God. It is because of his kindness, love, mercy and grace that he intervened on our behalf, he took the initiative, he came after us, and he rescued us from our hopeless predicament.

c. The ground of salvation

Granted that God's love is the source or spring from which salvation flows, what is the ground on which it rests? On what moral basis can God forgive sinners? It is true that in explicit terms this question is neither asked nor answered in Titus 3. Yet it is implicit in the antithesis of verse 4, which declares that *he* (God) *saved us, not because of righteous things we had done, but because of his mercy.* Not our righteousness but his mercy is the ground of our salvation. This sharp contrast between the false and the true way of salvation is hammered home in the New Testament by constant repetition.[19]

God does not save us because of his mercy alone, however, but because of what his mercy led him to do in the sending of his Son. His attribute of mercy is indeed the source of our salvation; his deed of mercy in Christ is its ground. This is implied in Paul's previous statement that *the kindness and love of God our Saviour appeared*

---

[16] *Out on a Limb* (Elm Tree, 1983), pp. 111, 166.
[17] *Going Within* (Bantam, 1989), pp. 27, 29.   [18] Lk. 6:35.
[19] *E.g.* Lk. 18:9ff.; Eph. 2:8ff.; Phil. 3:7ff.; 2 Tim. 1:9.

(14). For this saving 'appearance' clearly refers to the historical event of Christ's coming to save, as in 2:11 and 2 Timothy 1:10. Further, although there is no specific allusion to the cross, this must have been in Paul's mind, since twice elsewhere in the Pastorals he affirms that Christ 'gave himself' for our redemption (2:14; 1 Tim. 2:6). The ground of our salvation, therefore, is not our works of righteousness but his work of mercy in the cross.

d. The means of salvation

In order to clarify what the main verb is, on which this long sentence depends, the NIV repeats it in verse 5 (*he saved us . . . he saved us . . .*), although it occurs only once in the Greek text. On the one hand, *he saved us . . . because of his mercy*, that is, because of his merciful deed (the ground of our salvation); on the other, *he saved us through the washing of rebirth and renewal by the Holy Spirit* (the means of our salvation). Here is a composite expression containing four nouns – *washing, rebirth, renewal* and *the Holy Spirit*. What do they mean?

Washing (loutron) is almost certainly a reference to water baptism.[20] All the early church fathers took it in this way. This does not mean that they (or Paul) taught baptismal regeneration, any more than Ananias did when he said to Saul of Tarsus, 'Get up, be baptised and wash your sin away, calling on his name.'[21] Most Protestant churches think of baptism as 'an outward and visible sign of an inward and spiritual grace', namely of the washing away of sins, and of new birth by the Holy Spirit. But they do not confuse the sign (baptism) with the thing signified (salvation).

The next two nouns (*rebirth and renewal*) are variously understood. 'Rebirth' translates *palingenesia*, which Jesus used of the final renewal of all things,[22] and which the Stoics used for the periodical restoration of the world, in which they believed. Here, however, the new birth envisaged is individual (like the 'new creation' of 2 Cor. 5:17) rather than cosmic. It speaks of a radical new beginning, since 'God has not repaired us, but has made us all new'.[23] The other noun, 'renewal', translates *anakainōsis*. It may be synonymous with 'rebirth', the repetition being used for rhetorical effect. Or it may refer to the process of moral renovation or transformation which follows the new birth.

The Holy Spirit is of course the agent through whom we are reborn and renewed, and whom God *poured out on us generously*

---

[20] *Cf.* 1 Cor. 6:11; Eph. 5:26.
[21] Acts 22:16; *cf.* Rom. 6:3; Gal. 3:27; 1 Pet. 3:21.   [22] Mt 19:28.
[23] Chrysostom, p. 538.

through Jesus Christ our Saviour (6b). The use of both the verb 'pour out' (*ekcheō*) and the aorist tense suggests that the reference is to the effusion of the Spirit on the day of Pentecost,[24] and the statement that he was *poured out on us* denotes our personal share in the Pentecostal gift.

The question which perplexes all commentators is how these four nouns, which have been called a 'string of genitives',[25] are meant to be related to one another. The AV deliberately places a comma in the middle of them and translates: 'by the washing of regeneration, and renewing of the Holy Ghost'. The value of this rendering is that it distinguishes between the outward washing of baptism and the inward renewal of the Holy Spirit. But it also has the disadvantage of separating the Holy Spirit from the regeneration he brings about.

So other versions delete the comma and understand the expression as a single, complex phrase, not least because none of the nouns is preceded by the definite article. It could then be paraphrased that 'God saved us through a rebirth and renewal which were outwardly dramatized in our baptism but inwardly effected by the Holy Spirit'. Or, reversing the order, 'God generously poured the Holy Spirit upon us; this outpoured Spirit has inwardly regenerated and renewed us (or has regenerated us and is renewing us); and all this was outwardly and visibly signified and sealed to us in our baptism.'

Salvation means more than an inward rebirth and renewal, however. It also includes *having been justified by his grace* (7). We must decisively reject the RSV and JB version, which says that God saved us through rebirth 'so that we might be justified by his grace'. For justification is emphatically not the result, still less the object, of our regeneration. These two works of God are rather parallel and concurrent. Salvation includes both. Justification means that God declares us righteous through the sin-bearing death of his Son; regeneration means that he makes us righteous through the indwelling power of his Spirit. So we must never confuse justification and regeneration, our new status and our new birth. Nor should we ever attempt to separate them. For God always does both together. He never justifies people without at the same time regenerating them, and he never regenerates them without justifying them. The work of Christ in justification and the work of the Spirit in regeneration are simultaneous.

e. The goal of salvation

God saved us, Paul wrote, . . . *so that, having been justified by his grace, we might become heirs having the hope of eternal life* (7). All

---

[24] See *e.g.* Joel 2:29; Acts 2:17ff., 33; 10:45   [25] Knight (1992), p. 343.

those whom God has justified and regenerated become his heirs, because he has saved us for this purpose. We are 'heirs of God and co-heirs with Christ'.[26] And as his nominated heirs we cherish the sure expectation that one day we will receive our full inheritance in heaven, namely 'eternal life', an unclouded fellowship with God. During the present age, although we have received a foretaste of eternal life, the fullness of life is the object of our hope, and we are its 'heirs-in-hope'.[27] Yet our hope is secure because it rests on God's promise (1:2).

This is a trustworthy saying (8a), Paul adds. We have seen that the Pastorals contain five 'trustworthy sayings' (pithy statements which Paul endorses). This is the only one in Titus. In three of them the formula almost certainly relates to what follows.[28] But here in Titus (as probably in 1 Tim. 4:9), it seems rather to refer back to what precedes it, that is, to Paul's 'glowing statement' of salvation.[29] Whether it covers the whole of verses 3–7 or less, commentators differ. Though a longer 'trustworthy saying' than the others, it is still a concise, single-sentence utterance. And Paul endorses it. It is true, he says; it may be trusted.

f. The evidence of salvation

Although the 'trustworthy saying' formula seems to have concluded Paul's exposition of salvation, he has not yet finished the topic. He will not leave it without underlining the indispensable necessity of good works in those who profess to have been saved. *And I want you to stress these things* (that is, the essential ingredients of salvation), *so that those who have trusted in God* (and so have been saved by faith) *may be careful to devote themselves to doing what is good* (8b).

What kind of good deeds does the apostle have in mind? Because the verb translated 'to devote themselves' (*proïstēmi*) can have the almost technical sense 'to practise a profession',[30] the RSV margin translates it 'to enter honourable occupations', and the REB margin 'to engage in honest employment'. But the context does not require, or even encourage, this meaning. The reference seems to be a more general one to good works of righteousness and love. Although Paul has made it plain in verse 5 that God has not saved us 'because of righteous things we had done', he nevertheless now insists that believers must devote themselves to good works. Good works are not the ground of salvation, but they are its necessary fruit and evidence. It is in this way that *these things are excellent and profitable for everyone* (8c).

---

[26] Rom. 8:17.   [27] Hendriksen, p. 393.
[28] 1 Tim. 1:15; 3:1; 2 Tim. 2:11.   [29] Kelly, p. 254.   [30] Lock, p. 156.

The necessity of good works has been noted by several commentators as a major topic of the Pastorals. Robert Karris, for example, has called it 'the author's basic message'.[31] But it is Gordon Fee who has drawn particular attention to it, not so much in the Pastorals in general, as in Titus in particular. 'The dominant theme in Titus . . . is *good works* . . . that is, exemplary Christian behaviour, and that *for the sake of outsiders*' and 'in contrast to the false teachers'. It is 'the recurring theme of the entire letter'.[32]

The expression 'good works' (*kala erga*) occurs fourteen times in the Pastorals. Paul seems to emphasize five points. First, the very purpose of Christ's death was to purify for himself a people who would be enthusiastic for good works (Tit. 2:14). Secondly, although good works can never be the basis of salvation (Tit. 2:5; 2 Tim. 1:9), they are its essential evidence (Tit. 3:8, 14). Thirdly, it is therefore to be expected that all Christians will be 'equipped' and 'ready' to do good works,[33] women seeking this special adornment[34] and rich people accepting this special responsibility.[35] Fourthly, since pastoral oversight is itself a good work,[36] all Christian leaders should be conspicuous for the good works they do.[37] Widows should not be registered unless they have a reputation for good works,[38] and every pastor should be a model of good works (Tit. 2:7). All this is in contrast to the false teachers who 'claim to know God, but by their actions they deny him' (Tit. 1:16). Fifthly, it is above all by good works that the gospel is adorned and so commended to outsiders (Tit. 2:9–10).

We are now in a position to summarize the six essential ingredients of salvation. Its need is our sin, guilt and slavery; its source is God's gracious loving-kindness; its ground is not our merit but God's mercy in the cross; its means is the regenerating and renewing work of the Holy Spirit, signified in baptism; its goal is our final inheritance of eternal life; and its evidence is our diligent practice of good works.

We note what a balanced and comprehensive account of salvation this is. For here are the three persons of the Trinity together engaged in securing our salvation: the love of God the Father who took the initiative; the death of God the Son in whom God's grace and mercy appeared; and the inward work of God the Holy Spirit by whom we are reborn and renewed.

Here too are the three tenses of salvation. The past is justification and regeneration. The present is a new life of good works in the power of the Spirit. The future is the inheritance of eternal life which will one day be ours.

[31] Karris (1979), p. 120.   [32] Fee (1988), pp. 12, 200, 215. ·
[33] 2 Tim. 2:21; 3:17; Tit. 3:1.   [34] 1 Tim. 2:10.   [35] 1 Tim. 6:18.
[36] 1 Tim. 3:1.   [37] 1 Tim. 5:25.   [38] 1 Tim. 5:10.

Once we have grasped the all-embracing character of this salvation, reductionist accounts of it will never satisfy us. We shall rather determine both to explore and experience for ourselves the fullness of God's salvation and to share with other people the same fullness, refusing to acquiesce, whether for ourselves or others, in any form of truncated or trivialized gospel.

Titus 3:9–15
4. Final personal messages

So far in Titus 3 Paul has done two things. First, he has told Titus to remind the Christians in his care to be conscientious citizens (submissive, obedient and public-spirited) and to live consistent lives of peace, courtesy and gentleness (1–2). Whatever their national character or individual temperament, that is their calling. Secondly, Paul has elaborated the doctrine of salvation in its six ingredients (3–8), and so given Titus a ground for confidence that the people in his charge can be changed, so as to live the new life to which they are summoned.

Paul concludes his letter with a cluster of miscellaneous messages. What unites them is that they are all requests or instructions to Titus to do something.

But avoid foolish controversies and genealogies and arguments and quarrels about the law, because these are unprofitable and useless. [10]*Warn a divisive person once, and then warn him a second time. After that, have nothing to do with him.* [11]*You may be sure that such a man is warped and sinful; he is self-condemned.*

[12]*As soon as I send Artemas or Tychicus to you, do your best to come to me at Nicopolis, because I have decided to winter there.* [13]*Do everything you can to help Zenas the lawyer and Apollos on their way and see that they have everything they need.* [14]*Our people must learn to devote themselves to doing what is good, in order that they may provide for daily necessities and not live unproductive lives.*

[15]*Everyone with me sends you greetings. Greet those who love us in the faith.*

Grace be with you all.

a. Titus is to avoid profitless controversy

Having told Titus to 'insist on' certain things (8, REB), the apostle now tells him to 'avoid' certain others (9). *But avoid foolish controversies and genealogies and arguments and quarrels about the law.* George W. Knight terms these 'four errors' which Titus is to avoid, adding that 'each of these four errors is also mentioned in 1 Timothy'.[1]

The first (*foolish controversies*) cannot possibly be taken as a prohibition of all theological controversy. For Jesus himself was a controversialist, in constant debate with the religious leaders of his day. Paul himself was also drawn into controversy over the gospel, and could not avoid it. In addition, he had both urged Timothy to 'fight the good fight of the faith'[2] and told Titus that false teachers must be 'silenced' and 'rebuked' (1:11, 13).

So then not all controversy is banned, but only 'foolish' controversies. The noun is *zētēseis*, which could mean 'speculations'; its other occurrences in the Pastorals suggest that Paul is contrasting the false teachers' speculative fancies with God's revealed truth.[3]

The other three 'errors' are *genealogies, arguments,* and *quarrels about the law.* The references to genealogies and to the law show that a Jewish debate is in view, and the reader is referred to the exposition of 1 Timothy 1:3–11, in which the false teachers are said both 'to devote themselves to myths and endless genealogies' and to 'want to be teachers of the law'. It is evident that Paul regarded their treatment of the Old Testament as frivolous. Their speculations also led to 'arguments' and 'quarrels', which could be translated 'quibbles' and 'squabbles'.

To sum up, whereas good works are 'profitable' (*ōphelimos,* 8), being excellent and constructive, foolish controversies are 'unprofitable' (*anōphelēs,* 9), being pointless or futile; they get you nowhere.

b. Titus is to discipline contentious people

Warn a divisive person, Paul writes. The Greek word is *hairetikos,* which the AV and (surprisingly) NEB translate 'heretic'. But this is an anachronism, for the word had not yet assumed this meaning. *Hairesis* meant a sect, party or school of thought, and is applied in the Acts to Sadducees, Pharisees and Christians.[4] *Hairetikos,* however, meant somebody who is 'factious' (RSV), 'contentious' (REB) or 'divisive' (NIV).

Discipline was to be administered to such a person in three stages, beginning with two clear warnings. *Warn a divisive person once, and then warn him a second time.* Only then, *after that,* if the offender remains unrepentant, and refuses the opportunity of forgiveness and restoration, is he to be rejected. *Have nothing to do with him* (10).

---

[1] Knight (1992), pp. 353–354. [2] 1 Tim. 1:18–19; 6:12.
[3] 1 Tim. 1:4; 6:4; 2 Tim. 2:23. [4] Acts 5:17; 15:5; 24:14; 28:22.

Whether this refers to a formal excommunication (as in 1 Tim. 1:20) or to a social ostracism (as probably in Rom. 16:17) is not made plain. Yet to repudiate him is right. For after two warnings and two refusals *you may be sure that such a man is warped,* having 'a distorted mind' (REB), *and sinful; he is self-condemned* (11). One is reminded of the several-stage procedure laid down by Jesus.[5] An offender is to be given successive opportunities to repent; repudiation is to be the very last resort.

c. Titus is to join Paul at Nicopolis

Paul shares with Titus his intention to send someone to Crete, who would be competent to take Titus' place and so free him to join Paul. He may send *Artemas or Tychicus,* he says. Of Artemas we know nothing; nobody of that name appears elsewhere in the New Testament. Tychicus, on the other hand, is mentioned on five other occasions. These references tell us that he came from proconsular Asia, perhaps from Ephesus its capital, like Trophimus with whom he is bracketed.[6] He was one of those chosen to take the collection to Jerusalem. Paul called him a 'dear brother and faithful servant in the Lord',[7] and evidently had great confidence in him. He sent him to Colosse, perhaps with his letter, to tell the churches about him.[8] He is now proposing to send him to Crete to relieve Titus (verse 12), and will later send him from Rome to Ephesus, apparently to free Timothy to visit him as soon as possible.[9]

As soon as Artemas or Tychicus arrives in Crete, and has been able to take over responsibility for the churches, Titus is to do his best to join Paul *at Nicopolis* because he has *decided to winter there* (12). Although at least three towns with this name have been identified, scholars are largely agreed that Paul's reference is to the capital of Epirus on the west (Adriatic) coast of Greece.

d. Titus is to send Zenas and Apollos on their way

We know nothing of *Zenas* except that Paul calls him *the lawyer,* presumably meaning that he was a professional expert in Roman law. *Apollos* may well be the learned and eloquent Alexandrian, who had 'a thorough knowledge of the Scriptures' and who exercised a fruitful ministry in Corinth.[10] It seems likely that Paul had entrusted to Zenas and Apollos the task of carrying his letter to Titus on Crete. Once they had fulfilled their commission, they were to be given 'a good send-off' (JBP). Paul asks Titus to *do everything* he *can to help*

[5] Mt. 18:15ff.   [6] Acts 20:4; 21:29.   [7] Eph. 6:21.   [8] Col. 4:7–8.
[9] 2 Tim. 4:9, 12, 21.   [10] Acts 18:24ff.; 1 Cor. 1:12; 3:4ff., 22; 16:12.

them *on their way*,[11] equipped with *everything they need*, that is, all necessary supplies for their onward journey.

e. Titus is to ensure that 'our people' are dedicated to good works

Our people must learn, he writes, presumably from Titus their teacher, *to devote themselves to doing what is good*. The verb translated 'devote themselves' is the same as in verse 8 and could therefore be rendered 'enter honourable occupations' (RSV mg.). Moreover the reason given, *in order that they may provide for daily necessities and not live unproductive lives* (14), would be compatible with this. Yet, as we have seen, throughout the Pastorals *kala erga* consistently means 'good works' in the widest sense of fine actions or righteous deeds, so that it probably means the same here as well. 'Our people' must demonstrate that they are such, that they truly belong to Paul's following, by giving themselves to good works.

f. Titus is to arrange for an exchange of greetings

Everyone with me sends you greetings. That is, Titus must first receive the greetings sent to him by Paul and everyone with him. Then he is to convey Paul's greetings to others. *Greet those who love us in the faith* (15a). For the faith is 'our common faith' (1:4); it binds God's people together in love.

At the end of his letters it was the apostle's custom to take the pen from his scribe or amanuensis, and to write a word of personal greeting. He seems specially to have written a message which contained the word 'grace' and which so encapsulated his message.[12] He is referring to the grace which issues from the Father and the Son (1:4), which made its historical epiphany in Christ (2:11), and by which we have been justified (3:7).

As he pronounces his benediction, Paul looks beyond Titus to all members of the Cretan churches, indeed to all who would later read his letter, including us: *Grace be with you all* (15b).

Having now studied the three chapters which make up this short letter, it is evident that 'Doctrine and duty' has been an appropriate title for it. For in the church (chapter 1) Christian leaders, in contrast to false teachers, are to pass on the apostolic faith and practise what they preach. In the home (chapter 2) members of the household are

---

[11] For this meaning of *propempō* see Acts 15:3; Rom. 15:24; 1 Cor. 16:6; 2 Cor. 1:16; 3 Jn. 6.

[12] *E.g.* 1 Cor. 16:23; Gal. 6:11, 18; Eph. 4:24; Phil. 4:23; Col. 4:18; 1 Thes. 5:28; 2 Thes. 3:17–18.

to go about their different duties in this present age, motivated by the past and future appearings of Christ. And in the world (chapter 3) conscientious Christian citizenship is to be a spontaneous overflow of that great salvation which God – Father, Son and Holy Spirit – has won for us.

Thus doctrine inspires duty, and duty adorns doctrine. Doctrine and duty are married; they must not be divorced.

The Message of 1 Timothy and Titus

Study guide

Study guide

The aim of this study guide is to help you get to the heart of what the author has written and to challenge you to apply what you learn to your own life. The questions have been designed for use by individuals or by small groups of Christians meeting, perhaps for an hour or two each week, to study, discuss and pray together.

The guide provides material for each of the sections in the book. When used by a group with limited time, the leader should decide beforehand which questions are most appropriate for the group to discuss during the meeting and which should perhaps be left for group members to work through by themselves or in smaller groups during the week.

In order to be able to contribute fully and to learn from the group meetings, each member of the group needs to read through the section or sections under discussion, together with the passages in the letters to which they refer.

It is important not to let these studies become merely academic exercises. Guard against this by making time to think through and discuss how what you discover *works out in practice* for you. Make sure you begin and end each study by focusing on God in praise and prayer. Ask the Holy Spirit to speak to you through your discussion together.

The authenticity of the Pastoral Letters (pp. 21–34)

1. *The case for Pauline authorship*

1   Does it matter whether or not Paul wrote the Pastoral Letters? Why?
2   What evidence within the letters supports Pauline authorship? What alternative explanations have been put forward to explain these features? (See pp. 21–22.)

3 What external evidence is there? How does it contribute to the debate? (See p. 23.)

2. The case against Pauline authorship

4 In what ways do the historical details of these letters seem to contradict the framework set out in the Acts of the Apostles? How may such apparent discrepancies be accounted for? (See p. 24.)
5 What is it about the language of these letters that has led some scholars to cast doubt on Pauline authorship? How may such points be answered? (See pp. 24–26.)
6 In what ways have scholars been 'quite rude' about the theology and ethics of these letters? (See pp. 26–27.) How do you react to such statements?

3. The case for and against a pseudonymous author

7 What does 'pseudonymity' mean? What do you make of the assertion that 'forgery' is an inappropriate word to use? (See pp. 28–29.)

'Scripture lays constant emphasis on the sacredness of truth and the sinfulness of false witness' (p. 30).

---

4. The case for an active amanuensis

8 What evidence is there to support the suggestion that the writing of these letters was 'secretary-assisted' (pp. 30–33)?
9 Do you agree with John Stott that it is important to safeguard the 'leadership role and apostolic authority' of the author of these letters (see p. 34)? Why?

A. The Message of 1 Timothy

1 Timothy 1:1–2
Introduction (pp. 37–40)

1 What do we know about Timothy (see pp. 37–38)? To what extent are you able to identify with him?
2 In what ways is 'Pastoral Epistles' an 'appropriate expression' (pp. 38–39) for these letters?

3 On what particular features of apostleship does Paul focus in his opening greeting? (See p. 39.)

1 Timothy 1:3-20
1. Apostolic doctrine (pp. 41-58)

1 What is 'Paul's preoccupation' in this first chapter? Why does this strike 'a discordant note at the end of the twentieth century' (p. 42)? How do you feel about this issue?

1. The false teachers and the law (1:3-11)

2 In what ways was the law of God being misused by the false teachers about whom Paul writes? (See pp. 43-45.)
3 To what consequences of false teaching does Paul draw attention here? (See pp. 45-46.) In what ways have you experienced these?

'Speculation raises doubts, while revelation evokes faith' (p. 45).

---

4 What criteria do you use when assessing the Christian teaching which you hear? How do you think Paul would suggest you go about this?
5 What did the sixteenth-century Reformers teach about the right use of God's law? How does what they said reflect Paul's teaching here? (See pp. 46-48.)
6 'We must not therefore imagine that, because we have embraced the gospel, we may now repudiate the law!' (p. 50). In what ways are you tempted to do this? Why is it so wrong?

2. The apostle Paul and the gospel (1:12-17)

7 For what particular reasons does Paul *thank Christ Jesus our Lord* (12; see pp. 51-52)? How far are you able to identify with what he writes?
8 What four things does the *trustworthy saying* of verse 15 underline about the gospel (see pp. 52-53)? To what extent do these points feature in the way you seek to communicate the good news of Jesus?
9 What 'predisposed' God to be merciful to Paul? (See pp. 54-55.)

10 In what way does Paul's conversion remain 'a standing source of hope to otherwise hopeless cases' (p. 55)?

11 Do you tend to feel that 'liberty and liturgy' are incompatible (see p. 55)? Why is this? How can this problem be overcome?

3. Timothy and the good fight (1:18–20)

12 'Timothy possesses two valuable things which he must carefully guard' (p. 57). To what is John Stott referring? Why is it so important to hold on to both of them?

'A bad conscience is the mother of all heresies' (John Calvin, quoted on p. 57).

---

13 How might verse 20 be applied to the church today?

14 Spend time praying for those responsible for teaching the Word of God in the church today.

1 Timothy 2:1–15
2. Public worship (pp. 59–88)

1 How would you respond to someone who claimed that the church's first priority is evangelism? What are the serious consequences of such a view? (See p. 59.)

1. Global concern in public worship (2:1–7)

2 What 'stands out in this paragraph' (p. 60)? In what specific ways does the church to which you belong reflect this perspective? How do you think it could do so more effectively?

'I sometimes wonder whether the comparatively slow progress towards peace and justice in the world, and towards world evangelization, is due more than anything else to the prayerlessness of the people of God' (p. 62).

---

3 What is so 'remarkable' (p. 62) about Paul's instruction to pray for world rulers? Why is this so important?

4 In what ways do you, in effect, 'monopolize' God (p. 64)? What causes this?

5 In what ways have Christians down the years sought to reconcile God's desire that *all* people be saved with his election of *some* to salvation? (See pp. 65–66.)

6 How do you personally respond to this apparent contradiction between the 'all' and the 'some'?

7 What does verse 5 bring out as the 'fundamental basis' (p. 67) of the world mission alluded to in verse 4?

8 Why is the reference to 'one mediator' in verse 5 'indispensable to Paul's argument' (p. 68)?

9 What do the terms 'exclusivism', 'inclusivism' and 'pluralism' mean in this context? Which view do you hold? Why? What evidence is there as to which view Paul held? (See pp. 68–69.)

10 How 'dare' Christians claim that Jesus Christ 'has no competitors or successors' (p. 69)? What practical implications of such a claim can you think of?

11 What is meant by the terms 'limited atonement' and 'universal atonement' (pp. 70–71)? What are the holders of each position seeking to defend? What approach do you take to this debate? Why?

'Whatever we may decide about the scope of the atonement, we are absolutely forbidden to limit the scope of world mission. The gospel must be preached to all, and salvation must be offered to all' (p. 71).

---

12 What is distinctive about Paul's threefold description of himself as herald, apostle and teacher? In what ways do these terms apply to Christians today? (See p. 72.)

'It is the unity of God and the uniqueness of Christ which demand the universality of the gospel' (p. 73).

---

2. Sexual roles in public worship (2:8–15)

13 Hermeneutics is the study of how the truths of Scripture are to be applied today. What two hermeneutical principles 'of paramount importance' (p. 74) does John Stott draw attention to in this section?

14 How do you react to Paul's teaching on the role of women here? What do you make of the different approaches taken to how it should be interpreted today? (See pp. 75–78.)

15 What does John Stott mean by 'the principle of cultural transposition' (p. 78)? How does he apply it to this issue? Do you agree with him? Why or why not?

16 What three hindrances to prayer are highlighted by these verses? (See p. 82.)

17 How do you think Paul would answer someone who understood him to be saying that women should 'neglect their appearance, conceal their beauty or become dowdy and frumpish' (p. 83)?

18 What attempts have been made to soften Paul's teaching in verses 11 and 12? (See pp. 85–86.) Do you agree with John Stott that these efforts are 'unsuccessful'? Why or why not?

19 In what different ways has the promise in verse 15 been understood (see p. 87)? Which explanation do you find most convincing?

20 Pray for those caught up in contemporary conflicts concerning the ministry of women in the church today.

1 Timothy 3:1–16
3. Pastoral oversight (pp. 89–108)

1 In connection with church leadership, what are the 'unbiblical extremes' (p. 89) between which Christians have tended to oscillate? What evidence is there of either of these in your own experience of church life?

2 Why should the New Testament terms *episkopos* ('overseer', 'bishop') and *presbyteros* ('presbyter', 'elder') be viewed as 'two titles for the same office' (p. 90)? Why then were both terms used?

1. The overseers (3:1–7)

3 What does Paul mean by specifying that candidates for pastoral ministry *must be above reproach* (2)? How should this be evaluated? (See p. 92.)

4 Why has Paul's statement about the marital status of pastors 'been the subject of long and anxious debate' (p. 92)? What does he mean? And what doesn't he mean?

5 What different reasons lie behind the other moral qualities Paul mentions here? (See pp. 94–95.)

6 Why is being *able to teach* such an important qualification? (See p. 95.) How can someone's ability to teach be tested?

7 'What distinguishes Christian ministry is the pre-eminence in it of . . .' what (p. 95)? Why is this the case? What does it indicate about the church's role in deciding who should be appointed?

8 What are the benefits and the dangers of 'the modern western custom of ordaining people in their twenties straight from college' (p. 98)? How do you think this system might be improved?

2. The deacons (3:8–13)

9 What does Paul's teaching here imply about the role of deacons? What qualifications are emphasized? (See pp. 100–102.)

10 Does verse 11 refer to deacons' wives or deaconesses? What evidence is there either way? (See p. 101.)

11 In what way is the first half of this chapter 'a good example of the balance of Scripture' (p. 102)? How far does your own thinking about Christian leadership reflect this balance?

3. The church (3:14–16)

12 What three illustrations of the church does Paul set out here? What particular truths lie behind these expressions? (See pp. 103–108.)

13 What is 'the double responsibility of the church *vis-à-vis* the truth' (p. 105)? In what ways does the church to which you belong fulfil this?

'The church depends on the truth for its existence; the truth depends on the church for its defence and proclamation' (p. 106).

---

14 What three suggestions have been made about the meaning of the six statements in verses 14–16 (see pp. 106–108)? Which do you find most persuasive? Why?

15 'One of the surest roads to the reform and renewal of the church is . . .' what (p. 108)? How might this apply in your situation?

16 Pray for those charged with the responsibility of selecting and training the church's ministers.

1 Timothy 4:1 – 5:2
4. Local leadership (pp. 109–126)

1 Do you find theological debate 'uncongenial' (p. 109)? If so, why? Why does John Stott assert that it 'cannot be avoided'?

1. The detection of false teaching (4:1–10)

2 What does Paul describe as the threefold 'underlying spiritual dynamic' (p. 111) of erroneous teaching in the church? What evidence of these different aspects have you found in your own experience?

3 What two tests does Paul give for the detection of error (see pp. 112–115)?

4 Why is it vital to emphasize that 'everything *created by God* is good' rather than simply 'everything is good' (see p. 114)?

5 In what ways do you suffer from 'lingering evangelical asceticism'? (p. 115)? How might you go about putting this right?

6 'Jesus Christ has ministers of all sorts – good, bad and indifferent . . .' (p. 116). What sort are you? How do you know?

7 How can we train ourselves *to be godly* (7; see pp. 116–117)? Be as practical and specific as you can.

8 What does Paul mean by referring to God as *the Saviour of all men* (10; see p. 118)? Is he teaching universalism (the belief that everyone will ultimately be saved)?

'*We need have no hesitations about any teaching which glorifies God the Creator and promotes godliness*' (p. 118).

---

2. The commendation of true teaching (4:11 – 5:2)

9 What 'perennial problem' (p. 119) does Paul turn to in these verses? What experience have you had of such a situation?

10 In what six ways does Paul encourage Timothy to 'commend his ministry and gain acceptance for it' (pp. 120–126)? How do these apply to Christian leaders today?

'*The Christian leads by example, not force, and is to be a model who invites a following, not a boss who compels one*' (p. 120).

---

11 What are the three components which made up Timothy's 'ordination'? How do these apply today? (See pp. 122–123.)
12 Why is it wrong for Christian leaders to 'imagine that they have to appear perfect, with no visible flaws or blemishes' (p. 123)? What practical steps can leaders take to avoid giving such an impression?
13 'It is fatally easy to become so busy in the Lord's work that we leave no time for the Lord himself' (p. 124). How can this danger be avoided?
14 What is 'shocking' (p. 124) about verse 16b? How should what Paul says here be understood?
15 What implications does John Stott draw from the description of the church as a family? (See p. 126.)
16 Pray for Christian leaders, especially those who are young or who have recently been called into a ministry of leadership.

1 Timothy 5:3 – 6:2
5. Social responsibilities (pp. 127–144)

1. Widows (5:3–16)

1 What reasons does Paul give for children to support their parents and grandparents? (See p. 130.) How does this apply to you?
2 What are the principles which lie behind Paul's instructions here? (See pp. 131–132.) In practical terms, how does the church to which you belong put them into practice?
3 What 'lasting principles of social welfare' (p. 135) are found in this passage?
4 How might what Paul says here about widowhood be applied to the life of the church today?

'Christian relief should never demean its beneficiaries, but rather increase their sense of dignity' (p. 135).

---

2. Presbyters (5:17–25)

5 Is Paul specifying two different kinds of elder here? (See p. 136.) How do you arrive at your conclusion?
6 In what ways should appreciation be shown to the leaders of the church? (See pp. 136–138.) What do you think Paul would say about the way the church to which you belong supports its ministers financially?

7　How does what Paul says here about the disciplining of leaders apply today? (See pp. 138–139.)

'It is a safe rule that private sins should be dealt with privately, and only public sins publicly' (p. 139).

8　'In the work of a . . . Christian leader one of the worst sins is favouritism' (p. 139). What experience have you had of the consequences of this?

9　To what is Paul referring when he mentions 'laying on of hands'? Why is it so important to be cautious in this area? (See p. 140.)

'Attractive personalities often have hidden weaknesses, whereas unprepossessing people often have hidden strengths' (p. 141).

---

3. Slaves (6:1–2)

10　What do you think about slavery? Why doesn't Paul condemn it out of hand? (See p. 143.)

11　What lies behind what Paul *does* say about how slaves are to behave towards their masters? (See pp. 143–144.)

12　'Every human being is worthy of honour' (p. 144). Why?

13　Pray for those to whom you have difficulty in showing the honour which they deserve.

1 Timothy 6:3–21
6. Material possessions (pp. 145–164)

1. A charge about false teachers (6:3–5)

1　What characteristics of false teachers does Paul emphasize here? What does their teaching lead to? (See pp. 146–148.)

2　How does John Stott arrive at the conclusion that 'to disagree with Paul is to disagree with Christ' (p. 147)? Are there any areas where you find it hard to accept Paul's teaching?

'In the end, there are only two responses to the Word of God. One is to humble ourselves and tremble at it; the other is to harden our hearts, stiffen our necks and reject it' (p. 147).

3 What experience have you had of 'attempts to commercialize religion' (p. 148)? In what ways are you open to temptation in this area?

2. A charge to the Christian poor (6:6–10)

4 Would you describe yourself as 'content'? How do you think you would react if you had only food, clothing and shelter? How would what Paul says help? (See pp. 149–151.)
5 In practical terms, how is it possible to avoid austerity on the one hand and extravagance on the other?
6 What adverse results of covetousness does Paul point to here? (See p. 152–153.) Do you recognize any of these things in your own life? What can you do about them?
7 What is wrong with the statement that 'Money is the root of all evil'? Why is it important to hold on to what Paul really said? (See p. 152.)
8 How would you answer someone who claimed that Paul's teaching on contentment merely perpetuates the exploitation and continuing oppression of the poor? (See p. 153.)

3. A charge to a man of God (6:11–16)

9 What do you need to flee from as 'incompatible with the wholesome will of God' (p. 155)? What should you be pursuing instead?
10 When it comes to 'the faith' today, what needs to be fought for? How should we go about this?
11 What do you understand by the term 'eternal life'? What does Paul mean by telling Timothy to 'take hold' of it? (See p. 157.)

'Some fight for truth but neglect holiness. Others pursue holiness but have no comparable concern for truth. Yet others disregard both doctrine and ethics in their search for religious experience. The man or woman of God combines all three' (p. 158).

STUDY GUIDE

12 What two arguments does Paul use to buttress his appeal to Timothy? (See pp. 158–159.) What effect do these truths have on you?

4. A charge to the Christian rich (6:17–19)

13 Do you think of yourself as rich? How do you arrive at your conclusion?
14 What dangers does Paul associate with wealth? (See p. 161.) How have you found these to be true in your own experience?
15 What are Paul's positive instructions about wealth? (See pp. 161–163.) How do they apply to you?

'Simplicity, gratitude, contentment and generosity constitute a healthy quadrilateral of Christian living' (p. 163).

---

5. A charge to Timothy himself (6:20–21)

16 What exactly is it that has been entrusted to Timothy's care? How can he best go about guarding it? (See p. 163.)
17 What do you think Paul means by *godless chatter*? Why does he react to it in the way he does? (See p. 163.)
18 Pray for those who are held captive by possessions – either those they *do* have or those they do *not* have.

B. The Message of Titus

Titus 1:1–4
Introduction (pp. 168–172)

1. Paul introduces himself

1 What is significant about the way Paul describes himself? (See p. 168.)
2 Why do people sometimes suggest that faith and knowledge are incompatible? What is wrong with such a view? (See p. 169.)

'Any doctrine which does not promote godliness is manifestly bogus' (p. 169).

---

3 How would you describe your *hope of eternal life*? On what is it based? (See pp. 169–170.)

4 In practical terms, how can today's Christian leaders cultivate faith, hope and knowledge in those committed to their care?

2. *Paul addresses Titus*

5 What does the New Testament tell us about Titus? (See pp. 170–172.)

3. *Paul wishes Titus grace from God*

6 What does it mean to wish someone *grace and peace* from God? (See p. 172.)

7 Do you think the author of this letter displays 'a rather muddled soteriology' (*i.e.* understanding of salvation), as suggested by A. T. Hanson? (See p. 172.)

Titus 1:5–16
1. Doctrine and duty in the church
(pp. 173–184)

'The main way to regulate and consolidate the life of the church is to secure for it a gifted and conscientious pastoral oversight' (p. 173).

---

1. *The true elders (1:5–9)*

1 What four statements about the pastoral oversight of the church does John Stott draw out here? (See p. 174.) How does the church to which you belong put these into practice?

2 What exactly does Paul mean by requiring elders to be *blameless*? Why is this so important? (See p. 175.)

3 What are the three areas of reputation on which Paul focuses? (See pp. 175–179.) How do these apply today?

4 What does John Stott mean by the 'negative aspect of this teaching ministry' (p. 178)? Why is it so unpopular today? How might leaders be helped to exercise such ministry more effectively?

> *'A pastor needs two voices, one for gathering the sheep and the other for driving away wolves and thieves' (John Calvin, quoted on p. 179).*

2. The false teachers (1:10–16)

5 When false teachers increase, what is 'the most appropriate long-term strategy' (p. 179)? How should we put this into practice?

6 What does Paul tell Titus about false teachers? How is Titus to deal with the problem? (See pp. 180–182.)

7 What threefold test do these verses give us for assessing the teaching we hear? (See pp. 182–183.)

> *'True religion is divine in its origin, spiritual in its essence and moral in its effect' (p. 183).*

8 What 'two major lessons' (p. 183) are there for us in this chapter? How might these apply in your own situation?

9 Pray for those who carry the responsibility of teaching in the church to which you belong.

Titus 2:1–15
2. Doctrine and duty in the home (pp. 185–197)

1 What is to be 'Titus' distinctive role' (p. 185) in contrast to the false teachers? How does the Christian teaching you give and/or receive measure up in this respect?

1. The ethical duties (2:1–10)

2 What are the particular themes associated with each of the six groups Paul refers to here? (See pp. 187–192.) In what ways are these relevant for you?

3 What does John Stott suggest is the 'most important emphasis' (p. 190) in Paul's instructions to Titus himself? How do you feel about this?

4 'Our lives can bring either adornment or discredit to the gospel' (p. 192). How? Which of these has been dominant in your life today?

2. *The sound doctrine (2:11–14)*

5 What 'particular doctrine' (p. 192) forms the basis for Paul's earlier ethical appeal?

6 How exactly does the grace of God 'teach' us? (See p. 193.)

7 Does the end of verse 13 refer to two persons of the Godhead or to one? How do you arrive at your conclusion? (See pp. 194–195.)

8 How does verse 14 help us to understand that there is more to salvation than the securing of our forgiveness? What is significant about the words and images Paul uses here? (See p. 195.)

9 How would you answer someone who claimed that Christians are out of touch with the present and hopelessly preoccupied with the distant past and the remote future? (See p. 196.)

10 How do you think Christian leaders should go about putting verse 15 into practice?

11 Spend time praying for those Christian leaders whose relationship with those they lead is in difficulties.

Titus 3:1–8
3. Doctrine and duty in the world
(pp. 198–208)

1. Christians in public life (3:1–2)

1 Do you suffer at all from what John Stott calls 'the unhealthy lust for originality' (p. 199)? What is wrong with this?

2 Why isn't it enough for Christians simply to be law-abiding? What else is involved in our relationship with the state authorities? (See p. 199.) How might this work out in practice for you?

3 What four attitudes which Christians are to show to others does Paul draw out here? (See p. 200.)

2. Ingredients of salvation (3:3–8)

4 Why is it 'not enough to affirm that the grace of God that brings salvation has appeared to all men (2:11)'? What more do we need to say? (See pp. 200–201.)

> *'Without a personal experience of salvation we lack the right,*
> *the incentive and the confidence to teach social ethics to others'*
> *(p. 201).*

5 Why do people tend to react negatively to talk of salvation and being saved? (See p. 201.)

6 What are the 'six ingredients of salvation' (p. 201) which Paul deals with here?

7 Why is it impossible for us to save ourselves? How do you account for the fact that so many people try to do this? (See pp. 202–203.)

8 'God does not save us because of his mercy alone . . .' How does he do so, then? Why is it important to stress this? (See pp. 203–204.)

9 Paul uses four nouns to describe the means God has used to save us. What are they and what truths about salvation do they underline? (See pp. 204–205.)

10 Why is it so important to stress that 'justification is emphatically not the result, still less the object, of our regeneration' (p. 205)?

11 Why does Paul insist that 'believers must devote themselves to good works' (p. 206)? How does this apply to you?

12 In what ways are these verses 'a balanced and comprehensive account of salvation' (p. 207)?

13 What forms of 'truncated or trivialized gospel' (p. 208) are you aware of? How does what Paul says here counter them?

14 Pray that you may be more balanced and comprehensive in the way you go about communicating the good news of salvation.

Titus 3:9–15
4. Final personal messages (pp. 209–213)

1 How does verse 9 apply to you? Is Paul outlawing all theological debate? (See p. 210.)

2 Do you know anybody who could be described as a 'divisive person'? What do you tend to do about such people? What does Paul say you should do about them? (See pp. 210-211.)

3 What does it mean to live an 'unproductive life' (p. 212)? How productive is yours?